A WORD FROM GOD FOR THE CHURCH

Charlie O'Neal

CHARLIE O'NEAL

HFT PUBLISHING
Inc

Kindle eBook ISBN: 978-1-7351626-1-4
Paperback ISBN: 978-1-7351626-8-3
ePub eBook ISBN: 978- 1-953239-34-1

Exterior and Interior Design of the book by: _HFT Publishing, Inc._

eBook conversion by: _HFT Publishing, Inc._

HFT Publishing, Inc.
P O Box 1863
Brewton, AL 36427-1863
Email: HFT-Publishing@post.com

Printed in the United States of America

Paperback Book Cover and eBook cover designed by:

HFT Publishing, Inc.

This book is a message given by God
to the church for 2020 and the years to follow

This message was given on
December 3, 2019
to Charlie O'Neal

This message was before any knowledge of the coronavirus,
the pandemic, or the economic failure that
was to follow in the United States of America.

Read and see what God wants
out of us for 2020 and the years
(or days) that we have
until the rapture of the Church

CHARLIE O'NEAL

DEDICATION

This book is dedicated to all pastors who are seeking
the true directions of the Holy Spirit.

If your heart longs for the anointing of
God in your ministry and daily seeks for
the truth of God's word,
then this book is dedicated to you.

If you show love, compassion, empathy,
and forgiveness to all, then you are
ready to receive the blessings that will follow
in your ministry after reading this book
and acting on its recommendations.

CHARLIE O'NEAL

ACKNOWLEDGMENTS

A special thank you is given to the
Church of God ministers in the
States of Alabama and Florida that provided
editorial assistance and advice for this book.
Considering, I lived through these events as God
moved for us, they get lost in my mind with the
thousands of miracles he has performed.
Thanks for reminding me of events to share!

Because I am using a pen name as the author, I cannot list
your names. However, you know who you are and
how wonderful you have been to me.
I pray God blesses you 1000-fold for your
assistance in getting this book to publication!

With love and appreciation,
I am so grateful for the support of
my spouse and family.
Their support for my ministry
and understanding for the days
and weeks that I was "locked away"
writing was a valuable gift to me.

TABLE OF CONTENTS

CHARLIE O'NEAL

INTRODUCTION

A WORD FROM GOD FOR THE CHURCH

GIVEN TO CHARLIE O'NEAL
DECEMBER, 2019

This message was given through a series of dreams. (See the appendix section, "*Why and How This Book Was Written*," for the details of how this message was received). When Charlie woke up from the first dream at 2:00 AM, on December 3, 2019, the Holy Spirit said, "Write it down, now, so Satan cannot take it from you!" The dream had a long message. Charlie was anointed to write it all down. When the anointing came, Charlie was able to recall every point in the dream. It is amazing how God does that when he sends a word.

As Charlie began to study this word and research the topics God had given, specific scriptures started to take on new meanings. As you read this message, read it with an open mind. If you are not sure about a topic or comments, search the scriptures, and God will show you. If you have never heard a preacher cover these topics, then look up all of the scriptures Charlie provides. You should always verify anything that you read or any sermon you hear preached with God's word before accepting it as truth.

1

The spirits and problems discussed in this message are present in the Old Testament in detail. They are also mentioned in the New Testament. Most ministers never broach these topics because of fear that they might offend someone or impact their largest tithes payer in the church. However, God wants his church to know and understand in detail about these spirits, how Satan uses them, and why their impact on the church is so devastating.

In the appendix, you will find a section called ***Supportive Scriptures.*** This section discusses all of the Old and New Testament scriptures that support this word from God. To facilitate the ease of using this list of scriptures, we have categorized them. We want you to be able to practice what Charlie preaches; "anytime there is a word from the God or words of wisdom shared by any minister or prophet, set the words down as actually spoken, then search the scriptures to see if it aligns with God's word. If it is scriptural, date the message, fast, and pray. If that message is intended for you, then it will come to pass." Sometimes, God may give a word of warning to an individual, and it is years before it is evident in their lives, or the events prophesied come to light. God is a merciful God, who is longsuffering, and patient with us.

CHARLIE'S INTRO TO THIS WORD FROM GOD:

God's word is revealed to us as we read and pray. Each time I read through the Bible; I see things that I did not see before. Or God witnesses to me something that I need to know or never realized. It is amazing how the word of God is relevant to every generation and all situations. All we have to do is read it, and God will provide us with the insights needed.

There are a few key points that we must remember when accepting a word from God. When prophecies are given to a church or individual, the first thing we must not forget is that there is no time limit with God. He is a merciful and loving God. He always gives a warning in advance and allows plenty of time for people to repent. God never decides today to punish someone and kills them tomorrow without warning. God always deals with people multiple times. (Example: Jonah's message to Nineveh of pending destruction that God changed his mind about because the people repented).

Each time the children of Israel were taken into captivity, you read about numerous warnings and messages over forty years from the prophets before that captivity began. Remember, there is no time limit with God. One day is a thousand years with God. His timetable is not on our microwave, instant gratification schedule!

It is easy for people to hear a word of wisdom or a word of prophecy, and because it does not happen that week, month, or year, they reject it and declare it a false prophecy. I watched a church reject a word of prophecy given by a lady in their church one Sunday morning. She told them that she did not have any idea when the events she prophesied to them would take place, but to watch and pray. It was a hard word to give because it was not a "blessing prophesy." It was a prophesy that was a warning, or else wrath was coming. Several people openly rejected it and asked this lady and her family to leave the church and never return.

This prophecy was in early 2002, with the first component taking place in 2006. The main protestors/rejecters of this prophecy were dead by 2012, and two ladies that supported him were dealing with terminal illnesses, as the warning said would happen. By 2017, two more people in this church were dead. Homes were destroyed, marriages crumbled, and several of their children were in prison. They have gone through over 12 pastors since 2002, and the church's financial situation is severe. When this book went to press, this church was still without a pastor and in chaos. It never pays to put your hands or your tongue on God's anointed or reject God's word.

Never refuse a word from God, even if you feel that the man or woman is not of God, or you think that the message does not line up with God's word. Instead, write down the message word for word, add the date and time, plus the location where you were when this word was given to you. Then put the word up or in your Bible. Pray, wait, and see without accepting or rejecting the word! I have seen God use people who were not living right, like he used the "backslide prophet in the Old Testament, to prophesy doom on the man of God!" If you want to review a story where God used someone that would not have been "fit" to prophesy as we would deem it today, read the story of Balaam in the Old Testament. God gave him specific instructions about prophesying over Israel. Balaam was selling his prophecies to the highest bidder. Yet, God still used him to prophecy good over Israel.

When words of prophecy come, we see things happen immediately; other times, it is years. As I write this book, I share stories that will be significant for our ministry, church, and Americans from 2020 to 2023. However, the validity of this book may extend past that time frame for others. As we send this book worldwide, it may reach some people and churches later than 2023. We believe that the Holy Spirit will direct the sharing of this book according to God's plan. If you are reading this book and it is 2025 or 2030, know that this will be God's message for you in that time frame. God's word does not expire. However, it may speak to America in 2020 and Australia in 2022, or South America in 2025. Just know that if God has allowed this book to make its way to you, it will be appropriate for that time in your life or your church.

My purpose for sharing this word from God is to help as many people as possible around the world rapture ready! There is nothing else in life that matters more than going in the rapture. Fame, fortune, awards, careers, and world-wide recognition should not be the focus of our lives. It should not be the driving force behind the decisions we make for our lives and our churches, either. I pray that the Holy Spirit witnesses the areas you need to work on in your life from this book. I pray that it helps to motivate your church to move to the next level in their relationship with God.

Read and be blessed in Jesus' Name! Amen!

Charlie O'Neal

Chapter One:

THE MESSAGE FROM GOD FOR THE CHURCH

(Written as given by God in my dream)

I am a jealous God and a loving Father who desires to bless, honor, and favor his children. I want to give my children gifts, heal them, bless them, anoint them, and inspire them to work for me. I look down on my church, who will be joint-heirs with my son, Jesus Christ, as his bride. I desire to give them everything they need and want. However, my heart breaks when I see this "bride" (the church) living disloyal, greedy, and selfish lives. I have been longsuffering with the church, but I become angry when I see the works of the flesh active in their lives.

As a loving Father, I ask you, "why have my children turned their backs on me? Why are they no longer under a burden for lost souls? Why have they decided to play church? Why are they allowing deceitful spirits, the spirits of Python, Leviathan, Jezebel, and Moloch, to enter into my holy sanctuaries? Why are the pastors more concerned with entertainment, numbers, offerings, programs, and fame than winning souls?

For 2020 and the years to follow, I will no longer tolerate the hypocrisy, deceitfulness, and playhouse religion of the past decades to continue in the churches that declare they are honoring me! I am going to open the eyes of the preachers who believe me and who live righteous lives. I will give them a perfect spiritual vision so they can see the real condition of my church. I will anoint them with power to preach my word, rebuild the altars in my churches, and call my people back to the cross. I want my ministers to preach like my prophet Jeremiah did....with a bold yet humble and contrite spirit. I want my preachers to lead the church toward a lifestyle of victory and dedication, including integrity, honesty, love, and forgiveness.

5

For the past four decades, false prophets, teachers, and ministers preached the messages of prosperity, fame, and fortune. They convinced my children to compromise their standards and walk away from the precepts of my word. These false preachers have supported and promoted abortions, deceitfulness, jealousy, greed, and contention. They have refused to preach on sin for fear of losing their congregations or offending their members. Their sermons include compromised words and twisted messages that opened the doors for the spirits of Moloch, Jezebel, Leviathan, and Python to enter their churches. These spirits have convinced the church that it is okay for them to offer their unborn children to Moloch in abortion clinics worldwide. These spirits have convinced my children that it is acceptable to me for them to satisfy all of their fleshly desires. They laugh at my mercy and grace by continuing to corrupt themselves sexually. No one teaches discipline, self-sacrifice, and holiness anymore.

This corruption has resulted in me turning these individuals over to reprobate minds and allowing the demon, Moloch, to possess them. Yes, demon-possessed preachers and teachers are standing in pulpits across America. They have deceived the church and led it astray, as Ahab and Jezebel led Israel's children into idolatry and sinful living in Elijah's time.

I need preachers to teach the true, uncompromised gospel and draw my church back to the cross. I need preachers to help them get deliverance from the spirits that control them. They need to repent and do their first works over! No matter how much they claim to be "saved" and filled with the spirit of God, no matter how much they preach or teach, they are false prophets because they have compromised the gospel. They are standing in my house, claiming that they are delivering my words and operating in gifts I have given them. Yet, they are deceiving the people as they speak under the power of these demonic spirits. The miracles they work are not from me, but manifestations by demonic spirits to deceive the church.

In 2020, I will give the false prophets, preachers, and teachers that stand in my churches a chance to get their lives straight. If they do not heed my call to repentance, I will begin cleaning out the churches, starting at the pulpit. No matter what a person says, I know their hearts' intent and what they are secretly conspiring to do. After I have cleaned the pulpits, I will move to the pews. No one, pastor or member that is not right will be allowed to continue to hinder my word from going forth. If a church does not want to change or get right, I will give them over to Satan, write Ichabod over the door, and leave them alone. Do not be deceived by them; they are not rapture ready. Do not follow them!

When I begin this cleaning, I will forgive and help the pastors that try to lead their churches back to the altar. If their congregation does not want to change, I will begin the cleaning in the pews of those churches. If the congregations and boards refuse to accept my word, I will remove the pastors from their churches and place them where the people want to hear my word. I will write "Ichabod" over the door of the rejecting churches. They will be left here on earth to go through the tribulation period.

I cannot have a bride for my son that is oppressed or possessed with spirits, promoting sin, and concerned with their selfish needs and not souls! I will not tolerate boasting, arrogance, egos, pride, and haughtiness from anyone, including pastors. If any of these individuals refuse to heed my pleas with them, then they will be destroyed when I open the flood gates of wrath on these churches.

Only the true believers, founded in my word and with the fruits of the spirit operating in their lives, will survive what is coming over the next few years. I need to deal with my church and get it ready for the rapture. This will be a few years of tough love, but there will still be revival! I will bring revival and deliverance to those who desire a relationship with me and desire to be rapture ready. For the individuals and churches rejecting my pleas, they will face death, destruction, pain, suffering, and be left to go through the tribulation period. If I do not allow things to happen to turn my children back to the cross and the altar, my son may not have a bride to rapture because the numbers joining us in Heaven will decrease. I must stir-up my church to repent and have revival!

For the people who do not turn to me during this time of reckoning, I will shorten their days so the churches will not be destroyed if the members want a real move of God. I will help the repentant pastors who fell into these traps. They have turned my house of worship into a place of entertainment. If they make an effort to turn their churches back to the mission of soul winning, I will hear their cry, and I will heal their churches! For the ones that continue to "entertain" their congregations, and make them feel good, to get their money, I will deal firmly with them.

I desire to bless my children and bring forth ministries of honesty and integrity in these last days. I want to pour out my spirit on my churches and draw people to them to be helped. But I do not tolerate the "business and marketing scams" that bring in the numbers for attendance and finances. I am calling my pastors to stop prostituting themselves out to their congregation for an offering, numbers, and fame. The sins of the flesh, the pride of life, the lust of the eye, and the lust of the flesh, I will no longer tolerate from my pulpits. I want my pastors to turn their agendas over to me and give me total control of their lives and their church services.

Please beware of the people who say they are called by me and have the gifts operating in their lives. You need to try the spirits and ask me (God) for discernment, especially if there is a bragging spirit on those individuals. When people brag about their powers and spiritual gifts, they usually try to convince you how anointed they are when they are not. Men and women used by me (God) do not have to bring attention to themselves. My power in their lives attracts people to them. I never give my gifts to anyone for them to boast and make themselves look good. When they get recognition, I cannot use them. When a minister brags or selling their prophecies or blessings, run from them because my power is not anointing them!

Satan has a counterfeit set of gifts. So many preachers are operating under the assumption that they have received my gifts. They are engaging in a "play-house religion," causing me to turn them over to Satan. They are operating with his counterfeit, not my real gifts. Satan's counterfeits are so good, and it takes the gift of discernment to recognize what is not real. However, you can know that my children who are filled with my spiritual gifts will never boast about their gifts, offer their blessings of prosperity for a price, or compromise the word I give them to prevent offending someone.

For the pastors dealing with a congregation that is always begging for help and have their hands extended, asking for money, you need to enter into fasting and prayer and allow me to show you what to do to help these individuals. I have not called my church to take care of the slothful, lazy Christians who do not ever think of anyone but themselves. I have never blessed the lazy at heart, but cherish a merciful, humble giver who does without to help others. I want my church focused on winning souls, not buying members. Some individuals go from church to church, looking for handouts. If you stop meeting their monthly financial needs, they leave. For the sincere widows, orphans, and elderly that need the help and compassion of my believers, you will recognize them because of their spirits. They will be there and faithful regardless of whether or not they get help. They will be praying and looking to God, not to you, the church, or any other individual for their financial needs. Their attitudes will not become threatening if they do not get their way or the money, they think they should receive.

As their God, I desire for my church to repent and turn their eyes back to me. I want them to seek my face and to open their hearts to my word. Study your Bibles daily and let me, the God of heaven, fill you with understanding, knowledge, wisdom, and love. I am a God of love that requires my children to love their neighbors and love me with all of their hearts—not a partial but total commitment. I do not tolerate spirits of manipulation, controlling spirits, strife, conflict, discord, confusion, turmoil, gossip, and rumors operating in the church. If you see these spirits in individuals, separate yourself from them and their conversations!

My word teaches you that I will not tolerate an evil heart. I cannot live in a vessel with evil spirits or the works of the flesh. The heart of every man and woman must be "cleaned" and made new. I give new converts a time to learn of my commandments and submit themselves for a new heart of love. But I will not strive with them for years as they elect to ignore my words and fulfill the lust of their flesh and eyes. To have a victorious life, they must have a new heart of love. They cannot select who they will love, who they will reject, or curse. My children will always love everyone, even those who have hurt them and tried to destroy them. This attitude is how you will know my children; it will be because of their genuine, forgiving love!

If you have greed, pride, selfishness, arrogance, haughtiness, lust, hatred, or covetousness in your heart, you cannot go in the rapture. Hatred or unforgiveness is one of the works of the flesh and will keep you out of the rapture. The works of the flesh are not going in the rapture, no exceptions!

Go and preach my word, unadulterated, unaltered, and uncompromised, and I will anoint you as you have never seen before. Do not compromise, but preach the truth with love. I will use you to teach and train people on how to lead their churches back to Calvary and the altar. I will use you to show my ministers how to manage their churches and grow without compromising the gospel effectively. I want you to fast and pray for a renewal of the church, for revival, and that my children will have their desire to see souls saved restored. Pray that pastors will follow me, not man.

As a loving God, my desire is for my children to love me more than they love themselves or other people. I want my son's bride to return to Calvary by returning to the altar. I want them to do their first works over (salvation) and rededicate their lives to me while studying my word (The Bible) diligently. I desire for the preachers to preach my word (The Bible) to their congregations without compromise. My grace and mercy will be felt by all who turn to me. Then there will be a genuine move of God, and victory felt, then revival will come to their churches! Trust me, and know that I am God! Watch as I bless, protect, heal, provide for, and honor my children during the trials it will face in 2020 and the years to follow!

KNOW THAT I AM GOD, AND I DO NOT CHANGE!

End of the words of wisdom from the dream in which God spoke to Charlie O'Neal.

9

CHARLIE O'NEAL

10

Chapter Two:

THE FRUITS OF THE SPIRIT

This section was taken from my book, "Why am I not Living a Victorious Life?" If you want more information on this topic and how to live a victorious life, then contact us for a copy of this book. The Kindle Version is available through Amazon.com. The comments made in this chapter in message boxes like this one will indicate what new content was added to assist the reader with why this topic is relevant for this book.

The boxed content is NOT a part of the "Why am I not living a victorious life" book.

THE FRUITS OF THE SPIRIT

Many Christians wander through their lives, searching for what God wants out of them. Others make out long lists of "do's and do not's" that they preach to their congregations. Other pastors try to convince people to live by the Old Testament laws given to Moses for the children of Israel. They could not live by these laws while they were wandering in the wilderness for forty years, and they are impossible for people to live by in our world today. In his letters to the New Testament churches, even the apostle Paul kept warning them of the people who would try to put them in bondage to the law instead of walking in grace.

There is no reason why we have to ever worry about what man thinks or what a theologian has interpreted or devised as our requirements to make it to heaven. We have an incredible love letter from our Lord and Savior, Jesus Christ. It is called the Bible. It has the answer to every question or dilemma that we would ever face in our lives! However, we must open it and read it to understand what he desires for us to have in our lives.

In Galatians, Paul listed for us the fruits of the spirit. Then he described the works of the flesh. Paul gave these lists to us so that we would know what was accepted and what was not. If you look at these two lists as part of your job description, you will be amazed at how simple this Christian walk will become for you. When you accept a new job, your employer will provide you with a job description with the basic requirements for the job and the criteria on which you will be evaluated in 90-days, 6-months, and annually after that. Then they assign you to an orientation class. This class aims to share with you the company mission, vision, goals, and purpose. Then they follow with a discussion of critical policies and procedures. Somewhere in that day or week of orientation, you will be provided with a list of "no-never accepted, result in immediate termination" items. You are instructed on the disciplinary process. For most organizations, this includes two verbal warnings, then a written notice. If your behavior continues after three warnings, things get serious. You get suspended without pay, followed by termination if it occurs again. This orientation process prepares you so that you are not surprised when you are terminated.

Well, I like to look at the fruits of the spirit as our job description's mandatory skills requirements. We will be evaluated on these fruits of the spirit when we get to heaven. I look at the discipleship courses or classes offered by our churches for new converts as our orientation classes. I look at the works of the flesh as the "no-never tolerated" list. Paul said that the works of the flesh were an abomination and would not be allowed into heaven. So, this list is what will keep us from being rapture ready or keep us out of heaven if we die. This list is serious!

Before we get into the list of things that will not inherit heaven, let us look at what will go to heaven. If you know what to do or what is expected, then it is easier to understand why something is wrong or not accepted.

Galatians 5:22-23: But the *fruit of the Spirit* is love, joy, peace, long-suffering, gentleness, goodness, faith, meekness, temperance: against such; there is no law. (KJV, 2020).

There are ***nine of these fruits of the spirit*** listed in the scripture listed above. These are the attitudes and behaviors that God desires for the bride of Christ (Christians) to exhibit always. These nine fruits of the spirit are love, joy, peace, long-suffering, gentleness, goodness, faith, meekness, and temperance. These are the ***character traits*** that God says will inherit eternal life. If we want to be rapture ready, then we must exhibit these nine-character traits and lifestyles in our lives and none of the works of the flesh. To better understand each one of the characteristics, we need to define each one and discuss how God looks at this trait or lifestyle in us.

After you have studied and memorized this list, there will be no need for you ever to question if you are going to heaven again. This list will forever help you to understand what you must do to be rapture ready. No more guessing games, no more doubts!

THE FRUITS OF THE SPIRIT DEFINITIONS:

Each item listed below is a job requirement to be the bride of Christ. As you study each one, ask the Holy Spirit to witness to you how you can have more of these characteristics in your life. The Holy Spirit will also witness to you what you need to change to be more Christ-like each day that you ask! I will try to explain each of these fruits and encourage you to seek God for these character traits as you analyze your life, your pastor, and your church. You need to determine if you are in the right church for you and your family. In the process of victorious living, locating a church with leadership that does not exhibit the works of the flesh is essential.

FAITH: THE FIRST FRUIT OF THE SPIRIT

Faith: *Faith is a state or emotional condition where one learns to live wholeheartedly in confidence with trust in God that he will do what he has promised. Faith is a mental state where an individual learns to trust and rely on God regardless of what the circumstances appear to be at the moment.*

13

God has given each of us a measure of faith. He described it as a mustard seed, which is a very tiny seed. The scripture says that faith the grain of a mustard seed can move mountains and cast them into the sea. I do not know about you, but to me, mountain-moving faith is a lot! So, a mustard seed of faith is all that we need. But something is required of us to have this gift of faith. First, we must understand what faith is, then second, tell Jesus that we accept his gift of faith. Third, we must practice acting on that faith. If we know that acting on faith simply means that we agree to believe that God is bigger than all our problems, we are on our way!

God has given us several promises to help us stand on our faith. "I will not put more on you than you can bear, but make a way of escape" (I Corinthians 10:13, KJV, 2020). Hold fast and proclaim your "faith without wavering" (Hebrews 10:23, KJV, 2020).

Hebrews 11:1-3: Now faith is the substance of things hoped for, the evidence of things not seen.... through faith, we understand that the worlds were framed by the word of God so that things which are seen were not made of things which do appear. (KJV, 2020).

Hebrews 11:6-7: But without faith, it is impossible to please him, for he that cometh to God must believe that he is and that he is a rewarder of them that diligently seek him. By faith Noah, being warned of God of things not seen as yet, moved with fear, prepared an ark to the saving of his house; by the which he condemned the world, and became heir of the righteousness which is by faith, (KJV, 2020).

James 1:5-6: If any of you lack wisdom, let him ask of God, that giveth to all men liberally, and upbraideth not; and it shall be given him. But let him ask in faith, nothing wavering. For he that wavereth is like a wave of the sea driven with the wind and tossed (KJV, 2020).

I Peter 1:7: That the trial of your faith, being much more precious than of gold that perisheth, though it be tried with fire, might be found unto praise and honor and glory at the appearing of Jesus Christ (KJV, 2020).

Faith is a crucial component of our walk with Christ. You can now understand why it is the first fruit of the spirit to be listed. We must have faith. Without faith, we cannot do or ask for anything from God. Fear is the greatest killer of faith. If you are struggling with this characteristic, pray and ask God to show you what is killing your faith. Then assess your life for signs of fear or doubt. These are two of Satan's dynamic tools for hindering Victorious Living success and answered prayers. If you want scriptures to help build your faith, read the entire 11th chapter of Hebrews in the New Testament. You will see a list of Old Testament Patriarchs that were victorious because of their faith. Study the stories of each one and watch your faith be built!

GENTLENESS: THE SECOND FRUIT OF THE SPIRIT

Look at the definition of gentleness below. Then carefully ponder how this fruit is manifested in our lives.

> **Gentleness**: *Gentleness is a personality trait or character trait that one possesses that allows them to remain gentle, soft-spoken, kind, even-tempered cultured, and refined in his or her conduct even in the worst situations or discriminations.*

Jesus Christ is the best example of "gentleness" that I can share with you from the Bible. Father Abraham, in the Old Testament, is an excellent example of gentleness. He showed more love, gentleness, and longsuffering that most modern men could muster. Abraham accepted his wife's offer of her handmaiden; then, Abraham catered to every need or wish of his wife, including her jealousy of that maiden (Hagar) after giving birth to Ishmael. Abraham dealt gently with Hagar and Ishmael and blessed them after removing them from their camp. In the New Testament, Jesus was gentle with everyone he dealt with except the people in the temple selling goods. Jesus even remarked that we needed to be like a little child to enter heaven. What a perfect example of gentleness, goodness, and forgiveness!

GOODNESS: THE THIRD FRUIT OF THE SPIRIT

Look at the definition of goodness below. Then carefully exam your life to determine whether there is any goodness in you!

> **Goodness:** *Goodness is an emotion or character trait where an individual consistently stays in a state of being kind, considerate, compassionate, virtuous, benevolent, and generous while demonstrating a Christ-like attitude and conduct. This person controls their tongue as the apostle James outlines in the New Testament book named after him.*

The book of James gives us several examples of a person who demonstrates goodness. The first criterion is to control our tongues. If we are a "good person," we will not criticize, critique, or exam others' lives. We will not find fault, judge, defame or destroy another person's reputation. Instead, we will be kind, gentle, benevolent, and helpful. Gentleness and goodness are qualities that are easy for us to claim but very difficult to prove when faced with lazy employees, disgruntled customers, or hotheaded bosses. Gentleness and goodness require assistance from the Holy Spirit to accomplish.

JOY: THE FOURTH FRUIT OF THE SPIRIT

Look at the definition of joy below and try to remember when was the last time you felt true joy in your life! For your life to be graced with joy, there must be salvation, peace, and love. There is no joy without love. See how these fruits link to and support each other?

> **Joy:** *Joy is an emotion or state of mind where one experiences gladness, delight, excitement, etc., over blessing received, gifts, rewards, childbirth, etc. Joy is shared with others. Joy loves to give more than it longs to receive.*

16

When was the last time you felt joy, true joy? Was it the day you got married, the births of your children? The day you bought your new car? Or was it a few Sundays ago when three people came to the altar and gave their lives to God? When was the last time you rejoiced with real honesty about a co-worker's promotion? Have you ever gotten excited about someone else's success so much that you threw them a party? (Not talking about family members or children). When was the last time you were so excited about the blessing, healing, or miracle that your neighbor received that you prayed and thanked God for sending them that blessing?

If you have never thanked God for someone else's blessings and you have never helped someone not related to you celebrate a victory in their lives, then you have never known true joy. When was the last time you got excited about souls being saved? There is no joy like witnessing salvation. If you cannot remember, then you have NEVER experienced real joy. So, you need to ask God to help you learn how to demonstrate real joy!

LOVE: THE FIFTH FRUIT OF THE SPIRIT

Look at the definition of love below and then read John the 15th chapter. Love is what Jesus demonstrated and what God expects from us. We need to love and forgive like Christ did while he was here on earth.

> **Love:** *Love is a feeling or emotion that expresses how one feels about another person. It is a feeling or sense that shows kindness, patience, and long-suffering with another individual. Here are many types of love; the kind of love a parent has for a child, the love between a husband and wife; the love between two friends or colleagues, and the love between family members or church family. There is divine love that is a reliable yet tender and compassionate type of love. This divine love is willing to give* **everything**, *including their life, for the person they love. This agape type of love is what Jesus did for us. He gave his life so that we could be forgiven and have eternal life and a home in heaven!*

John 15:9-13: As the Father hath loved me, so have I loved you: continue ye in my love. If ye keep my commandments, ye shall abide in my love; even as I have kept my Father's commandments, and abide in his

17

love. These things have I spoken unto you, that my joy might remain in you and *that* your joy might be full. This is my commandment, that ye love one another, as I have loved you. Greater love hath no man than this that a man lay down his life for his friends. (KJV, 2020).

LONGSUFFERING: THE SIXTH FRUIT OF THE SPIRIT

Look at the definition of longsuffering listed below. Longsuffering is one of the virtues that Jesus demonstrated to his disciples. He also told his disciples that they were to forgive 70 times 70 per day. That display of forgiveness is one of the most outstanding examples of longsuffering that I can think of in the scriptures. Longsuffering requires patience. So many of the fruits of the spirit work hand-in-hand as a team. We need to love and forgive, as Christ demonstrated for us.

> **Longsuffering:** *Longsuffering is a virtue or character trait that displays patience. It endures offenses, injuries, and provocations by others. The person with the gift of longsuffering does not murmur, gossip, rant, rave, or complain. An individual with this character trait does not show resentment to others or seek revenge when they suffer because of others' actions.*

Below are a couple of my favorite scriptures on longsuffering. Pay special attention to the scripture of God's love, mercy, grace, and longsuffering show in Noah's time.

I Timothy 1:16: Howbeit for this cause I obtained mercy, that in me first Jesus Christ might shew forth all longsuffering, for a pattern to them which should hereafter believe on him to life everlasting. (KJV, 2020).

II Timothy 4:2: (*This verse is Paul's instruction to Timothy about how to correct and rebuke with longsuffering*). *Preach the word; be instant in season, out of season; reprove, rebuke, exhort with all longsuffering and doctrine. (JKV, 2020).*

I Peter 3:20: *Which sometime were disobedient when once the longsuffering of God waited in the days of Noah, while the ark was a preparing, wherein few, that is, eight souls were saved by water. (KJV, 2020).*

II Peter 3:9: *The Lord is not slack concerning his promise, as some men count slackness; but is longsuffering to us-ward, not willing that any should perish, but that all should come to repentance. (JKV, 2020).*

MEEKNESS: THE SEVENTH FRUIT OF THE SPIRIT

Meekness is the one that most of us struggle with almost as much as longsuffering; like longsuffering, **meekness** requires patience and mercy. The easiest way to explain meekness is to look at the definition and Paul's explanation in Galatians' sixth chapter.

> **Meekness:** *Meekness is a condition or character trait whereby one under pressure displays a pleasant attitude with gentleness, kindness and displays a balance between tempers and passions. This individual is patient when suffering injuries, persecutions and would never feel a need for revenge, even if they have been falsely accused like Jesus.*

Galatians 6:1-10: *Brethren, if a man be overtaken in a fault, ye which are spiritual, restore such a one in the spirit of meekness; considering thyself, lest thou also be tempted. Bear ye one another burdens, and so fulfill the law of Christ. For if a man thinks himself to be something, when he is nothing, he deceiveth himself. But let every man prove his*

19

own work, and then shall he have rejoicing in himself alone, and not in another, for every man shall bear his own burden. Let him that is taught in the word communicate unto him that teacheth in all good things. Be not deceived; God is not mocked: for whatsoever a man soweth, that shall he also reap. For he that soweth to his flesh shall of the flesh reap corruption, but he that soweth to the Spirit shall of the Spirit reap life everlasting. And let us not be weary in well doing: for in due season, we shall reap if we faint not. As we have, therefore, opportunity, let us do good unto all men, especially unto them who are of the household of faith. (KJV, 2020).

Trying to maintain a balance between temper and passion is difficult for anyone who is a workaholic or a perfectionist! Many ministers' lives can be defined as workaholics with a little narcissistic and selfish behavior added to the mix. The other key component is the desire to avenge ourselves. That is human nature and comes to our minds without us having to do anything. Satan loves to give us thoughts of "poor me, why me, or how dare they do this to me!" It is normal to feel this way. Do not beat yourself up over it, but also, do not let these thoughts rent out a room in your mind and take up residence! If Satan can turn our minds into his battlefield, he won the battle and eventually won the war. We must stop this type of thinking. We have to rebuke Satan with the scriptures as we remind him of these verses in Galatians. We cannot display meekness if we have a grudge in our hearts or desire revenge on the person who hurt us. We have to forgive and forget!

PEACE: THE EIGHTH FRUIT OF THE SPIRIT

This is one of the fruits that so many Christians struggle with within their personal lives. Some people do not desire to function in peace. They are happiest when they are stirring up trouble, getting people told off, or spreading rumors and gossip. If you are this type of person, you need to meet with your pastor or associates and get counseling. The uncontrollable desire comes from the control of either the Jezebel, Leviathan, or Python spirits in your life. If you do not get control over this personality disorder, either one of these three spirits can possess you and bring with it seven more spirits.

There is nothing to be ashamed of about admitting that you have let a spirit take control. The shame comes if you do not take action and allow it to possess you. Through the years, I have counseled people with these spirits in control in their lives that wanted deliverance. They tried to be patient, kind, gentle, and longsuffering toward others. They tried to show meekness and goodness to others. They wanted to be used by God. However, if they did not get this spirit under control in their lives, it eventually destroyed their careers, followed by their homes. Satan does not care how he stops you from having an effective witness or testimony. He just wants to keep you from having a victorious life and helping others get rapture ready or living victoriously. Peace is defined as:

> **Peace:** *Peace is a feeling, state, or condition where a person is at ease, relaxed, non-stressed, or in perfect harmony with their environment, themselves, families, or colleagues. It is a state of quiet, rest, and security exhibited during turmoil, strife, and temptations.*

TEMPERANCE: THE NINTH FRUIT OF THE SPIRIT

Temperance is mentioned in Paul's writings to the Galatians. When you look at this definition, you must consider that this fruit of the spirit is also a personality or character trait like meekness that can destroy your peace if left unchecked. When we allow fear, despair, revenge, and hate in our lives, we destroy our peace. When the peace in our lives is attacked, we lose our gentleness, meekness, goodness, and then we lose temperance! It is human nature to go into "defense mode" when others attack us, our families threatened, or our worlds rocked with trouble and problems.

There is nothing sinful about having the thoughts run through your mind. The sin comes when we sit and ponder how we will implement those thoughts of revenge. If we have our sins under the blood, our prayer life intact, and our minds made up that we will walk daily in the fruits of the spirit, then the Holy Spirit will help us have self-control, which will result in intemperance.

21

It is hard to control our tempers and walk away when someone is in your face screaming at you in a fit of road rage as they tell you that you stole their parking spot or you cut them off when you turned into the parking lot. But temperance will manifest itself with a smile and a comment similar to "Sir, I am so sorry. I did not mean to cut you off or steal your parking space. I will be happy to move my car if you give me just a moment. You can have this place. I do not mind walking a few extra feet; I need to get my steps in today anyway!"

If you do not have temperance, your response will not be soft words spoken with meekness. Instead, your words will be like, "Sir, I was here first. I did not cut you off earlier; you were the one who flew through that stop sign and cut in front of me. I got here first, and I am parking here. There are plenty of other empty spots that you can get in. The longer you stand here fussing at me, the longer it will take you to get inside. It is not me wasting your time; it is you. You are your problem; you need help! You could have been in the store and got what you needed in the time you have been fussing at me! Sir, you have a serious problem. Leave, or I am calling 911!"

Does this second comment sound like you? If not, I am proud of you! If it is you, then you are in like company. That was me a few years ago. I did not have revenge in my heart for others, but I would stand my ground. I thought I had the right to defend myself and not be anyone's doormat. There is something about the culture we are raised here in America that programs this into us in high school and college. We develop this attitude, not realizing its impact on the rest of our lives. It can be a simple, smart remark we make to people who do not put their buggies in the cart racks in the parking lot or the person who straddles two parking spaces to protect their new car. Whatever Satan can use to get us started is what he uses.

The problem with these smart remarks is the fact that this condition will grow to something bigger. Then you find yourself judgmental and irritable all of the time. After a couple of years, my spouse said something one day when I had one of these smart-back at someone episodes to someone in a store. I noticed that my spouse just disappeared to the back of the store.

After we got in the car, I asked what happened. It was the words that came in answer to that question that forever changed me. It sent me to my "prayer room—my war room" to find out what was going on with me. That remark was, "Honey, you know I love you. I think that you are the best gift that God ever gave to me. However, there are times that this gift scares me to death. There are times that I see you say something like you did today, with the intent of balancing discrimination and standing up for the less fortunate person, but I wonder how God looks at what you did. I walked away because I was embarrassed about how you handled it. It needed handling because that employee was wrong treating that elderly man that way. I know the intent of your heart, but your words were so harsh that if Jesus had been standing beside you, he would have left you like I did today. If the rapture takes place when you are in one of these 'crusades' that you have, I fear he is going to skip over you and leave you behind!"

Those words cut like a knife right through me. No matter the intent, even standing up for an elderly minority citizen, who was being discriminated against by a pharmacist in a big box store, was the right thing to do; the way I executed that stance was wrong! I found myself praying and asking God to take control back in my life. I needed all nine of the gifts in my life, not all of the gifts except temperance. Look closely at the definition below and ask God to show you any areas where you need more temperance!

Temperance: *Temperance is a personality trait or character trait whereby one displays self-control in all things. Moderation with regards to any indulgence for self-pleasure is always maintained. This self-moderation includes drinking, food, play, and other passionate pleasures.* **Self-Control** *is the best word to describe a person with temperance.*

Galatians 6:1-4: Brethren, if a man be overtaken in a fault, ye which are spiritual, restore such a one in the spirit of meekness; considering thyself, lest thou also be tempted. Bear ye one another burdens, and so fulfill the law of Christ. For if a man thinks himself to be something, when he is nothing, he deceiveth himself. But let every man prove his own work, and then shall he have rejoicing in himself alone, and not in another. (KJV, 2020).

This scripture, written by the apostle Paul to the Galatian church, correctly states temperance's impact on a Christian's life. If we have the true love of God in us (Agape Love), then we will want to see our fellow Christians restored, sin removed from their lives, and desire to help them become victorious in their Christian walk. There is more to living a victorious life than securing it for yourself. Our duties as a Christian are to help those around us become rooted in their faith, learn the precepts, and find ways to help them get their lives in alignment with God's word. This is love, forgiveness, mercy, longsuffering, and temperance combined!

The fruits of the spirit and the works of the flesh are specific and clear. Once you understand each word's definitions, there is no question as to what will enter heaven. This path of "holiness unto the Lord" is not a laundry list of "you shall NOT do this or that," but it is a lifestyle change that results in a productive and happy spiritual life. The works of the flesh will destroy any spiritual, physical, emotional, and financial success that God has planned for you. We must work daily to keep the works of the flesh out of our lives. It takes a conscious effort to demonstrate the fruits of the spirit at all times in our lives. We need to start each morning with God, reading the Bible, and praying before we start our workdays.

If you have a long commute to work each morning, I recommend that you get the Bible on CD, mp3 format, or jump drive so that you can listen to the word while commuting. Even on public transportation like taxi, bus, or subway, you can listen to the Bible through an audio Bible app on your phone. The beauty of the technology that we have access to eliminates any excuses for not listening to the word of God. Wireless earbuds are fabulous!

Reading other Christian books or listening to audiobooks while traveling will also boost your faith, keep you encouraged, and help you put good things into your mind to meditate daily. We are the gatekeeper of our minds. If we do not control what comes into our minds, then we will not control what goes out of our mouths. Our tongues are our worst enemies! (Read the entire book of James, then read your Bible commentary on this topic). We cannot have spiritual success if bitterness, negativity, and complaining are flowing from our mouths. We must be able to apply the word of God to each problem that we are facing. God desires for us to have victory in all things every day. Trust him and watch him change things for you this year as you implement the needed lifestyle changes in your life!

As you grow spiritually, your lifestyle will change from an evil heart to one that demonstrates the fruits of the spirit. This book will help you assess (for spiritual planning for yourself and your purpose, not gossip or judging) your pastor's spiritual lifestyle, church leaders, and Sunday School teachers where you attend church. If you see the fruits of the spirit in their lives and none of the works of the flesh, then you are in a church that is trying to keep God front and center. However, if your assessment reveals that the pastor has the works of the flesh active in his life and his or her family is not living victorious, then you need to find a new church to attend. You must have your family in a church promoting a spiritual relationship with God, which is focused on the word and not entertainment. It must be a church that supports the adoption of concrete, Bible-based Christian standards and convictions.

If the pastor and senior church leaders live victorious lives, but other church workers and teachers do not, you will need to discuss this with your pastor. I do not recommend sending your children to any classes or youth groups where spirits may attach to them. You want to be the spiritual steward over your children. Discuss this also with the pastor. It may be that these workers are in counseling with the pastor and working on the issues. Pray, and God will let you know where to stay or to go. If the pastor covers for those individuals and makes excuses for them, he is compromising to appease these spirits. Leave that church! It is only a matter of time until those spirits are controlling him and the leadership team.

Learning to live a victorious lifestyle is a choice that you and your family must make and commit to wholeheartedly. You cannot make it for you and your spouse and leave out your children or your church. This lifestyle choice is an all or nothing path that you chose to walk. The fruits of the spirit are the minimal requirements on our job description as a Christian. If we look at the fruits of the spirit as a job description, it makes it easier for us to eliminate the works of the flesh from our lives. If we love our jobs, we do our best to make sure that we follow our job description. We do not get involved in any tasks (works of the flesh) that would cause us to lose our jobs (miss heaven or the rapture). This viewpoint is a powerful way of looking at these required lifestyle changes that the Apostle Paul mention throughout all of his writings as he encourages the churches to keep God first!

Now, let us take a detailed look at the works of the flesh and define each one that the Apostle Paul has listed for us in Galatians, the fifth chapter. Knowledge and understanding are of God. Knowledge provides us power in our lives that helps us be victorious over Satan and is essential for engaging in spiritual warfare.

REMEMBER:

God has a plan for your life. He will reveal that plan to you if you seek him. Read first the King James Version. Then read the Message version that follows. Does this scripture now speak to you? The entire Bible will speak to you in this same way each day if you will pray and ask God to reveal his plan and purpose for your life!

Jeremiah 29:11-13: (King James Version). *For I know the thoughts that I think toward you, saith the LORD, thoughts of peace, and not of evil, to give you an expected end. Then shall ye call upon me, and ye shall go and pray unto me, and I will hearken unto you. And ye shall seek me, and find me when ye shall search for me with all your heart.* (KJV, 2020).

Jeremiah 29:11-14: (The Message). *This is GOD's Word on the subject: "As soon as Babylon's seventy years are up and not a day before, I'll show up and take care of you as I promised and bring you back home. I know what I'm doing. I have it all planned out—plans to take care of you, not abandon you, plans to give you the future you hope for. When you call on me, when you come and pray to me, I'll listen. When you come looking for me, you'll find me. Yes, when you get serious about finding me and want it more than anything else, I'll make sure you won't be disappointed." GOD's Decree. "I'll turn things around for you. I'll bring you back from all the countries into which I drove you"—GOD's Decree— "bring you home to the place from which I sent you off into exile. You can count on it."* (MSG, 2020).

Chapter Three:

THE WORKS OF THE FLESH

This section was taken from my book, "Why am I not Living a Victorious Life?" If you want more information on this topic and how to live a victorious life, then contact us for a copy of this book. The Kindle Version is available through Amazon.com. The comments made in this chapter in message boxes like this one will indicate what new content was added to assist the reader with why this topic is relevant for this book.

The list of the "works of the flesh" is a great starting point for our personal convictions list. We should not *have* the "works of the flesh" in our lives. We should strive to have all of the fruits of the spirit, the character, conduct, and behaviors of Jesus Christ in our lives. We should demonstrate the exact opposite of the works of the flesh in everything that we do. God desires us to live lives that honor him and cause other people to want the same type of relationship. A person with the works of the flesh active in their lives will attack other people verbally, emotionally, and physically. If we are continually demonstrating the works of the flesh, not only will people be embarrassed by us, they will not desire to be around us. No one wants to spend time with negative people that always have tons of drama in their lives!

Let us review the scripture where the apostle Paul shares the 17 works of the flesh that are forbidden to enter heaven. Then we will review the definition of each of these seventeen terms.

Galatians 5:19-21: The <u>works of the flesh</u> are manifest, which are these adultery, fornication, uncleanness, lasciviousness, idolatry, witchcraft, hatred, variance, wrath, emulations, strife, seditions, heresies, envying, murders, drunkenness, and reveling, and such like, of the which I tell you before, as I have also told you in time past that they which do such things shall not inherit the kingdom of God. (KJV, 2020).

I have defined each of these works of the flesh as listed in this scripture. Hopefully, this will help you to understand this elusive list. As we discuss each of these "no-never behaviors and attitudes," I will provide you with examples of this characteristic in modern 21st Century terms. My goal is to make this list of unrecognizable terms become a list that you can understand and relate to in your lives. Satan loves that this list is so complicated with strange words not utilized in our modern vocabulary. Many people have told me that this list was not comprehendible, so they skip it when they get to these verses in their Bible reading. No part of this love letter from our Lord and Savior should be overlooked or ignored. He gave it to us for a reason. Let us read and learn today how to understand this list and recognize when these actions, behaviors, or attitudes are present in our lives.

THE WORKS OF THE FLESH DEFINED

ADULTERY:

The **_first_** "*work of the flesh*" listed in this scripture is **adultery**. In religious organizations, adultery is defined as a sexual relationship (association, connection, or affiliation) with a person other than the person you are married. Adultery can also be considered any behavior where a married individual engages in fondling, inappropriate sexual talk, or behavior with a person other than their spouse. In other words, engaging with sexual talk or teasing with someone of the opposite sex on Twitter or Facebook that is not your spouse would be considered committing adultery according to the apostle Paul's teachings.

To assist with understanding a word, I always look at similar (synonyms) of a word. The synonyms of adultery are *infidelity, betrayal, disloyalty, falseness, or treachery. Deceitfulness and faithlessness* are considered the same as adultery. As a child of God, we should be honest, faithful, loyal, and respectful of our spouses in addition to being sexually faithful to our spouse. Even though some of these characteristics may not initially lead to sexual impurity, they will lead to sexual acts resulting in adultery if left unchecked. (Google, 2020).

Let us take a more in-depth look at the definition of adultery. Any unfaithfulness in our marriage violates the vows taken. Most people do not realize that adultery can include pornography, prostitution, internet sex, masturbation, petting, or fondling. Some religious organizations classify engaging in sexually inappropriate talk with someone other than your spouse, involved with sexually provocative communications, or flirting on social media with a person other than the individual married to as an act of adultery. When not used in a sexual context, the word adultery is defined as betrayal, disloyalty, infidelity, falseness, and treachery.

Sexual sins enjoyed by the LGBT community are listed in this category, even though most feel this lifestyle choice is not indicated here because these individuals are were not married. However, now that same-sex marriages are acceptable and legal in America, yes, this term adultery applies even when one from this group has sexual relations with someone other than the person they are married. Having added this to this definition, please do not send me letters telling me that I am wrong for including then, in this definition, that it makes it appear that I am supporting same-sex marriages. Know that I am not defending them or promoting them.

As you read through the rest of this list of the works of the flesh, it will be evident to you my stand against same-sex marriages. Even though I am against their sins, we cannot hate them or mistreat them. How will these individuals ever know the gospel's truth or understand the awesomeness of

God's grace and mercy if we do not show them God's love? Remember the "Agape Love" we discussed earlier in this chapter? This is one of those areas where we are required to show agape love to our neighbors. They need to see something in us that is such an accurate representation of Christ that they long for a relationship with him.

As Christians, we are not to accept same-sex marriages as they are scripturally ok, because they are legal. Just because something is legal like abortions, marijuana (in most states), and same-sex marriage does not mean that it is ok with God. We have to live in America and obey the laws of the land, but we do not have to conform to those laws nor practice them. God wants us to respect the rules and the individuals who are required to enforce those laws (like cops and officers of the courts), but that does not mean that we have to accept them or engage in them.

We can have convictions against abortion, preach against abortions, yet accept people in our churches who have had abortions. Yes, we will encourage them to ask God to forgive them for that sin and teach them not to engage in it anymore. We will not promote anyone in our churches having abortions. Yet, we will forgive those who have and help them get deliverance from the spirits attached to them, make lifestyle changes to prevent the need for abortion in the future, and help them grow in grace! This is another example of the longsuffering that Christ expects in us as one of the duties of our Christian job description.

As Christians, we can commit *spiritual adultery* in our relationship with Jesus Christ. If there is anyone or anything that we give first place over being faithful in our relationship with God or following the commandments of God, then we are unfaithful, disloyal, deceitful, and ultimately guilty of infidelity in our relationship with God. God is a jealous God that does not share us with anyone else. He desires to have a relationship with us daily. God wants us to meditate on the Bible (his love letter to us).

Most theologians consider spiritual adultery as a "turning away" from the one true God to do the bidding of false gods. Most people's mind immediately goes to immorality. However, spiritual adultery can be much broader. It is easy to fall for the allurement of horoscopes, tarot cards, fortune-telling, psychic hotlines, and other lures of the "occult" that will tell you the future. It is easy for Satan to make you feel that you need to know the future.

Most Christians today will tell you that reading your horoscope is not wrong. They will even defend *The Harry Potter book series and movies.* I have heard missionaries that claimed to be filled with the Holy Ghost give the author of this book series "Sainthood" for her excellent comparison of good morals and attitudes in these books. However, these stories for children are full of witchcraft, sorcery, and evil deeds. I realize that the Harry Potter series' author always ends each book with a "good moral" and allows the "good person" to win. But we are not to have other gods before our Heavenly Father. We are not to engage in witchcraft, so why use it to teach our children? We are not to have any other gods before our heavenly father. Witchcraft is one of the 17 works of the flesh that will not enter into heaven. We need to take time and seriously consider what we are promoting. Are our choices lining up with the word of God?

Reading your horoscope is opening the door for divination in your life. If you are a Christian and playing with horoscopes or calling psychic hotlines, you are opening the door to be demon-possessed. You are playing with fire that is going to destroy you. Some drugs, potions, charms, and magic items can have the same power because they operate through the realm of sorcery. Drug addiction to prescription pills, as well as street drugs, also opens the door to possession. As a Christian, you should never play with or take medicines, magical potions, spells, or martial arts. Martial arts originated from pagan practices and can honor other forms of worship. If you are learning the skills for self-defense, the method of teaching and practicing is essential. Ensure you are not practicing or letting down a gap in your spiritual hedge or armor for Satan to enter. The same is valid for yoga.

Be not deceived by who promotes actions, activities, and programs that directly contrast with God's word. Do not let your church, denomination, or colleagues convince you to believe that some of the works of the flesh are okay because they do not hurt anyone else, just the person partaking (example: masturbation). Know that the scriptures say that God will not be mocked. He will not allow people who go in his name to continue to spread a false doctrine or use evil devices like sorcery and witchcraft to explain the Bible.

I realize that the benefits of yoga stretching exercises for relaxation, core bodybuilding, and muscle toning are great. Practicing yoga or martial arts without allowing divination can be productive. However, the methods of teaching, delivery, and the environment practiced in is crucial. If you have questions about these two, you may need to talk with a pastor or prayer partner who can go with you to check out these facilities and the environment.

I once heard a southern minister say that the word BIBLE stood for "Basic Instructions Before Leaving Earth." I do not know where he heard that word or phrase. I have never heard anyone else use the name Bible as an acronym. However, if it is our instructions for what we need to do before we leave earth, we could call the Bible a love letter from God to us. In this awesome love letter that God has decided to share with us, he warns us of the early church's mistakes and problems, gives us some history about the Jewish people (his chosen people), and prophecies about what is in our future. The Bible has instructions for all the things that we could ever face while motivating us to want to be rapture ready.

The Bible warns us of Hell (a lake of fire) and what it would be like to go there. As we study this love letter (the Bible), we realize that God desires for us to want him more than anything else in life. He wants us to be the bride for his son Jesus at the "Marriage Supper of the Lamb" in heaven. (Revelation, KJV, 2020). He wants us to desire to be his bride more than any earthly possession. If we love God this much, and we are grateful for his son taking our place on the cross, we will study the Bible and try to help others avoid the tribulation period and hell. We need to ensure that we are just as faithful in our relationship with Christ as we are in our commitment to our marriage.

FORNICATION:

The **second** "work of the flesh" that Paul list is **fornication**. Fornication is the same act as listed under adultery, with one exception. Fornication occurs between two non-married individuals. This work of the flesh can also include sexual acts by the LBGT community, rapists, sexual predators, and others. These individuals are having sex with someone that they are not married.

Some people believe that if you are single and you have sex with another non-married individual, that you are not committing adultery, so it is okay. Some ministers even teach that it is acceptable for two non-married individuals to cohabitate for up to one year as a trial to see if they are compatible for marriage. Though this may be acceptable in the world today, it violates God's word and his commandments for us. We need to set our minimum standards and convictions for full avoidance of all of the works of the flesh!

The interchanging of fornication with words and terms like the definition of adultery occurs in the United States a lot. However, in most areas of the world, fornication is singled out as inappropriate sexual acts between two non-married individuals as fortification and adultery as sex between a married person with someone other than their spouse. Galatians, the fifth chapter, list fornication as one of the 17 works of the flesh.

Each scripture that applies to adultery also applies to fornication. Jesus promised us that he would return for us and that he was sending to us the comforter (the Holy Spirit) to be with us, to lead us, and to guide us in all that we need to do each day of our lives. (Matthew 24-25, & Acts, KJV, 2020). However, if we claim that the spirit of God is living in us, but we are involved in sins of the flesh and lustful actions, then we are telling Jesus that his spirit is no good and incapable of doing its job. To engage in sexual acts like adultery and fornication, we are telling Jesus that his gift is not good enough to keep us clean or that we do not respect that gift enough to make every effort to keep ourselves clean.

Jesus promised that he would be with us always to provide for us and meet our needs. (Luke, KJV, 2020). If we are not trying to live lives free of adultery and fornication, then we are telling Jesus that is not what we need or that he is incapable of meeting our needs. To step out on your spouse or significant other, and have sexual relations with someone else, tells your significant other that they are incapable of meeting your needs. Stepping out on Jesus to engage in sexual activity other than what is acceptable within the confounds on marriage is saying the same thing to Jesus. That is why spiritual adultery/fornication is just as devastating to your relationship with Christ as it is in a physical relationship with someone you hope to marry or have married.

Hopefully, now you can understand why sins of sexual immorality are prohibited and why God will not allow them into heaven. Think about how you would feel if your significant other or spouse had an affair with someone else. Then add to that fact Jesus gave his life for us. He suffered more than we can imagine so that we could be free. So, Jesus' hurt has to be more severe than the wounds you and I would feel if a spouse cheated on us. Sexual sins will separate us quickly from Christ, just like they will separate you from the one you love here on earth!

Jude 1:7: Even as Sodom and Gomorrah, and the cities about them in like manner, giving themselves over to fornication, and going after strange flesh, are set forth for an example, suffering the vengeance of eternal fire. (JKV, 2020).

[The above scripture list same-sex immorality in the category of fornication. The word fornication is in the list of the works of the flesh].

Revelation 2:20-22: *Notwithstanding, I have a few things against thee because thou sufferest that woman Jezebel, which calleth herself a prophetess, to teach and to seduce my servants to commit fornication, and to eat things sacrificed unto idols. I gave her space to repent of her fornication, and she repented not. Behold, I will cast her into a bed, and them that commit adultery with her into great tribulation, except they repent of their deeds. (KJV, 2020).*

[This scripture deals with the spirit of Jezebel and its sexual spirits. This verse proves God's stands on the issue of fornication entering heaven].

UNCLEANLINESS:

The *third* "work of the flesh" that Paul list is ***uncleanliness***. It is considered a condition of impurity. This category includes but is not limited to the prevalent acts in Paul's day under the Roman rule. The common types of uncleanness that Paul preached against were: sodomy, homosexuality, lesbianism, pederasty, bestiality, bisexual, and transgender lifestyles and behaviors. This includes all sorts of sexual perversion, especially those resulting in physical harm to the human body or abnormal use and abuse of the human body. In Paul's day, with pagan temple rituals and orgies, uncleanliness included molestation, incest, sex trafficking, rape, and sexual abuse of minors. Paul listed uncleanliness as one of the 17 works of the flesh.

Uncleanliness covers a vast territory. I have heard so many people say that the LGBT (Lesbian, Gay, Bisexual, Transvestite) Community's lifestyle choices are not in the New Testament. Therefore, it is not a sin. Well, know you know it is listed and where to find it. Paul said these sins were an abomination and would not enter heaven under any circumstances. You may claim salvation while involved in these lifestyles but not enjoying

34

the benefits and protection of Salvation. Regardless of a person's lifestyle choices, we reach out to them in love and witness.

These individuals need to know that we love them, even if we do not accept their lifestyle choices. They need to know that we are here to help them when they need it. As Christians, we should be praying for them and their souls. These individuals need to see Jesus in us and know that we are different from the Christians who do not love God's word or follow his commandments. They need to see the real character of God through us. We love and accept people from all walks of life and all lifestyle choices. We show them Calvary and teach them of this remarkable Grace and Mercy of our Lord and Savior, Jesus Christ! Then we work with them to understand what they need in their life (fruits of the spirit) and what they need to get rid of or separate themselves from (all types of uncleanliness). As they feel our love and the love, hope, grace, and mercy of God, they will begin to change. We cannot turn our heads, ignore and overlook their sins.

Ephesians 4:19: Having the understanding darkened, being alienated from the life of God through the ignorance that is in them, because of the blindness of their heart: who being past feeling have given themselves over unto lasciviousness, to work all uncleanness with greediness. (KJV, 2020).

Ephesians 5:3-5: But fornication, and all uncleanness, or covetousness, let it not be once named among you, as becometh saints; neither filthiness, nor foolish talking, nor jesting, which are not convenient: but rather giving of thanks. For this ye know, that no whoremonger, nor unclean person, nor covetous man, who is an idolater, hath any inheritance in the kingdom of Christ and God. (KJV, 2020).

Colossians 3:5-6: Mortify therefore your members which are upon the earth; fornication, uncleanness, inordinate affection, evil concupiscence, and covetousness, which is idolatry: For which things' sake the wrath of God cometh on the children of disobedience: (KJV, 2020).

I Thessalonians 4:7: For God hath not called us unto uncleanness, but unto holiness. (KJV, 2020).

II Peter 2:10: *But chiefly them that walk after the flesh in the lust of uncleanness, and despise government. Presumptuous are they, self-willed, they are not afraid to speak evil of dignities. (KJV, 2020).*

As you can see with these scriptures, the New Testament is full of references to uncleanness, lasciviousness (defined below). The LGBT community's lifestyles are specifically identified as a work of the flesh that shall not enter into heaven. These scriptures disperse the myth that this was just a sin of Sodom and Gomorrah that was used to identify the town in Old Testament scriptures but did not indicate that God killed them because of the sin.

I have heard several preachers speak, justifying same-sex marriages by saying that sin was just an identifier of the cities of Sodom and Gomorrah, but did not indicate that was the reason for their instructions. I guess these ministers overlooked the portion of Abrahams' bargaining with God to save the city if there were at least ten righteous people in it. These same preachers declared that to be against same-sex marriages was to be "small-town minded and old-fashioned like the Old Testament that so many holiness people live out of," which you can see is wrong based on these scriptures. Same-sex marriage lifestyles are condemned in the New Testament in numerous verses. Several of the works of the flesh include same-sex marriages as part of the definition. Many people get these concepts confused because they read the works of the flesh without understanding the meaning of each word. They do not look up the scriptures associated with those words either.

LASCIVIOUSNESS:

The *fourth* "work of the flesh" that Paul list is *lasciviousness*. Lasciviousness is a behavior that is lustful, sensual, and lewd. Lasciviousness is also considered the promotion of or the partaking in actions, events, etc., that tend to produce vulgar emotions (like heavy petting between non-married individuals) or viewing things that make one desire, or lust after sex, or lewd things. Lasciviousness is the primary reason that most Christians must avoid so many worldly pleasures. Galatian's fifth chapter lists lasciviousness (lust) as one of the 17 works of the flesh.

Lasciviousness covers a large group of sins, activities, and all types of sexual behaviors, including the gay and lesbian communities, sexual predators, child molesters, rapists, bondage, open marriages, all kinds of passions of the flesh, and bisexual relationships. Lasciviousness includes three partner marriages, transgender, the lust of the eyes, and immoral sexual pleasures.

The desire to dress lewd (both men and women) is provocative and considered lascivious. Pride and the lust of the flesh causes a woman to show off her body parts that should be reserved for her husband only to see. Lasciviousness can affect a man too. If he desires all the women to want him or wants every man around him to envy his endowments, this person has the spirit of lust in his heart. Any man or woman fighting these feelings and desires needs deliverance from this spirit. Remember, the Christian is modest in all things, Christ-like in their behavior and attitudes, and do not have the lust of the eye, the pride of life, or the desires of the flesh controlling their lives.

Ephesians 4:17-19: This I say, therefore, and testify in the Lord, that ye henceforth walk not as other Gentiles walk, in the vanity of their mind, having the understanding darkened, being alienated from the life of God through the ignorance that is in them, because of the blindness of their heart: who being past feeling have given themselves over unto lasciviousness, to work all uncleanness with greediness. (KJV, 2020).

I Peter 4:2-3: That he no longer should live the rest of his time in the flesh to the lusts of men, but to the will of God. For the time past of our life may suffice us to have wrought the will of the Gentiles when we walked in lasciviousness, lusts, excess of wine, revellings, banquetings, and abominable idolatries: (KJV, 2020).

Jude 1:4-5: For there are certain men crept in unawares, who were before of old ordained to this condemnation, ungodly men, turning the grace of our God into lasciviousness, and denying the only Lord God, and our Lord Jesus Christ. I will, therefore, put you in remembrance,

37

though ye once knew this, how that the Lord, having saved the people out of the land of Egypt, afterward destroyed them that believed not.

These scriptures leave no question about the definition of lewdness, lasciviousness, and uncleanliness or uncleanness. The best modern-day example that I can give to you is reality television. Most of the reality programs, especially *Big Brother* and *Love Island,* are complete demonstrations of lasciviousness. Most reality TV programs include the majority of the works of the flesh in their programming. Hollywood is convinced that "sex sells!"

However, God desires holiness from his children. One of the best ways to understand what lasciviousness includes is to understand the definition of holiness fully. **Lasciviousness is the exact opposite of Holiness.** I realize this term, holiness, has been used numerous times in different texts in the first half of this book. So, I will define it for you because you will see it many more times before you finish reading this book series.

Holiness: *This word has multiple meanings and is used in specific geographical areas to mean various things in religious circles. This is one of the most misunderstood and most inappropriately used words in Evangelical communities.*

The word holiness is best described by looking at the synonyms that it represents. (bless, consecrate, purify, approve, hallow, virtue, devoutness, and devotion). Holiness is a way of life.... a pure, virtuous lifestyle, consecrated to God, and his will....not a dress code or list of "thou shall not's."

However, I want to share with you a couple of popular online definitions of the word holiness. These definitions are what people have made popular, not what the scripture defines as holiness, nor the true dictionary definition of Holiness. Paul said that "holiness was godliness." Godliness is when a person lives his or her life trying to be more like God or trying to have more of Jesus' characteristics that he demonstrated while he was here on earth! That is true holiness.

Holiness is defined by google as a "state of being holy. [It is also used as] a title given to Pope Orthodox patriarchs and the Dalai Lama when addressing them. Holiness is a Christian renewal movement originating in the mid-19th century among Methodists in the United States, emphasizing the Wesleyan doctrine of believers' sanctification. (Dictionary.com, 2020).

According to Carlsbad Current-Argus (2018), true holiness has true worth….literally, holy living means that the Christian lives a life set apart, reserved to give glory to God. It is a life of discipline, focus, and attention to matters of righteous living.

WE ARE IN GOD'S ARMY—NOT IN THE
SECRET SERVICE—SO WITNESS FOR
JESUS CHRIST, EVERYWHERE YOU GO!
DO NOT BE A SECRET AGENT!
---T. D. Jakes

To help people understand this word from God, I decided that the word holiness needed more research. As a result, I found the following characteristics when I began to study the synonyms. It resulted in a more detailed definition of this word that I want to share with you to help you.

Now let us take an in-depth look at the synonyms of the word *holiness*. We will define each one: ***sanctify, sacredness, purity, holiness, piety, righteousness, godliness, and religiousness***. To further understand each of these words, I want to look at the synonyms of each one. The definitions of these terms are frequently misused. This misuse completely changes the meaning of some of these words. Then I will tie all of this together for you with a formal definition of holiness at the end. Bear with me and read all of these synonyms.

SYNONYMS

Sanctify: bless, consecrate, purify, approve, hallow
Sacredness: purity, holiness, blessedness, inviolability

Piety: virtue, piousness, religiousness, devoutness, devotion
Godliness: divinity sacredness, holiness
Religiousness: devoutness, spirituality, faithfulness, piteousness, and
                        conscientiousness

FURTHER SYNONYMS AND DEFINITIONS

Conscientiousness: thoroughness, meticulousness, carefulness,
                        scrupulousness, and assiduousness

Devoutness: religious fever and religious zeal

Inviolability: holiness, blessedness, purity, and sacredness

Assiduousness: persistence, tirelessness, diligence, industriousness,
                        perseverance, and attentiveness

Meticulousness: care, strictness, diligence, perfectionism, and thoroughness

THE DEFINITION OF HOLINESS
BASED ON THE SYNONYMS

It is a lengthy definition covering your personal life, work-life, church-life, and a life filled with honesty and integrity. You will notice that there is nothing about clothes, religious do's and do not's. If you follow this definition of holiness in your life, all other things in your life will come into alignment with God's word without me trying to preach it to you. The animals around your home will know that you have changed. Your family will recognize it, even if they do not acknowledge what is happening. Your church family and colleagues will notice the difference. If you follow my definition below, your attitude, actions, vocabulary, and work-ethic will change as you began to live a life of holiness. Remember, this is a lifestyle change, not a religious transformation. It is a lifestyle, moral choice to make changes that God will honor and bless.

CHARLIE'S DEFINITION OF HOLINESS:

To live a life of holiness is to live a life consecrated to God, seeking God's approval, blessings, and purification through saving grace of the blood of Jesus Christ. To live a virtuous life devoted to God, seeking his favor, blessings, and purity in all things. While living a life that is continuously demonstrating holiness through cleanliness (from sin), devotion to God, diligence in reading and praying, and faithfulness to the statutes and commands of God. It is a respectful life to God and man, making a conscientious effort to living virtuously and peacefully with all men.

A holiness person who lives a life that diligently seeks to care for oneself and others with thoroughness and perfectionism that results in quality care with compassion and empathy is a person demonstrating holiness. This person will live a conscientious life that demonstrates thoroughness, follow-through, persistence, and promotes meticulousness.

A holiness person demonstrates their devotion to God through their religious fervor and zeal by doing their best at all jobs given to them. They desire for their works to promote the growth of the church, not destruction or control. A person with a zeal for the great commission....winning souls!

A holiness person demonstrates perfectionism, industrious behaviors, and attentiveness to the job's details with tireless diligence and strict adherence to the rules and regulations. This is a person who gives 110 percent to God, their families, and their careers. They diligently perform to the best of their abilities in all tasks.

AN EXAMPLE OF WHAT "HOLINESS" SHOULD BE VERSUS WHAT IT IS NOT:

While I was writing this book, I received a series of nasty, judgmental emails and text messages from a group of Holiness ministers who had read the book I had written, *Why am I not Living a Victorious Life?* The text messages that stand out the most were from holiness pastors in Nigeria and Kenya. Both had been training under a world-renown prophet from Africa. US Missionaries from the Holiness denominations had trained this prophet from Africa. He is a huge "You-Tube" hit with his end-time prophecies.

This prophet and the pastors drawn to him tend to relate holiness to "clothes-line" regulations for Christians. Lewdness (indecent dress) is a work of the flesh. It should be preached on, but continually judging and rebuking every individual you meet because they do not look like you think they should always drive away the new Christians that do not understand. Wisdom is necessary to know when and how to preach on dress codes!

The first text from the pastor in Kenya simply stated, "Are you a born-again Christian?" Considering he had just read my book, I thought that was a strange question but decided to play along and see where he was going. I replied, "Yes, I have accepted Jesus Christ as my personal Lord and Savior. I am filled with the gift of the Holy Spirit with the evidence of speaking in tongues. By accepting God's grace by faith, he has washed away my sins with the blood that Jesus Christ shed for me on Calvary, granting me eternal life with Him in Heaven."

There was a several hours pause, then the following message, "Sir, you are so deceived, you are not ready, you are not saved, you are in the wrong ministry, God is not with you! You need to repent, turn to God, and change your ministry, or it is going to be bad for you!"

Well, that felt like a threat! However, I am not jumping to conclusions, especially with words from individuals that I know probably use online translation software to send their text to me. So, I replied, "What do you mean that it is going to be bad for me? I do not understand. Can you clarify?"

The response to that question was written in anger and fiery! I could feel the demonic presence as I read the words on my phone. "You are not going to Heaven. You are one of the preachers that the New Testament talks about that will teach false doctrine to convince people to follow them!" At this point, I was confident that he had crossed up email addresses and phone numbers with the wrong person. So, I asked who he was trying to reach.

He replied, "I am trying to contact Charlie O'Neal. You have written a book called *Why am I not Living a Victorious Life?* You are on Facebook, and your account profile photo is a picture of an Angel and a Demon fighting! I know who I am talking! You are not of God."

I asked a question that I probably should have left alone. The best thing that I could have done at this point was to block that number and ignore the previous text. But I am the type of individual that wants to make sure people understand and that no one is offended. I am so afraid that I will be someone else's stumbling block. Satan uses that against me and wastes my time, which is what he did on this day. My question was, "why do you have a problem with the profile photo. Is the front cover of the book you are inquiring about?"

"Sir, let me tell you something. Anyone who puts a photo of God, angels, demons, or Mary, the mother of Jesus, on their Facebook page is of Satan. You are deceived and an 'Idol Worshipper.' You are making that photo your idol. Most people who identify themselves with God or angels are also making themselves a God!" Now, I was in shock. How could anybody be this delusional?

My reply was, "I am sorry if my Facebook Profile photo offends you. It was not my intent to offend anyone. This book is currently being marketed around the world. Next month, the profile photo will change to the front cover of my next book, *A Word from God for the Church*. Maybe that photo will be less offensive. However, if you have read my book, *Why am I not Living a Victorious Life?* Then you should understand why that photo is so important. Remember the story in Daniel, where he is praying for 21-days seeking an answer from God and wondering why God had not answered? When the angel showed up with the message, he said he had been delayed fighting the principalities of darkness. Yes, I agree. We may not know what God looks like, what angels look like, or even demons. We may all be shocked when we get to Heaven. However, to market a book, it is best to choose a cover photo that people will recognize. Not only did I want a cover that Christians would recognize, but I wanted one that sinners would recognize. I wanted a cover that would catch people's attention when they walked past the book stand. I feel that the photo with Satan or the demon (whichever one you choose to call it) is on the ground, and the Angel of the Lord holding a flaming sword has his foot on him holding him down is a perfect depiction of being spiritually victorious! Besides, the only thing we have to go on is that God said, 'let us make man in our own image,' so I am sure that God looks like a man. So, an angel that looks like a man, with wings, appears appropriate."

"Yes, sir, I have read your book! You are teaching people that they can be victorious, that they can pray and God will answer their prayers, that he will heal them, deliver them, and bless them! You cannot preach that! If you are a real God-ordained preacher, all you can preach is repentance, holiness, and deliverance! You are teaching people in this book the keys to being successful, but you never mention holiness. You do not tell them how they need to dress, how they need to look and act! You do not tell them that they have to get saved and sanctified! You are teaching them how to pray and what to look for in a pastor and church! Therefore, I am rebuking you in the Name of Jesus! I am calling you out and demanding that you confess your sins to the world and let the world know that you are wrong! I am rebuking you as the New Testament directs so that you can be reconciled to God and join in a true ministry! You need to close this ministry that you have yourself involved in, stop giving money, and royalties to a ministry to help preachers and missionaries. You need to put that money on the mission field. You need to take that money and give it to preachers like me, who is getting souls saved! You need to build churches and sponsor pastors who will get the lost saved and stop worrying about making people comfortable in their later years when they are no longer of use to God. When preachers are no longer of use to the ministry, God takes them if they are ready. If a preacher or his wife is still around and needs help in their old age, they have only been left here by God because God hopes they will change. Instead of helping them, you should be rebuking them, pointing out their sins, and getting them to repent, so that they will be ready to die!"

This series of text messages sent shockwaves of anger through me and fear of God's wrath for this minister. I wanted to fire back a response immediately and point out that he was the one deceived. Instead, I laid my phone down, went back to my desk, and began looking over the student test papers from the class for that day. After an hour of distraction, I asked the Lord to help me respond with mercy.

It is amazing how a person can support another minister and feel that that person is doing God's work and rejoice with them when souls are saved. At the same time, other ministers cannot rejoice at all with anyone else getting the money or the limelight. Then have that person turn on you like this pastor did on me, had me asking questions of God and reviewing what I had written in the book, *why am I not Living a Victorious Life?* Since he mentioned a couple of points that I knew were discussed in that book, I decided to reread those chapters before responding to his text. As I read this definition of holiness, I immediately knew what had generated this pastor's rebuke. Condemnation gripped him as he read about his need to demonstrate humility, temperance, patience, longsuffering, etc. He was presenting a demanding, controlling, haughty, arrogant, and prideful spirit. Yes, a spirit that feels like no one else is preaching the true gospel-like you are, or that others are not as holy as you, is the Jezebel spirit. It has wrapped and twisted around him along with the Leviathan spirit. I realized that those spirits severely oppressed this pastor. That was the reason he was lashing out at me!

Anytime a minister preaches the true, unadulterated word of God, with anointing and power, false prophets, preachers, and teachers will lash out. Anytime the Holy Spirit convicts the hearts of a man or woman oppressed by demons, those spirits will try to take over with a spirit of self-righteousness and convince the individual that they do not need to change. In this case, these spirits were trying to convince this pastor that the book's writer was wrong! This is a defense mechanism by the demons to keep you from accepting the word from God. Satan's job is two-fold. 1) Keep you from hearing the word of God; 2) If you listen to it, Satan will keep it from taking root in your life and bringing forth fruit!

Before I had finished praying and outlining my answer to this pastor, I received a text from the Nigerian pastor. I had listened to this pastor's prayer requests for the past few months and knew that his church was struggling. He wanted God to help him get through to his church about the works of the flesh operating in their lives. He was feeling the pressure to compromise and overlook a few indiscretions. Even though I was aware of these prayer requests, they had been received months after completing the manuscript for *Why am I not Living a Victorious Life?* So, none of the words or recommendations in that book were written based on his prayer request.

This Nigerian pastor's text me to say, "Brother, as I was looking at your ministry and reviewing the information on your book, I wanted to write to you and rebuke you in Jesus' name for the ministry that you have set up. (Strange that for over nine-months of asking me for prayer, he had never checked my ministry out!) That is a poor ministry! Do you not understand that Jesus is coming? Why are you helping widow and widower pastors? Why are you trying to help them with their medical needs, housing, and food? You should not be doing that at all. You should be out there preaching to everybody that Jesus is coming. Don't you know that? Don't you understand the importance of that message? Brother, I am rebuking you, not judging you, because your ministry does not glorify God. Instead, you involve yourself in activities that do not matter to the Lord. Is it a small thing to preach or do works?"

I gave a short answer, hoping to buy time to respond. "Pastor, we are a ministry that is focused on getting as many people saved here in America and around the world through the missionaries we support. We feel that we are in the last days. We are praying for revivals, souls saved, lives delivered, hearts healed, and people/pastors restored. I have written this seven-book series on *The Keys to Victorious Living* to help individuals and preachers worldwide understand the key concepts provided in the New Testament. God has provided us with the blueprint for living victorious, engaging in spiritual warfare, and learning how to put on the whole armor of God each day." I shared those details because I wanted to make sure that our mission and vision were not lost in translation from English to your native tongue.

I was not prepared for the response that came, "Brother, what do you mean by getting souls saved? What is getting saved? Is this some effort you make? So, you think that you are the ones getting people saved? What is that? It is not you! Why are you giving yourself glory? You are to preach repentance and holiness only."

I was confident that the phrase "getting saved" did not translate to his native language. So, I replied, "To clarify, since I feel certain that my choice of words 'helping people around the world to get saved' did not translate appropriately with your conversion software, let me clarify. We are preaching that every person needs to repent of their sins, to ask Jesus Christ to become their Lord and Savior, by faith. We preach that if you ask Jesus to be your Lord, you have accepted him into your heart and life. We call this accepting Jesus as 'getting saved or born-again' as the apostles taught. Once a person receives God's grace and mercy by faith, their sins are forgiven. If a person is saved, then they are rapture ready!"

He gave a rapid reply, "Brother, you are deceived and teaching a false gospel. We cannot accept salvation by faith. You cannot be born-again. You have to get in there and get sanctified. You are not saved, no matter how much you repent or accept grace until you are sanctified. You have got to preach holiness. Without repentance and holiness, you are not going to Heaven! Brother, you are on dangerous ground; you are no longer safe. I have called you out, rebuked you, and you have refused to accept. So, you need to get ready; you are not safe. You are a poor excuse for a preacher, who is in a false ministry!"

At this point, I felt pains go through my heart. Not aches of fear because I felt threatened, but pains, because my heart broke that some person had been to Nigeria preaching a false doctrine and this man had been deceived. I began to pray for him, asking God to open his eyes. My heart broke for the false prophet that went from America or any other country to the African continent, taking a doctrine of men, based on legalism, that destroyed the effectiveness of grace and was damning people to hell because they did not understand grace. I began to pray for God to give this pastor dreams and visions, to show him the truth. To provide a way for him to get deliverance in his life from the religious spirits that oppressed him.

It is sad when you encounter a minister that does not understand the saving grace of God. I have listed in the Appendix (Supportive scriptures)— all scriptures quoted to these two pastors. Including that we are not "saved by works that any man should boast" (KJV, 2020). We are saved by grace.

John 3:16 says that "For God so loved the world that whosoever believes on him could be saved. For God sent not his Son into the world to condemn the world, but that through him, they might be saved" (KJV, 2020).

This verse *alone* would have informed this pastor what salvation was and explained what it meant to "be saved." It is a spiritual crime for ministers to get into the pulpit without an in-depth knowledge of the word of God.

Well, I spent a few hours praying before I responded to both of these pastors. I am one who never rejects a message from anyone until I have evaluated it and determined whether or not it aligns with God's word. Here I was researching two messages and looking in the Bible for the answers to provide to them. I asked God that if there was anything in their messages, I needed to understand that it was a truth to show me in the Bible. I am always willing to accept spiritual education or training and ready to learn what God has said in his word. I try with humility to admit when I am wrong, confess, and change my ways when the Holy Spirit convicts me of something that I have done wrong. So, with humility and contriteness of spirit, I sought God's word to prove what this preacher had said, not to disprove it. However, the word of God disproved the majority of both pastor's theories.

I am sure that you are reading these two stories I have shared with you are wondering, "Why is Charlie sharing these texts? All preachers get 'hate' mail, judgmental comments, and we just throw them to the side and keep pressing forward for God!" Well, there are a couple of reasons. Not everyone reading this book is a minister and understands how to pray and discern the spirits. I want to go through the analytical steps on how to determine if a message is from God. So, I am using these two pastors' text to show you how to research the scriptures and to determine if a word is from God or not. Sometimes, God will speak to an individual to share a word of wisdom or guidance with another person, but when they get in the middle of the delivery, and they add their "two-cents," or they put their viewpoint onto the word from God, it changes the meaning completely. When this happens, the message becomes distorted, confusing, and misleading. That is why I have dedicated a chapter in this book (Is this message from God Scriptural) and the appendix section with supporting scriptures in the Bible for the message from God. I do not want my viewpoints, personal convictions, or community ties to sway my delivery of this word from God for the church. I want to make sure that I am not adding to it!

If you are confronted with a rebuke, constructive criticism, judgmental emails, critical phone calls, or text, you need to know how to handle the situations. Do not fall into the snare of an immediate response. If the person has confronted you face-to-face, tell them that you appreciate them "obeying God and delivering the message." Then tell them that you will take what they said and spend some time in prayer and fasting, and then you will get back with them later to discuss this further. Spend some time praying before you respond. I recommend waiting overnight, if possible. I find that God talks to me in dreams, and he also wakes me up at night with the answer to my dilemmas by giving me a scripture to check. Know that a "hasty answer" is never the best choice!

If you have been confronted face-to-face by the person, write down every word that they said as soon as you get back to your car. If you have a pen and a piece of paper on you, ask them if it is ok for you to write down the word or message, they have brought you. You do not want to miss any keywords. Especially in the English language, leaving out a 'but or and' can completely change the sentence's meaning while impacting the entire message. If a person is sharing a word from God with an honest heart, they will not be offended if you write it down. They will be glad that you are taking it seriously. Read the message back to them to make sure that you heard them correctly. Sometimes, when preachers share words from God, they forget that the person they are talking to may not understand the words or may not know the scriptures they are referencing. So, they fail to share critical points. If that has happened, when you read it back to this man or woman of God, they will clarify those points. Feel free to ask questions in a spirit of humility to help you understand their word.

Once you have arrived back at your home, get your Bible, notepad (iPad, laptop, etc.), and go to your "War Room or Prayer Room." In the place where you meet God each day, read this message to God and ask him to help you to understand it or show you why it is a false word from God. You must remember that a false prophet is a counterfeit prophet or preacher. If it is a good one, a counterfeit will be so perfect that the average person will not recognize that it is a counterfeit. Any word that Satan sends to you through a false prophet will be approximately 90 percent true or backed by the word of God. I have seen words of prophecy given to people that were all true but one sentence! That one sentence was the one thing that would have gotten them out of the will of God if they had not been discerning!

Satan is diligently working his job in these last days to deceive us! He will work over-time to get you out of God's will if possible! To help you understand how to discern good verse evil, true words of wisdom versus judgmental words, and true prophecies versus false prophecies, let us walk through my two messages received from these two pastors.

First, always begin by outlining the word you received from God. This will help you identify keywords to look up in the Bible, your dictionary, or concordance. I have outlined these two messages and ask as you read them to pay close attention to the topics. I gave all of the scriptures to support each point that I addressed. I did this type of response to both ministers and informed them that I would be praying for them that God would help them to have the fruits of the spirit in their lives and God's favor on their ministries. I asked them to read my response, study it, and pray over it. But to never contact me again, unless they were contacting me to repent for their arrogant, prideful, judgmental spirits. I informed them that I did not have time to debate topics with pastors oppressed by the spirit of Leviathan. When souls needed to be saved, and lonely, hurting people needed love, plus the forgotten and rejected needed to hear of Christ, and there were millions not ready for the rapture, why would I waste my time debating false prophets? (Neither of these pastors responded to any of the Bible facts or the supportive scriptures I sent! My daily prayer is that they will see the truth soon!)

But it was apparent they were offended because the book showed them where they were living…not in a victorious relationship with Christ. They were judgmental of the outreach ministries that we were supporting because of greed. They wanted the money for themselves and were jealous of the money being used to help the elderly, retired ministers, or their widows! Jealousy and greed, combined with a judgmental attitude, are not attractive qualities and show a lack of true love. When we have God's heart of love, we do not desire to destroy other ministers or ministries or to have revenge or jealousy. When these traits present themselves in our lives, homes, and churches, then it is time for us to make a trip back to Calvary!

Let us take a look at what this pastor said and how it lines up with the word of God. You will notice that approximately 90% of a deceived person's words or concepts will be accurate. Satan never sells you a bad counterfeit. He always sells his best products! This makes the deception easier to sell. This is why we have to be in God's word daily and know it!

Kenya Pastor's word of rebuke outline:

Deceived and demon-possessed
Engaging in idol worship while making yourself a God
Putting other Gods before God
Preaching victorious living and claiming the promises of God.
You can *only* preach on salvation and the coming of the Lord
You should be preaching repentance, holiness, and
           deliverance.
Teach the people how to dress, look, and act.
You cannot teach people how to pray
You cannot teach people what to look for in a pastor or church
I am rebuking you by the New Testament instructions.
Stop this ministry; it is not of God.
Pray, repent, and join a true ministry!
Ask God to forgive you for starting this ministry!
Then get a new ministry of soul-winning

Preach only on salvation, sanctification, holiness, and the
rapture

Outline for my response to the Kenya Pastor:

What does God look like…man? We are created in his image!
Flaming sword at the Garden of Eden
The warrior angel speaking to Daniel after 21 days of battling
the principalities of darkness
Knowing to do good and doing it not…is a sin
Jesus taught the disciples to pray.
Jesus gave us a model prayer
What did Jesus say was necessary to be saved?
How did Paul say to rebuke a person?
Jesus gave us the 1st commandment to love God
Jesus gave us the 2nd commandment to love our neighbor as
ourselves.
Jesus said we needed to be humble as children
Jesus taught that we should take care of the widows and
orphans, to visit the sick, those in prison, etc.
Paul said that we are to have the fruits of the spirit present at
all times in our lives, because this is what will inherit
Heaven!
Paul said that the works of the flesh were an abomination and
would not enter Heaven!
Since the works of the flesh WILL NOT enter Heaven, then
these must be preached on, in addition to salvation
and the first two commandments by Jesus.

Nigerian Pastor's word of rebuke outline:

You are in the wrong ministry.
You are not safe. If you continue this ministry, you will not go
in the rapture. Get out of this ministry!
You do not understand the gospel.
What should matter most to you is what God wants
Souls are not crucial to you.
You had better do the work of God
Man licensed you; God did not call you, not to this ministry!

You need to repent and preach only repentance and
    holiness.

Outline of my response to the Nigerian pastor:

What is salvation?
God's love, mercy, and grace is not dependent on what man
    thinks
God's mercy and grace are accepted by faith, not by works.
James teaches that by faith, we produce works (fruit). He said
    faith without works is dead. To not have works in our
    local church and community is to be disobedient to
    God's commandments to help the widows & orphans
Jesus said to tarry until he comes.
Jesus told Peter to be "fisher of men."
Jesus said to take care of the widows, orphans, visit the
    sick, and those in prison, etc.
It is more blessed to give than to receive
How to rebuke someone according to the Bible.

If you use my model of outlining the word given to you, then research the topics to find scriptures to support or contradict the message, you will always know the truth and never be deceived. At times I share this strategy when I am ministering in other churches, only to have someone tell me after the service, "Preacher, I do not have time to do all of this research. That is why I come to church, so the pastor can research this stuff and just tell me how to live or what to do!" People, this is a dangerous place to allow yourself to go.

You should never put that much faith in a pastor, preacher, or missionary. Yes, they may love you, and they may live lives of honesty and integrity, but they are human. They can misunderstand or misinterpret something. They can have an off day or week. I know because it has happened to me; no preacher is perfect. That is why we must always go back to God's word with everything that we hear.

I do not know who started the slogan back in the 1990s of "Too busy not to pray," but later, Bill Hybel wrote a book with this title (Hybel, 2008). This message is powerful because people claim that their day was too hectic or too tired to pray when night comes. They may feel that they can pray tomorrow or next week, but not now. You CANNOT afford to skip praying every morning and night. Your prayer time should be planned and organized and include your spouse if married. If you have small children, you should have Bible story reading and prayer with them before you, and your spouse read and pray privately. I pray with my spouse every morning and night. Our children are grown, married, and have children now. They are now following through with this same practice. Sometimes, I go with a prayer in my heart all day as I search for answers or seek God for the next sermon. Just like you cannot afford to skip praying today, you cannot afford NOT to research words that you hear, messages that are received, etc.

If we attend another church service as guests (not the ones we are ministering at), I always take notes while the preacher delivers his sermon. The next week during my private devotional times, I review those notes and reach the scriptures and topics that the preacher provided. Not for the purpose of "recycling" that preachers' sermon, but to make sure that I got "all" of God's word for me. Yes, preachers have to be preached to, and we have to be corrected. Yes, God has to talk to us about secret sins and attitudes! I know he is continually working on me every day, dealing with me on topics, issues, and deeds that I have omitted. To be obedient to God, I search the word and double-check my life according to the Bible every day! More than anything else in my life, I must be ready.

So, I feel that not only should I say that "I am too busy not to pray, but I am too stressed not to research God's word!" If I do not research the word and correct what has been fed to my mind, it might take root in my heart and produce fruit that I do not want to harvest!

Before we move on to the fifth work of the flesh, I now want to *redefine lasciviousness for you based upon it being considered the opposite of holiness*. The opposite of holiness would be uncleanliness, impurity, and a non-holy life.

CHARLIE'S DEFINITION OF LASCIVIOUSNESS

Lasciviousness is a lifestyle choice. It causes an individual to engage in lustful, sensual, and lewd behaviors. It causes people to act and dress to promote immorality, vulgar emotions, lustful desires, evil desires, and actions. Lasciviousness makes us desire to be involved in activities and music that supports lustful pleasures. Once this spirit hangs around for a while, you find that it becomes easier to be revengeful. It is also easier to go about life without considering the disrespect or hurt we are causing others.

Lasciviousness covers a large group of sins, activities, and all types of sexual behaviors, including those of the LGBT community, sexual predators, child molesters, rapist, individuals utilizing bondage, open marriages, all kinds of passions of the flesh, bisexual relationships, including three partner marriages, transgender, the lust of the eyes, and sexual pleasures.

Lasciviousness drives people to have desires for everyone to lust after them and want them. These desires result in them provocatively dressed while parading in pride body parts that should be for the pleasure and viewing of their spouses only. This spirit also causes people to lose their desire to live according to God's statutes and commandments. Lasciviousness instills a desire to be rebellious against the rules and seek every way in their life that they can defy God's commandments and making them reject rules. This is manifested by their defiance to follow dress codes, show respect to teachers, reverence the pledge of allegiance, respect those in authority at work, at home, or in the church.

The lascivious or passionate individual will not be seeking to be pure and holy before God but will be trying daily to scheme a way around the rules or what God desires for their lives. Instead of seeking God's favor, they are concerned with popularity, the majorities' opinions, and having everyone like them. Lasciviousness causes pride to enter your heart and life. As these spirits become more prevalent, you see an increase in arrogance and egotistical behaviors. They will not demonstrate respect for man, God, God's house, or the preachers. Living peacefully with all men will not happen if it results in any inconvenience to them or requires any additional work from them. They will not demonstrate any empathy or compassion for anyone unless it brings them money or recognition.

The lascivious person does not maintain a work ethic that includes thoroughness or perfectionism. This type of employee will work harder, trying to get out of work, than they would have worked to complete the task in the first place. They show no respect for the boss or more senior employees. They do not show respect to elders in the workplace or at home. Providing a meticulous work product that they were able to complete is never a goal.

The lascivious individual does not demonstrate passion or zeal in their work for God. They treat what they do for God, including church attendance and a daily devotion, as something on a "to-do-list" that must be checked off each day. Having a burden for lost souls, fasting a meal, visiting the sick and elderly, or taking the time to do something for someone who will not ever be able to pay them back never crosses their minds. Words like industrious, attentiveness and perfectionist never come to mind when you think about them.

The one factor that stands out about these individuals is their self-centeredness. It is always about what they need, want, or desires. If I do X for you, when will you be able to do Y for me? For the millennial generation, they approach things with I need you to do X for me because you owe me! Their attitudes do not promote collaboration or community. They never have the time to help others, especially if there is no pay in it for them. These individuals never pray and ask God to show them what they can do for others. Their prayer is a "Santa's wish list" for God each time they feel that they must pray to keep God happy. They are concerned with what they need, what God can do for them, and how God can bless them!

The lascivious person is a selfish-self-centered individual who promotes everything they want and desires that fulfills their desires, makes them feel good, promotes them, and defames others. They believe that whatever actions they have to take (whether lewd, sinful, hateful, vindictive or illegal) are justified because they desire to have their wishes granted! The fruits of the spirit that you will NEVER see in their lives are patience, longsuffering, unconditional agape love, and gentleness. The lascivious person will continually add the works of the flesh into their lives to get what they desire. They will continue demonstrating these behaviors until they get what they want or meet their end (like life in prison or death). So, if you do NOT have lasciviousness in your life, then you have holiness. Holiness is the opposite of lasciviousness!

Paul taught about how it is man that makes the law impossible to keep. When he told us to keep the first commandment, love him with all our hearts and the second commandment, love our neighbors as ourselves, he gave us the first two keys to victory. The apostle Paul then provided us with the next two keys. Be filled with the fruits of the spirit...having none of the works of the flesh present, for they are an abomination to God.

IDOLATRY:

The **fifth** "work of the flesh" that Paul list is **idolatry**. Idolatry is the admiration, adoration, worship, and idolization of an object, person, or god. Most theologians consider idolatry the act of worshiping an image, thing, or person. In the Bible times, they worshipped idols made of wood, stone, gold, silver, bronze, and other precious stones. Today, people worship possessions and things that they hold dear to their hearts. An idol to a Christian is anything that takes first place in our hearts. God is to have first place, family second, and all others last. You can make an idol out of a car, boat, or even money. If your job and the desire to make money keep you out of the church and from reading and praying, then it is your idol. Galatians, the fifth chapter, list idolatry as one of the 17 works of the flesh.

There are numerous examples of idolatry in the Old Testament. But I want to share with you a powerful story from the New Testament on idolatry. You may remember the story of Ananias and Saphira and how they lied to the Holy Ghost. We always say that their greed drove them to prepare this deceitful story to give to the apostles. But there is something more substantial here. God did not kill them over a simple case of greed or deceitfulness....but idolatry and blaspheming the Holy Ghost would anger God enough to kill them! This couple had made money, things, and possessions their god. The day that their possessions took hold of them strong enough to make them construe a lie, it became their idol. No one made them sell their property. However, their self-centeredness and need to be considered as generous as the people giving land or money; they decided to do something that would make them look good. But they did not want their generosity to cost them!

Acts 5:1-11: *But a certain man named Ananias, with Sapphira, his wife, sold a possession, and kept back part of the price, his wife also being privy to it, and brought a certain part, and laid it at the apostles' feet. But Peter said, Ananias, why hath Satan filled thine heart to lie to the Holy Ghost and to keep back part of the price of the land? Whiles it remained, was it not thine own? And after it was sold, was it not in thine own power? Why hast thou conceived this thing in thine heart? Thou hast not lied unto men, but unto God. And Ananias hearing these words fell down, and gave up the ghost: and great fear came on all them that heard these things. And the young men arose, wound him up, and carried him out, and buried him. And it was about the space of three hours after, when his wife, not knowing what was done, came in. And Peter answered unto her, tell me whether ye sold the land for so much? And she said, Yea, for so much. Then Peter said unto her,* *how is it that ye have agreed together to tempt the Spirit of the Lord? Behold, the feet of them which have buried thy husband are at the door, and shall carry thee out. Then fell she down straightway at his feet, and yielded up the ghost: and the young men came in, and found her dead, and, carrying her forth, buried her by her husband. And great fear came upon all the church, and upon as many as heard these things. (KJV, 2020).*

It does not pay to have other idols or gods before the Lord God Jehovah. We can make a god or idol of anything or anyone in our lives. If you love something so much that you would lie to God to cover up your involvement, then it is a sin to you. If you allow selfishness and greed to control your lives, then greed or money has become your god!

There are numerous scriptures in the New Testament that you can read later about how "idols" destroyed people. Money was Judas' idol. See the scriptures below from Luke's recollection of this story.

Luke 22:1-6: *Now the feast of unleavened bread drew nigh, which is called the Passover. And the chief priests and scribes sought how they might kill him; for they feared the people. Then entered Satan into Judas surnamed Iscariot, being of the number of the twelve. And he went his way and communed with the chief priests and captains, how he might betray him unto them. And they were glad and covenanted to give him money. And he promised and sought opportunity to betray him unto them in the absence of the multitude. (KJV, 2020).*

Romans 2:17-24: sacrilege—Paul puts sacrilege equal to idolatry. He said that the priest and scribes would not think of committing idolatry, but they would show disrespect to the things of God or the temple. Verbal sacrilege is also known as blasphemy. When a person verbally blasphemes the things of God by disgracing them and esteem something else or someone else above God, desecration has occurred. This error is so easy to be committed in our fast-paced society of technology.

Revelation 9:20: idols of gold and silver—John speaks of how men repented not of the works of their hands, worshiped devils, and idols of gold, silver, brass, stone, and wood. Even though idols in the New Testament times were made from these natural resources and worshipped, in our 21st Century lives, we have different types of idols. We have idols made from metals (technology, vehicles), stones (jewels), woods (homes, businesses, real estate holdings), gold and silver (bank accounts, cash, assets, holding, funds, stocks, savings), brass, and other precious metals (possessions, décor), and jobs. Yes, jobs and spouses can be idols. Anything that separates you from God is an idol to you. Anything that takes first place in your life is an idol. If you allow your clothes, shoes, makeup, and accessories to come before you going to church, helping others, or showing love, kindness, goodness, or gentleness to another, then those items have become idols to you!

WITCHCRAFT:

The *sixth* "work of the flesh" that Paul list is *witchcraft*. Witchcraft is the practice of sorcery, dealing with evil spirits, magic, magical incantations, enchantments, séances, casting of spells, and charms by casting evil spirits or using mind-altering drugs or potions. These are all evil, regardless of the desired outcome. In other words, it does not justify the use of these methods if one is seeking love, good, health, or blessings for themselves or others— Galatians, the fifth chapter, list witchcraft as one of the 17 works of the flesh.

The everyday witchcraft items of the 21st Century are horoscopes, science-fiction books, and works of spells and powers, not of God. Enticement and enchantment of other eastern religions (ex: Hinduism, Buddhism, etc.), reading tea leaves, palm reading, tarot cards, voodoo dolls, Wiccan practices, and other forms of white witch activities are a common lure for the young person who is trying to gain control of his or her lives and careers. There is the lure of movies and TV programs like *The Good Witch, Lucifer, The Blair Witch Project, The Harry Potter Series,* and other programs where witchcraft and sorcery are shown in an attractive light. It is so easy for young impressionable teens or young adults who have never heard their pastors preach on idolatry, sorcery, or witchcraft to fall prey to this work of the flesh.

Witchcraft stories are scattered throughout the Old Testament books, with a number of stories that are still relatable today. Especially the story of King Saul in I Kings and his visit to the witch to call up the prophet

Samuel for him. The only time this word is listed in the New Testament is in Galatians, the fifth chapter.

HATRED:

The **seventh** "work of the flesh" that Paul list is **hatred**. Hatred is a feeling or mental state where a person desires to hate, detest, abhor, or loathe a person, place, or thing. Hate is also a state of mind or attitude whereby one is not forgiving or refuses to let go of ought, grudge, or desire for revenge against an individual. This attitude is also characterized by bitterness, malice, ill-will, anger, hatred, loathing, abhorrence, hate, aversion, or dislike toward another person. Galatians, the fifth chapter, list adultery as one of the 17 works of the flesh.

Galatians, the fifth chapter, is the only mention of the word hatred in the New Testament. There are numerous stories where hatred caused pain and disrupted lives. In Genesis, the story of how Jacob and Esau have torn apart because of inheritance and deception. Joseph sold into slavery because of his jealous brothers. Hamman, who hated Mordecai so much that he built gallows to hang him on them, then died on his gallows. In King Saul's story, he was jealous of David that he tried to kill him; we see hate at the ultimate level here for another human being. So much hate in so many circumstances in the Bible is generated because of greed or jealousy. The same is true in our society today.

We see so much hate each time we turn the news on at night. The *Black Lives Matter* versus *Blue Lives Matter* or we *Back the Blue* campaigns are just a few of the events we see actions from frequently. Law Enforcement officers beating up, abusing, wrongfully imprisoning, and killing individuals of all races and ethnic groups, not just blacks, is on the new weekly. The groups that are rioting in America as they support the Black Lives Matter organization spiral out of control at times because one persons' hate interprets what someone else says incorrectly. So many hate crimes are committed across America each day because of ignorance and prejudices.

We should not be taking sides in the "*Lives Matters*" campaigns. If we are true Christians, ALL LIVES MATTER to us! There is no room in heaven for segregation or controlling ethnic groups. There will not be elections every four years in heaven to determine who will control the business operations. We are not going to heaven if we have these feelings and thoughts. Our feet will not leave the ground if we cannot keep the first two commandments God gave in the New Testament (love God with all your heart and love your neighbor as yourself)!

In our 21ˢᵗ Century society with so many clashes, including walls to keep people out of our country, citizenship, healthcare benefits, financial assistance, etc., we do not have to look back into the Bible for any examples of hatred. We see so much on our nightly news. If there is not a riot or storm somewhere each night, there are church shootings, school shootings, mass suicides, hate crimes against specific ethnic groups, lifestyle choices, or legal rights disputes.

God is going to hold preachers responsible for teaching on this topic. Hatred, grudges, conflicts, disputes, etc., are not going to heaven. If you cannot forgive and forget, you will find yourself left behind! The fruits of the spirit do not leave any possible ways for hatred to sneak into the life of the true born-again Christian.

VARIANCE:

The *eighth* "work of the flesh" that Paul list is *variance*. Variances are differences, alteration, discrepancy, and modification. Variance is a personality trait or character trait that evil individuals love to demonstrate. Variance shows as dissensions, debates, clashes, disagreements, disputes, discord, quarreling, arguing, fighting, debating, and conflicts. A person with a spirit of variance in their spiritual life will thrive on chaos and confusion in groups or churches. You could describe this person, even if it means stirring, as an individual who feels that they must be in control or authority. A person who must get his or her way, mess-up things, creating lies, telling lies, or by sabotaging another person's efforts. Galatians, the fifth chapter, list variances as one of the 17 works of the flesh.

The spirit of variance loves to destroy churches. The demons of Leviathan and Python love to stir this spirit up in as many members as possible. If it can get two families in a church disagreeing on whether their two children should date or not, it will be happy. It does not have to be a doctrinal issue or legal issue. If that is not possible, an argument over how the churches' money is spent will serve several purposes for Satan. When the spirit of variance makes way for Leviathan, it opens the door through sabotage, deception, and lies. Then the spirit of Leviathan takes over. This is not a spirit to play with...it is not going to heaven in any shape or form!

EMULATIONS:

The ***ninth*** "work of the flesh" that Paul list is ***emulations***. Emulations are rivalries, simulations, and imitations. Emulations are personality traits or character traits that are demonstrated by extreme displays of envying, jealousy, and deviant behavior to put down another person for the sake of lifting one to the top. In other words, a person who is always stepping on others, hurting them to get the promotion, the publicity, the reward, or raise, etc. Some people call these individuals "zealous." However, their zeal goes above the bounds of motivation. Galatians, the fifth chapter, list emulations as one of the 17 works of the flesh.

I met a Christian lady that had been raised in a minister's home. She had never made a true confession of Christ as her personal Lord and Savior. She identified herself as a Christian because her dad had pastored the church, she attended all of her life. From the age of four, she was signing in the church and playing the piano around the age of 12. She was kind and appeared to be extremely compassionate when I met her.

I was the guest speaker for a three-night revival. By the third night, I had seen every demon that possessed her acting out. The sad part was that no one in the church, including her pastor-father, knew that she was possessed. This was a very religious group of people that believed that outward appearances were the ultimate sign that you had been forgiven. I was shocked as I heard the words of hate that were expressed by her to her husband. There was no respect for him or his position in the family. She did everything except curse him. She openly cut-him-down, criticizing everything that he said. She told everyone that would listen about his past sexual affairs and how her father covered for him and his immorality. Her husband was on the deacon board and was the adult Sunday school teacher.

This lady has a story to tell about every member that was not flattering. Finally, I asked her why she was even wasting her time to attend if she felt so negatively about every member. She dropped her head and did not answer. There was one thing that I noticed about all of her stories. She was never present with the "crap would hit the fan," or the episodes would result in a church disturbance. So, I began to ask questions. I realized she was always present talking to everyone about how they felt about each situation, but she was never present when they took the actions, she was instigating with them. This is what I call a "stirrer." The spirit of Jezebel loves to stir things up, add fuel to the fire, then disappear while it explodes, but bask in the heat and the light from the explosion as the instigated events mushroom. The Jezebel spirits love to utilize the Leviathan and Python traits to accomplish their goals. It loves to see this spirit control a church. If you like to see confusion and you love to see people get "caught" in their sins, then you have the spirit of emulations in your life. This is a work of the flesh, and it WILL NOT enter Heaven!

WRATH:

The **tenth** "work of the flesh" that Paul list is **wrath**. Wrath is a demonstration of anger, rage, or fury. Wrath may present as madness. Wrath is a personality trait or character trait that is very noticeable due to the person's anger, indignation, resentment, and fierceness. They seek revenge or the public destruction of another individual. Galatians, the fifth chapter also lists wrath as one of the 17 works of the flesh.

Every time we turn on our local news, we see wrath, anger, hostility, revenge, and self-made justice! Satan uses Christians just as much as sinners to discuss their indignation, anger, and resentment with a passionate viewpoint in public. Satan desires for there to be discord, confusion, strife, deception, anger, hostility, and civil war all the time!

In this 21st Century, wrath is a daily medication fed by national network and cable network news. Each news cycle proposes topics that will induce confusion, rioting, or deviant behavior to discuss on the nightly news. If there is not something handed to them by their bosses, some reporters will create their conspiracy theories or wildly interpret a statement made by local or federal government officials to get an online discussion or debate started. Many of these "discussion starters" result in anger, wrath, rioting, and hostile open arguments on social media.

I have spoken with several reporters who have informed me that they did not intend for the discussion to go how it did or for the innocent people to be hurt. Their network bosses gave them a topic and some questions to ask for a discussion. Most admitted that they thought the discussion would be different. I am confident that their bosses knew precisely what would happen or what discussion would occur from each topic list. This is the controlling spirit of Jezebel that is not happy unless the Leviathan spirit has something to twist and Lucifer has something to deceive people with each day! As Christians and church leaders, we have to be on guard for this trap of Satan to get us involved in "wrath and riot initiations."

STRIFE:

The *eleventh* "work of the flesh" that Paul list is **strife**. To demonstrate strife is to cause discord, animosity, disagreements, contention, conflict, hatred, trouble, and fighting. A person who loves to generate strife is a person who has a personality trait or character traits that love to see contention, disputing, and conflict. It is usually a person who loves to publicly display angry words or start arguments and sit back and watch them mushroom. A person who loves strife also likes revenge and display bitterness and hatred. Galatians, the fifth chapter, list strife as one of the 17 works of the flesh.

Strife is a subtle tool that Satan loves to use in churches. He will get one person to disagree with another person, then use Jezebel and Leviathan's spirits to stir or poke the fire. As the fire grows and the smoke begins to rise, the "in secret" disagreements or conflicts become openly discussed strife. Most strife within a church results in a church split. God did not create us to have strife or to try to straighten everyone out. He created us to worship him and get souls saved. If we are doing God's will, we will not have time to be involved in strife!

SEDITIONS:

The *twelfth* "work of the flesh" that Paul list is **seditions**. To display seditions, a person will cause subversions, cause agitations, inflict treason, rabble-rousing, or incite a riot. Divisions and cliques in churches are the demonstrated characteristics of sedition. A person with a spirit of sedition loves to cause divisions, mutiny, insurrection, rebellion, revolt, treason, revolutions, and strife in a group or church to control the situation or outcomes. A popular definition is a person with a spirit of sedition is an individual who loves to cause disorder, disarray, revolts, and strife in religious groups, government, or the home. Galatians, the fifth chapter, list seditions as one of the 17 works of the flesh.

In this 21st Century of "feelings," almost any words or comments made by a pastor can generate conflict in the church. Any words not carefully weighed, once spoken into the media, can create a rebellion, revolt, revolution, or riot. Now we feel that we have to walk on eggshells verbally around generations x, y, millennials, and now generation C. God does not want us changing his word, our sermons, and our teachings to appease these younger generations. He wants us to preach the word of God with passion and accuracy. God wants us to help these generations to understand that he is a God that DOES NOT CHANGE! He wants consistency and integrity out of us, not seditions, rioting, and heresies!

HERESIES:

The *thirteenth* "work of the flesh" that Paul list is *heresies*. When a person is guilty of heresies (paganism), they resort to behavior and language that includes profanities, sacrilege (blasphemy), and results in deviations and sacrilege. Heresies are considered false witnesses and false accusations (made up or not real). Heresies can also include spreading gossip and rumors as though they are facts. They are defaming another person's character, integrity, or honesty.

Heresies are Satan's tool to use on professing Christian to cause church trouble. Satan is a liar and the Father of Liars, according to the Bible. He loves to scatter lies and deceptive truths to the point that church splits, disputes, discord, and confusion ensue!

If you are getting involved in church gossip, sharing on social media things that you have not fact-checked, or you have a fault of sharing things in a fashion to make people believe what you want them to think, even if you did not say that fact, then you have heresies active in your life! Know that this work of the flesh is NOT going to Heaven. You need deliverance! If you do not want to change, get ready 2021 is not going to be your year. You are going to see the wrath of God as he becomes your judge, not your savior. God is no longer going to allow jealous and self-righteous individuals to destroy his church anymore!

ENVYING:

The *fourteenth* "work of the flesh" that Paul list is *envying*. For an individual to demonstrate envying in their life, you will notice that they are portraying the actions of coveting (*wanting, craving, hankering*), begrudging (*to be envious or jealous*), resenting (to *have bitter or hard feelings*). These individuals crave the thing or person that they are lusting after. Envying is a character trait or emotion displayed by an individual that causes pain or ill will to others. It is an emotion that is jealous of the good or blessings that others are enjoying. It is the inability to show joy or thankfulness when others win or get what they desire or deserve. Envy is the base of all degrading and disgraceful passions in a person's life. Galatians, the fifth chapter, list envy as one of the 17 works of the flesh.

Envying and jealousy walk hand-in-hand in most people's lives that are bound by this spirit. Some Christians are master deceivers and keep the church leaders from seeing their jealous sides. They enjoy in private and under the umbrella of "compassion." They spread lies and half-truths about the individuals they are jealous or envious of to destroy their testimony, impact, or standing in the church.

This spirit is entirely disruptive and destructive to a church. If a pastor and his leadership team do not see this spirit for what it is and get control over it, this spirit will destroy the church from the inside, which is Satan's goal. If Satan cannot get outside persecution strong enough to close our doors, he will use the people inside to destroy it for him!

MURDER:

The **fifteenth** "work of the flesh" that Paul list is **murder**. (_Synonyms_: kill, slay, slaughter, or assassinate). A murder is a person with an attitude or personality trait that desires to mar or destroy others' happiness and peace. A murderous attitude is an attitude of hate, so strong that a person wants to "kill" good things for others. This mentality can also try to kill physically (murder other human beings). Galatians, the fifth chapter, lists murder as one of the 17 works of the flesh.

There are more ways to "murder" a person, their life, career, or ministry than with knives, guns, and weapons. The worst form of murder in the church is gossip, jealousy, envying, and heresies. When we share information that we have not fact-checked, we attempt to murder our fellow brothers and sisters in Christ. We are destroying their testimony and effectiveness.

There may not be a prosecutor and detective investigating your actions, but you are as guilty of murder as the person who shoots another person dead! Over the years, I have seen many self-righteous, self-centered Christians murder the new converts with judgmental accusations and gossip. The Lord witnessed to me in the 1980s to teach my church that this was spiritual murder and that God would judge it as such! I would hate to arrive in Heaven to have God turn me away from the gates with this remark. "Sorry, Charlie, you cannot enter Heaven. You violated my commandments and had the spirit of murder inside of you. That is one of the works of the flesh, and it shall not enter here. Sorry, but you are going to be cast into the lake of fire!" I do not want any appearance of the "spirit of murder" in my life on any level. I have to make it in the rapture!

DRUNKENNESS:

The *sixteenth* "work of the flesh" that Paul list is *drunkenness*. Drunkenness is a state of being drunk. Drunkenness (Alcoholism/ Intoxication) is also a condition where the individual is out of control of their normal functions due to alcohol or mind-altering drugs that have caused a total loss of inhibitions. Galatians, the fifth chapter, list drunkenness as one of the 17 works of the flesh.

I will not debate the issue of social drinking or drinking a couple of tablespoons of wine before and after a meal for your stomach condition. That is another topic for another book. However, I will say that this scripture is referring to drunkenness. Being intoxicated with drugs, alcohol, and prescription drugs to the point that you pass out, do not recall what you are doing or have done, or lose control of your inhibitions, is a sin. It does not matter whether it is legal or illegal.

Public drunkenness leads to lewd and lascivious behavior and dress. Those behaviors do not please God. They do not bring honor and glory to God, so they should not be present in our lives. Allowing one work of the flesh to have a small hold in your life is extremely dangerous. All of these spirits bring other spirits with them.

REVELING:

The *seventeenth* "work of the flesh" that Paul list is *reveling*. Reveling is considered partying, delighting, and drinking. A person who is a reveler or involved in reveling is an individual who is engaged in rioting, lewd, and boisterous feastings with obscene music and their sinful activities like orgies. A ubiquitous display of lewd behavior during the Roman Rule over Israel, during Paul's days, were sexual orgies committed in the temples for the idol Gods. Galatians, the fifth chapter, lists reveling as one of the 17 works of the flesh. God expects us to demonstrate the fruits of the spirit daily in our lives. God also desires for us to walk away from situations and ignore the works of the flesh. This behavior is the minimum acceptable behavior for a Christian.

Reveling for the 21st Century includes partying, drinking, drugs, alcohol, sexually promiscuous behavior, sexual orgies, cohabitation, sexual perversion. The obscene and vulgar language used in many rap songs and R & B songs is embarrassing to a moral person. Those songs promote a lifestyle that supports all 17 of the works of the flesh. Those songs, words, and lifestyles are not entering Heaven. God placed us here on earth to worship him. We have drifted very far away from that purpose. However, to enter Heaven or be rapture ready, we will need to be worshipping God, not promoting the actions and lifestyle of Satan or evil!

Songs that threaten our policy and government are not scriptural. Songs that incite anger, hate, hostility, wrath, and vengeance are not godly. They are promoting revellings and will not enter Heaven. To some, this may seem harsh. But do not get justified just yet. I am not through. The same holds true for country music, bluegrass, pop, rock-n-roll, and other secular music. If the music promotes lifestyle choices that do not support God's purpose for your life, then it is wrong! If your music destroys lives instead of building them up, it is wrong. If your music choices promote any of the works of the flesh, like adultery, fornication, lewdness, envy, jealousy, and pride, it is wrong too! Our minds do not need to be Satan's garbage can. Our minds should be meditating on scriptures, praise and worship, uplifting Christian songs, and the work or purpose God has designated for us.

My interpretation of the works of the flesh may appear to be too strict to some reading this book. If you feel this way, do not throw this book down. Keep reading. Make a note in your journal to conduct your own research on this topic. If you will read, pray, search God's word, and sincerely ask God to show you what he wants in your life, he will answer you! You will be amazed at what God shows you. Your list of convictions may be stricter or more lenient than mine. That is not for me to judge. That is between you and God. Remember, approach God openly and honestly. You do not want anything to keep you out of the rapture!

It is easy to let pastors and other Christians convince you that a Christian's life is hard and almost impossible for you to live. So many pastors preach with a list of "do's and don'ts." If you listen to their list of requirements, you will give up and never follow Jesus Christ. If you decide to push forward and try to be a Christian because of your fear of hell or fear of missing the rapture, you will never know spiritual success and happiness! The way to salvation is not a "slave's" path. It is not a miserable lifestyle of poverty and dread.

Instead, a Christian's life should be one of peace, hope, love, forgiveness, happiness, and success. It is not God's desire for you to be homeless, sick, dirty, and ashamed to present yourself in public. God is a God of love! He loves to bless his children and help them. God wants us to prosper and be in good health, "even as our soul prospers!" (KJV, 2020).

Salvation is so simple. It is not hard to accept, nor challenging to live. It is a lifestyle change that takes time when we get saved. This transition period is not because it is hard, but because it is a different focus. When you begin making this transition, you will find that your friends who are not Christians will not understand. They may decide not to be friends with you anymore. Salvation is a gift that God freely gives to us. We do not earn it or work our way to that promotion. It is freely given the moment we ask for it. Each day of our lives, we will make mistakes. We are human, and we do not always think like our heavenly Father. However, the more we read and study his word, the more we desire to be Christ-like.

Once we accept Christ as our Lord and Savior, we should begin studying his word and praying each day. The more we read and pray, the more we will desire the will of God for our lives. Our Christian walk does not have to be a walk of fear of a taskmaster God. We do not have to walk in fear of damnation, punishment, or lightning striking us. I met a lady about twenty years ago that told me she prayed for every hour during the day, asking God not to punish her for her sins because she was afraid that God would kill her on the spot for her thoughts and deeds. She felt like God would do to her what he did to the boys who made fun of the prophet of God, Elisha, in the Old Testament. God sent an animal to kill them. We must understand that to err is human. To receive forgiveness is our birthright!

You can lay aside all fear and condemnation that Satan has tried to place on your life. Simply strive each day to have the fruits of the spirit in your life. When you do not demonstrate humility or longsuffering, ask God to forgive you and help you the next time. If you keep having a problem with one particular person, ask God to show you how to handle that individual or control your reactions around them. Remember, this Christian walk is a walk or lifestyle to be more like Jesus. We want to show love, mercy, hope, and forgiveness to everyone like he did while he was here on earth!

The next step is to study the work of the flesh. Try each day not to have any of these in your life. If you have habits that you feel fall into one of the categories of the works of the flesh, it may take time to get deliverance—notably, drug and alcohol-related habits. You may even require professional help. Do not let negative, narrow-minded individuals cause you to drop out of church. Keep praying daily. God will help you make it through the withdrawals.

Salvation is a gift received by faith that creates a new heart in us. That new heart longs for the things of God. We want to serve God, love him, get closer to him, and pursue His will for our lives. As we make these lifestyle changes, changes will come that affect our personality, appearance, attitude, actions, and habits. We gradually change as we grow in God's word. If you do not have the works of the flesh in your life, you have accepted Jesus Christ as your Lord and Savior, and you are demonstrating love toward your neighbor as you would yourself, you will portray the fruits of the spirit. And you will be rapture ready if you are obedient to what God lays on your heart or impresses you to do for him.

Isaiah 41:10: Fear thou not; for I am with thee: be not dismayed; for I am thy God: I will strengthen thee; yea, I will help thee; yea, I will uphold thee with the right hand of my righteousness. (KJV, 2020).

Remember, *fear* creates doubt. *Doubt* causes faith to leave. Without faith in God, we have fear, no peace, and no blessings. We want to ensure that we keep doubt out of our lives. We want to walk in faith. The Apostle Paul said that we must put on the *shield of faith* daily to fight off Satan's darts. When you visualize our faith keeping Satan from hitting us with his darts like a shield, it becomes easy to understand why knowing god's word and using it in our lives each day is essential! Our spiritual armor is crucial to us living a victorious life and reaping God's blessings that he has for us for this decade (2020 through 2030)!

Chapter Four:
THE PYTHON SPIRIT

This section was taken from my book, "Why am I not Living a Victorious Life?" If you want more information on this topic and how to live a victorious life, then contact us for a copy of this book. The Kindle Version is available through Amazon.com. The comments made in this chapter in message boxes like this one will indicate what new content was added to assist the reader with why this topic is relevant for this book.

Several scriptures discussed in the Bible about spirits mentions the python spirit using different terms. All spirits can possess a person. However, in most cases, if the spirit can influence or oppress the person and accomplish what it desires, then there is no need for possession. However, after a long period of controlling an individual, these spirits automatically move into the individual and possess them. Under possession, a spirit can thoroughly control an individual and cause them to do things that their family and friends would think impossible for them to do. An example would be a loving, happy, care-free person who becomes so angry that they go to work one day and kill all their co-workers.

Contrary to popular opinion, I have seen people that were possessed and did not realize it. It is rare for a person raised in the church and understands the true gospel of Jesus Christ to be possessed and not know it. But it is prevalent for people to be influenced and oppressed without realizing it. I have seen pastors with 40-years of ministerial experience oppressed and controlled by demonic spirits without recognizing that these spirits had taken them over.

I do not share these things with you to put fear in you. I share them so that you can learn to recognize these spirits and prevent them from controlling your lives and churches. As you study the next couple of chapters, I want you to keep an open mind. Know that it is not an unforgivable sin to be influenced by spirits, but it is the spiritual damnation of your soul to not do anything about it once you recognize the signs.

As you carefully examine your life with honesty for any signs of influences by these spirits, God will show you what is attached and what is trying to attach to you. If you see any signs of attachment or influence, make sure you begin fasting and praying for God to help you get deliverance and freedom from their power. You can break free once you learn how to recognize them. Ignorance is the key that Satan uses to keep the church in the dark about these spirits. So, defy Satan and learn all that you can to be set free and live a victorious life.

Acts 16:16-24: And it came to pass, as we went to prayer, a certain damsel possessed with a spirit of divination met us, which brought her masters much gain by soothsaying: The same followed Paul and us, and cried, saying, these men are the servants of the most high God, which shew unto us the way of salvation. And this did she many days. But Paul, being grieved, turned and said to the spirit, I command thee in the name of Jesus Christ to come out of her. And he came out the same hour. And when her masters saw that the hope of their gains was gone, they caught Paul and Silas, and drew them into the marketplace unto the rulers, and brought them to the magistrates, saying, these men, being Jews, do exceedingly trouble our city, and teach customs, which are not lawful for us to receive, neither to observe, being Romans. And the multitude rose up together against them: and the magistrates rent off their clothes, and commanded to beat them. And when they had laid many stripes upon them, they cast them into prison, charging the jailor to keep them safely: Who, having received such a charge, thrust them into the inner prison, and made their feet fast in the stocks. (KJV, 2020).

The python spirit can attack anyone, especially spirit-filled Christians that it hates. Being attack by the python spirit is not the same thing as being oppressed or possessed. A person who is oppressed or possessed by the python spirit will be the person who attacks the church. In most cases, it is an influential Christian that attacks the church leaders or the pastor. As you see in this scripture, Paul and Silas were attacked by the python spirit on this damsel. It was not because Paul and Silas were not praying. This spirit wanted to stop them because it knew if Paul and Silas got the people in this area praying and dedicated in their walk with the Lord that this spirit was about to lose control. Plus, the owners of this damsel were going to lose money.

I am sure this python spirit was planning to attack Paul and Silas, knowing that Paul would try to cast it out. This spirit knew that once the magistrates lost their "cash cow," that they would humiliate Paul and Silas in public and would stop them by throwing them in jail. This spirit hoped that Paul and Silas would curl up in the fetal position in prison, lick their wounds, and have a self-pity party. However, this spirit did not realize that Paul and Silas were going to do the opposite. They were going to praise God for the trial, sing, and pray.

The python spirit gets its hold on most ministers because they complain and gossip instead of going to God in prayer. It is easier to complain when attacked than to enter into spiritual warfare. It is human nature for us to withdraw when attacked and lick our wounds. But God is our deliverer and avenger. All we have to do is give our spiritual attacks from Satan to God. He will fight our battles. However, Satan knows that his most powerful battlefield, the one where he usually has the home advantage, is our minds! He loves to remind us of our past, all mistakes made over the years, and to convince us that God is upset with us! We cannot give Satan this level of power in our lives. We must remain firm in our faith in God.

In one of the dreams, God showed me how to determine who in the church was severely oppressed by demonic spirits and who was possessed. God showed me the struggles of the current church (world-wide) and various well-known ministries across the United States. These evangelical ministries' specific actions were pointed out in the dreams, especially why they displeased God so much. God also showed me that the focus that he intended for the church was "winning souls," not numbers, programs, buildings, and lavish lifestyles for the leadership teams. God also shared with me about Christians' evil hearts that Satan had trapped them into accepting their evil hearts without realizing it.

After these dreams, I began searching the scriptures for directions on presenting this information in this book. I realized that this Python spirit oppresses and depresses Christians while controlling the pastors in so many churches. As God kept giving me dreams that explained what he wanted in this book, I began to fast and pray. As I researched the various stories from the Bible and other Christian patriarchs that had moved on to their heavenly homes, I realized that there were specific characteristics for how this spirit works and destroys.

It became apparent that this message that God wanted to be delivered to his people was instructing them to take back control of their churches from Satan, train their congregations in spiritual warfare, and lead them into victorious living. It was never God's intention for his church here on earth to be beaten down, depressed, stressed, financially struggling, sick, and emotionally stunted. God wanted the church living in victory, even amid trials and tribulations. He wanted his "bride" to have something that the world would desire so much that they would be attracted to come to church. However, we find ourselves witnessing to people who reply, "Why should I go to church? I am in better shape mentally, physically, emotionally, and financially than anyone in that church! What is their God going to do for me that I have not already accomplished?" We must have something that the world longs for and desires enough to step out of their comfort zones and join us!

In addition to sinners not wanting to step down to the level of defeat that the church is putting on display, they are not impressed by how we are letting spirits control our churches. Recently I have been in two churches where the pastor admitted to me that "several families that had been in the church since it started" had managed to run off all of the recent converts.

Some churches make Christianity so hard that no one can live it, not even the individuals preaching this legalistic doctrine. On the other side, we see churches that are so liberal in their viewpoints that they act abusing grace. The pastors in these churches are afraid to preach on sin because they might run the new convert off or lose the tithes of more senior church members who have these sins in their lives or the lives of their children who are attending.

Both sides are wrong. God expects a "middle of the road" approach out of all Christians. Our character expectations cannot be ultra-liberal nor legalistic. Instead, we must reach the lost, disciple them, and help everyone to grow spiritually. We have to learn how awesome God's grace is, how to use it, and the beauty of humbly submitting to God's will in our lives. Then we need to learn about our "job descriptions as Christians," which is the fruits of the spirit. These are the expected outcomes in our lives.

After we have mastered an understanding of the fruits of the spirit and prayed until we have a desire (hunger) for God's word (the Bible), we need to learn about the works of the flesh. Paul told the Galatians that the 17 works of the flesh were an abomination unto God and would not enter into heaven! Yes, Christianity is this simple! We are the ones that make it so hard and unmanageable. God wants us to live victoriously. The Bible has given us all of the tools that we need to accomplish a victorious life!

As I began researching these spirits and demons, it became apparent what the Apostle Paul was talking about when he discussed the works of the flesh. Paul shared with us about the spirits that loved to oppress and control churches. He talked about the spirits that caused preachers and pastors to alter their sermons to please people and keep them happy. So, Paul brought us back to remembrance of a few simple truths…God wants us to forgive and love without limits….plus demonstrate the fruits of the spirit in our lives. No sin…no works of the flesh….no demonic oppression or possession, just simple, pure love and forgiveness!

As I began to list the results, I began to notice a list of characteristics forming. After a detailed review of this list, I realized that these are the character traits or behaviors present in the lives of anyone who is demon-possessed. These traits may not be present at all times, just when the demon acts out through that person. If a person has more than 50% of these characteristics, they are evil, and they are not a born-again Christian, even if they profess to be one. There is a 90% chance that this individual is not only oppressed but possessed. As you read this list of characteristics, pray and ask God to show you if you have any of these characteristics in your life or ministry. If you conclude that you some of these characteristics in your life, pray and seek the help of your pastor or trusted prayer partner to get deliverance. If you are symptom-free, but these characteristics are present in your pastor or church leaders, begin praying to know where to go to church. You need a new church!

To understand the python spirit, we need to define what this spirit is, how it attacks, how it attaches itself to Christians, and how it possesses individuals. This spirit is best described by looking at the characteristics of this spirit.

The characteristics of demonic oppression and possession listed below will be present in the lives of any person who has allowed these spirits to take control of their lives and ministries. As you review this list, put a checkmark beside the ones that are present in your life. If one of these characteristics is present in your pastor or church leadership team, put an asterisk (*) beside the characteristic. <u>If you mark at least five of these characteristics as being present in your life, you need to seek ministerial help because you are oppressed. If you have ten or more, you are possessed and need deliverance</u>. If you have put an asterisk more than ten asterisks marked, you need to find a new church. Do not have that pastor pray over you. He will not be able to help you get deliverance because he is possessed.

CHARACTERISTICS OF THE PYTHON SPIRIT:

To be successful in spiritual warfare against the python spirit, you must be able to recognize the characteristics of this spirit. Many Christians are ignorant of Satan's deceptive tools, and they do not understand how to bind Satan or why it is essential to bind him. You cannot be victorious without binding Satan through the blood of Jesus Christ. You cannot bind a spirit or guard against it if you do not recognize the spirit in action. Especially when these spirits are "under-cover."

1) Deceitful to the extreme and very good at their game of deceit
2) Irritable, excitable about the least thing, losing control easily
3) Arrogant and Egotistical
4) Selfish and controlling
5) Self-centered, all about them
6) Never see them happy when others are being blessed
7) They can do everything better than anyone else
8) Always finding fault with others in the church
9) Always seeking praise for what they do
10) Feel that no one can sing as good as them or cook better than them. They must feel that they are the best and will argue with you if you think you are better than them
11) They must have their way always. It does not matter what the majority wants. They must get their way, or they will not participate
12) They are two-faced with everyone. Appearing to be your best friend, they will get all of the info they can from you and then tell everyone.
13) They are compulsive liars that lie without thinking. They love to make lies. They get excited when their lies start a confusion.
14) They are compulsive individuals
15) Most demonstrate aggressive compulsive behaviors
16) Most do not like animals or anything or anyone that requires them to show love and patience. They are never good with special needs children or individuals with mental issues.
17) Those who profess to like animals will be cruel to them when others are not watching. They are also abusive to children in private.
18) They talk to others with a loud, condescending voice
19) They will speak to their children and grandchildren by calling them names and speaking doom over them. For example, a Grandfather in anger may call a grandchild a devil, "Oh my God, Jonathon is just

a little devil." Or say to their child, "Come here, you little devil, I am going to teach you a lesson." This person is demon-possessed, even if they do not have any other characteristics on this list.

20) They have a spirit of compromise concerning personal convictions. They agree with whoever they are talking with, then spread rumors about them behind their backs.

21) These individuals are usually racist and sometimes demonstrate dogmatic type behaviors. It may not initially be present, but if you stay around them in settings away from the church, you will see the judgmental looks and hear the rude comments they make about other ethnic groups.

22) They love to see strife and confusion in the church.

23) They love to control the pastor, his wife, and the board.

24) If they cannot control the members, they will want them to leave.

25) Clings to new members trying to control them, get them in their clique, or run them off.

26) They love to spread rumors and gossip about the pastor and his family or others working in leadership positions in the church.

27) They are master manipulators that are always jealous when others are blessed or receive miracles, evident by envy and covetousness.

28) They are always showing signs of jealousy because they can never be happy when others are being blessed.

29) Always showing signs of envy because they cannot stand to see any miracles occur to those who are not in their clique.

30) It always wants to control the money, how it is spent and loves to see confusion started over money in the church.

The feelings that the python spirit can generate when attacking you (listed above) can be overwhelming at times in our lives. These feelings can manifest with physical conditions and ailments. This is one of its covers. It can attack you while making you think that there is a medical condition in your body. If you have been experiencing aches and pains that the doctors cannot find a "cause" for or there is no medical reason for those symptoms, begin fasting and praying. God will show you what is in your life or home that is causing those spirits to have control in your life.

The python spirit's primary goal is to stop you or at least make you ineffective. If this spirit can achieve this hindrance level by making you physically incapable of performing your ministry duties, it has won! If you are around a person possessed by this spirit, you can easily recognize this spirit in action because it will always be on the prowl to attack. It will always be looking for faults in people and programs that it can criticize. These attacks have one goal, stop the work of God!

Contrary to the popular new age teachings, a professing Christian and pastor can be demon-possessed. If they are genuinely living righteous lives, dedicated to God's word, possession is not possible. However, remember how I mentioned the counterfeit prophets earlier? Well, pastors can be men or women of God who were at one time truly anointed (Just like Balaam), but as they began to compromise for money, things began to happen, until they are deceived, and the spirit of God has left them like it did Samson. We must remember that to be successful in our spiritual war against the python spirit, we must know and recognize all of the above characteristics in those around us. This spirit is very creative, and it can hide in plain sight for years without being detected in most churches.

Judges 16:20: And she said The Philistines be upon thee, Samson. And he awoke out of his sleep, and said, I will go out as at other times before, and shake myself. And he wist not that the LORD was departed from him. (KJV, 2020).

Another Old Testament story talks about the anointing or the power of God departing from someone, and they did not even recognize it was King Saul. God anointed him through the prophet Samuel to be the first King of Israel. He was anointed in battles and blessed by God on many occasions over the years that he was king. But Saul disobeyed God, and the power and anointing departed from him.

Whether you believe everything as strictly as I do, is not the issue here. I am sharing my thoughts and personal convictions as I explain what God showed me. Know that I want you to be rapture ready too. I want you to have a relationship with God as I enjoy. I know that God talks to me almost daily. He will do the same for you if you approach him with the right attitude! God desires a relationship with you. He will show you what he wants in your life!

I Samuel 16:14: But the Spirit of the LORD departed from Saul, and an evil spirit from the LORD troubled him. (KJV, 2020).

The **python spirit's characteristics** listed above describes the most common spirit that affects churches today. The python spirit wraps around a church and chokes the very life out of it. It can do the same thing to a minister or church member. If you are a pastor and you have been struggling with your church board or membership, pray and ask God to show you who in your church has these spirits operating in their lives. Hopefully, they are only oppressed by this spirit, and you can help them get a deliverance. The longer you let this spirit control, the harder it will be to get rid of it.

If this spirit has made its way into your church leadership team, you will need to have God's direction and guidance to get it out of your church. This spirit loves to control and can destroy a church from the inside quicker than anything else. Do not make any efforts to rid your church of these people until you have spent time fasting, reading, praying, etc. This spirit does not give up just because you ask. You have to get aggressive through the blood and name of Jesus with this spirit to see it cast out of your church. Study this book and pray; God will show you which steps to take next.

Luke 10:20: *Notwithstanding in this rejoice not that the spirits are subject unto you; but rather rejoice, because your names are written in heaven.* (KJV, 2020).

BEING ATTACHED BY THE PYTHON SPIRIT:

Satan loves to use individuals that are oppressed by spirits to keep confusion, dissension, strife, and confusion in each church that has a pastor who is trying to lead people to live victoriously and get souls saved. When I visit churches where the pastor has asked us to come minister and help encourage the "core membership" of his church to hang-on through the trials, I see church leaders that are being attacked by this python spirit.

If your pastor has been acting a little "off" lately, stressed, sick, and extremely tired, review this list below. See if you recognize any of the symptoms of being attacked listed below. Suppose you see any of these signs because praying for your pastor. Fast if you feel led to and enter into intercessory prayer.

77

WHEN THE PYTHON SPIRIT ATTACKS OR TARGETS SOMEONE, THEY WILL EXPERIENCE THE FOLLOWING PHYSICAL AND MENTAL SYMPTOMS

1. Public humiliation
2. Slander and false accusations against them
3. Depressed feelings that you are not sure where they originated. For ministers, if this spirit is in the church, it can make it hard to minister at times.
4. Feelings of dread on the inside daily, including panic attacks.
5. They have to "pump themselves up" or use various mental strategies to "psych themselves" into even going to church
6. Feeling like something is squeezing the life out of them
7. Weariness, fatigue, mental, and physical exhaustion
8. Desire to run away from all of the confusion and the church
9. Desires to give up on the church attendance, or ministry
10. Loss of your passion or desire to read and pray
11. Feelings of being overwhelmed and helpless
12. The helplessness that leads to hopelessness and loss of faith
13. Loss of desire to attend church or socialize with other Christians.
14. Feelings that lead to contemplating suicide
15. Feelings that lead to contemplating giving up their minister's license and walking away from everything church related
16. Difficulty preaching or teaching when this spirit is attacking
17. Feeling of choking, being stifled, or chest pressure while you are preaching can indicate that this spirit is in the audience trying to block you from delivering God's word

If you know someone experiencing these symptoms, get a copy of this book into their hands. Talk to them about what is happening so they can engage in spiritual warfare and get loose from the hold that this spirit is trying to get on their lives. These spirits' number one targets are preachers, teachers, and church leaders. Remember that prayer is the key to victory over this spirit, and fasting is the key to deliverance!

Suppose a person is oppressed or possessed by the python spirit, and it is using that person to destroy the church. In that case, those individuals will demonstrate specific behaviors that you can easily identify. You do not have to know the person, spend time with them, or accept them into your inner circle to know if they are possessed. You can spend 15 to 20 minutes observing them in, before, or after a church service and know if they are possessed or not.

THE PERSON OPPRESSED OR POSSESSED BY THE PYTHON SPIRIT WILL DEMONSTRATE THE FOLLOWING BEHAVIORS

When you are in the presence of a person who has become possessed or oppressed by the python spirit, you will see those individuals demonstrate the following behaviors and attitudes. These spirits are master-minds of deceit. They can hide in plain sight and deceive you. Make sure you keep your spiritual eyes open at all times for the following behaviors.

1. It always has an *arrogant* and *egotistical* spirit. If you observe closely, you will notice severe, deep-rooted *narcissistic* behavior. No one does it better than them!
2. A *religious* spirit that is very *self-righteous*, always feeling that it is saved, and rapture ready, while demonstrating at least five of the works of the flesh in their lives at all times.
3. An extremely *self-centered* spirit that requires them to be the center of attention at all times. They put themselves in the limelight all the time, making every issue and situation about them.
4. They will *interrupt the move of God* in the service with their self-righteous demonstrations, usually under the pretense of "Pastor, the Lord witnessed to me that Sis. B needs to sing song x!" This type of interruption usually occurs when the pastor has decided to sing another song or change the order of the service to prayer, etc. However, out of fear of being accused of being disrespectful, the pastor will agree to the suggestion. This *compromise* results in the suppression of the Holy Spirit. God may have planned to heal people in a prayer service, save souls at the end of the sermon, or

deliver several people from habit. This spirit's goal is to prevent the move of God in the service!

5. This spirit *distracts and acts out* in an attempt to blow up situations and keep individuals from doing what God has planned for them to do in the service.

6. This spirit can even speak "truths and scriptures," as this damsel did when Paul was preaching. This spirit will speak truths to deceive the pastor and other members into thinking that it is a real move of God when all it wants to do is destroy the church's prayer life or the real move of the spirit that God had planned.

7. The purpose of this spirit attacking you or your pastor is to distract you and upset you, where you will not have time to pray. He does not want you reading and prayer. He wants you to be stressed and frustrated so he can keep you away from your purpose.

8. If this spirit can stop your lifeline (reading and praying), then it can squeeze the life out of the members until it kills the church. It prefers to use grumbling, complaining, negative talk, and confessions of defeat to stop us your "spiritual well" so that you cannot receive the blessings intended for you.

9. This spirit loves to remind people of their past and beat them down over their past to keep them out of God's will.

10. The python spirit is a coiling spirit, just like the actions of the snake it is named after. It loves to wrap around a church and squeeze the life out of that church by cutting out the prayer lives of Christians.

11. It loves to convince pastors that there is no need for an altar in the church. Once we eliminate our lifeline to God (prayer), then this spirit becomes a stronghold in our churches controlling and possessing as many members as possible.

12. This spirit paves the way for the leviathan spirit and the jezebel spirits to possess the person. So, you may see some of the characteristics of these two spirits also present in this person's life.

If you enter the home of a person who has allowed this spirit to attach itself to them and to control them, their house, family, and marriage, you will feel a "life squeeze" like the snake it is named after. The python snake squeezes the life out of its prey. This demon spirit squeezes the life out of a home or family. When a born-again, spirit-filled, praying Christian walks into their home, you will feel something oppressing you, and it will feel like something is trying to squeeze the life out of you. This feeling is because you have entered the "home" of this spirit. It is territorial. It does not want you there. It wants this home to remain in darkness and under its control.

Earlier this year, just a few months after the COVID-19 pandemic began, I had to go by the home of someone who was a church leader in a church I had pastored several years ago. This person had called and asked if I could write a recommendation letter for them. It was an insignificant matter in my eyes, but this former church member felt that she needed this recommendation letter. As I was writing the letter, I kept feeling the Holy Spirit say no. I did not understand why. So, I continued to write the letter. However, when I arrived at this person's house, I wanted to talk to her and her husband before giving them the letter. I have learned to "try the spirits" and allow the Holy Spirit to guide you.

I stood outside talking with her (compliance with our state's social distancing-stay-at-home orders). I wanted to speak to her and her husband. After about 10 minutes, I asked if her husband was at home. I explained that I wanted to talk with him for a few minutes. She finally said, "Well, come inside. You have your mask on, and I have my mask. I will have my husband put his mask on. He is in his recliner and does not feel like coming outside. So, come in." At that point, she opened the door and hollered at her husband to put his mask on.

Almost immediately upon sitting down on the couch in their living room, I recognized that the wife was possessed with the Leviathan spirit. The husband was under the control of the Leviathan and Python spirits. I began to ask questions, and I realized why the Holy Spirit told me not to provide this recommendation letter. While I was pastoring this church, I never entered their home, so I do not know if this spirit was inhabiting their house during my tenure at that church or not. I know that at times, I felt that the Leviathan spirit was trying to oppress this woman's husband because of things he would say in church meetings. However, I never paid attention to his rants. He was not a church leader.

After about five minutes, the Holy Spirit answer my prayer and let me recognize why he did not want me to give them this letter of recommendation. This woman began telling me how their current pastor was acting and what he was doing wrong. She said that they had to get him out before he bankrupted the church and it split. She said that half of the members were on the pastor's side. Then she went into detail about why they were wrong. We know that we will lose those members when he leaves, but that is ok. If they are going to be for a pastor like him, then we do not need them in our church."

At this point, it was my time to be shocked. This was an Assembly of God minister that I had worked with in years past. When I was the pastor of this Assembly of God church, he had visited and ministered in the church. I did not know a lot about his personal life or the operation of the gifts of the spirit in his ministry, but I felt like he was a true man of God. I advised them against this type of attack on their pastor. Then the truth came out. "Well, preacher, we wanted a letter from you to give to the district officials. We know that they know you and will trust what you say. We know that we are right, but they do not. They only know what the pastor is telling them. The district wants to put us out of the church, not the preacher!"

With the truth out, I had my answer. I politely told them that I could not get involved. My reason was that this would be against the Assembly of God's operational policies for a former pastor to be involved in the current politics. I also quoted the scriptures about honoring and respecting those in authority. Then I left, went home, and began fasting and praying. I prayed for their pastor that God would open his eyes and let him know that he needed to leave that church. In less than six weeks from me walking out the door of their home, their pastor had resigned. This lady was diagnosed with cancer and her husband with a severe heart condition and cancer. It never pays to put your tongue on God's anointed or to see harm toward the pastor of your church. If you do not like him or her, leave! Do not talk about them, defame them, or try to control them. This will bring the wrath of God upon your life quicker than anything except blaspheming the Holy Ghost.

Spiritual warfare is not for the faint at heart or the Sunday only Christian. Spiritual warfare requires commitment, dedication, and integrity. Most Christians and a large number of ministers never learn to walk in spiritual victory because they will not make the sacrifices and commitments needed to engage in spiritual warfare. Some victories are only won on the spiritual battlefields of our mine. Others are only won on our knees in fasting and prayer!

HOW THIS SPIRIT GETS CONTROL IN OUR CHURCHES:

Years ago, in our public-school system, prayer was eliminated from the daily routine. As this python spirit began to wrap around our schools and apply pressure to the staff, who feel overwhelmed, helpless, and desperate. Once hopelessness sets in, despair takes up residence. This is the number one reason that there has been so much teen suicide in the past two decades. The increase of illegal drugs, prescription drugs, and alcohol use by teenagers and college kids has also impacted the suicide rates of the 14 to 28-year-old group.

The python spirit loves to remind people of their past mistakes or things that they have done. It likes to attach itself by placing guilt, self-pity, selfishness, and depressive spirits on the person it is attacking. This spirit specializes in opening old wounds and gouging in them to the point of causing severe pain and situations that tempt you into compromising. It desires to squeeze the life out of your church, ministry, and your personal spiritual life!

This spirit works very hard to try to get you involved in grumbling, rumors, complaining, gossiping, separations, dissensions, quarrels, isolations, bondage, sulking, withdrawal, disobedience, hopelessness, and suicidal behavior. Know that the python spirit can cause you to commit suicide or have a nervous breakdown if it is not dealt with or cast out.

The python spirit has a few goals that it strives for when it is attacking an individual or church. Its top priority is to cut off or at least rendered ineffective your prayer life. Your prayer life is your spiritual oxygen. It serves the same purpose as oxygen to your heart and lungs. Oxygen is the critical ingredient that keeps your heart functioning and beating properly. Prayer is the oxygen that keeps your spiritual life alive and pumping.

WHY GOD WANTS THIS MESSAGE TO THE CHURCH TO INCLUDE THE INFORMATION ON THE PYTHON SPIRIT:

The python spirit is not a spirit that you should play with, appease, or try to negotiate within your life or church. This spirit is extremely deceptive and religious. It is a master of deception and destruction. When pastors compromise to keep this spirit happy or calm in their churches, it always destroys the church and their ministry.

I have witnessed numerous ministers give up their ministerial license and walk away from the call of God on their lives because they played with this spirit, trying to keep the money it brought into their churches flowing. You can never win against this spirit, except to allow God to excise it from your church!

Do not allow Satan to "choke" out your prayer life or the move of God in your churches. Protect your altar services and the gifts of the spirit that are operating in your church or ministry. Satan does not want the church to experience the power of God. Satan does not want us to live in victory! But remember, "He that is in you is strong that he that is in the world!" (KJV, 2020). See the scriptures below:

I John 4:4-6: Ye are of God, little children, and have overcome them: because greater is he that is in you than he that is in the world. They are of the world; therefore, speak they of the world and the world heareth them. We are of God; he that knoweth God heareth us; he that is not of God hearth, not us. Hereby know we the spirit of truth and the spirit of error. (KJV, 2020).

We can have power over any spirit that comes into our lives and our churches if we do not compromise or play with the spirit. The goal that Satan desires for your church is for it to lose its power! Therefore, from 2020 forward, we need our goals to ensure that our churches return to God's real power and keep it operating at all times in their churches.

When you study, fast, and pray, God's anointing will be present. The true anointing will always upset the possessed and oppressed individuals in your church. When they begin to act out (they will!), do not back down, but stand firm in the faith, knowing that the God that lives inside of you is stronger than the demons attacking you or acting out through these individuals. Do not compromise, to keep the peace, church attendance, and tithe payers coming. Allow God to send who he wants. Stand firm with love and humility on the word of God! Then God will have your back!

The Apostle Paul, in Ephesian 6:10-18, shares with us about the "Armor of God" needed for spiritual battle. We need to make sure that we are putting on this full armor each day before leaving our homes. See scripture below:

Ephesians 6:10-18: Finally, my brethren, be strong in the Lord, and the power of his might. Put on the whole armour of God, that ye may be able to stand against the wiles of the devil. For we wrestle not against flesh and blood, but against principalities, against powers, against the rulers of the darkness of this world, against spiritual wickedness in high places. Wherefore take unto you the whole armour of God, that ye may be able to withstand in the evil day, and having done all, to stand;

Stand, therefore, having your loins girt about with truth and having on the breastplate of righteousness. And your feet shod with the preparation of the gospel of peace. Above all, taking the shield of faith, wherewith ye shall be able to quench all the fiery darts of the wicked. And take the helmet of salvation and the sword of the spirit which is the word of God. Praying with all prayer and supplication in the spirit and watching thereunto with all perseverance and supplication for all saints. (KJV, 2020).

The study of our spiritual armor, the power it provides, and the anointing are essential for every Christian believer. Most Christians have heard about spiritual armor, even discussed it in detail in Sunday school classes, but never implemented it in their spiritual lives. This book is not large enough for me to explain this topic thoroughly. However, book number 11 of "*The Keys to Victorious Living Series*" titled "**The Spiritual Warrior**" covers this topic in detail. Once you master this book and the "**Why am I not Living a Christian Life?**" book in 2020-2021, know that in January of 2022, "**The Spiritual Warrior**" and "**The Prayer Warrior**" books will be available to help you through a detailed study on being a spiritual warrior and a prayer warrior. This spiritual journey is not something you read once, master, and go into battle next week. It takes months to study and years of practice to perfect. Daily spiritual warfare is essential, so please keep studying God's word and asking for the Holy Spirit's help with this gift that God has promised to every Christian who will ask and commit to the learning process.

THE BIBLE HAS THE ANSWER TO ALL OUR QUESTIONS:

It has instructions for all our spiritual battle needs. It is imperative to read our Bibles daily and read through the Bible at least once per year! When Satan comes to you with a spirit of fear or doubt, turn to your Bible and begin to search for scriptures that will help you fight this mental battle.

If you do not have a reference Bible or Bible concordance to help you search scriptures, then use the internet. I prefer to use Google Chrome to search. If Satan is trying to convince me that I will not receive my healing, then I will type into the search bar, "KJV scriptures regarding physical healing." The reason I use the term KJV-King James Version is so that it will pull a list of scriptures from the Holy Bible, not the Quran and other religious books and Bibles. If I cannot understand the KJV language, then I will type in the desired verse using these reference versions.

"John 17:5 MSG" or
"Jeremiah 29:11-13 NIV."

The Message and New International Version are my two favorites for comparing word choices with the King James Version. It is like reading a sentence Thesaurus instead of looking up synonyms of each word in the sentence. As a Christian, you will need to use all educational tools at your disposal. Do not let people tell you this is not necessary. Ignorance is one of Satan's favorite tools to use on the church and pastors. It is second only to his use of guilt. Satan loves to guilt us by reminding us of our past.

Having the power of scripture search on the internet and translation or version searches empowers us to feed our minds the word of God. This search engine is an excellent tool for young Christians struggling to get through the Bible their first few times. The more you search topics and scriptures, the more comfortable you will become with this task. You must learn how to "research" the scriptures not only to put good words in your mind but to double-check what you hear preached in your church or on television. Do not accept something at face-value because a TV minister shared it. Make sure that is the correct translation of the scriptures. Know that you are getting the "truth of the gospel" and not a compromised version of God's word.

For example, if Satan is trying to convince me that I will not receive my healing, I quote the healing scriptures that I have searched. If he is telling me that I am not worthy to receive my healing, then I search the following.

Goggle Chrome Search Bar: **"KJV scriptures that prove that I am worthy to be healed."**

As I click on each scripture listed, it will pull up that text. I read it to determine if it applies. If it does, I write on my legal pad. I read those scriptures to Satan and bind him. I tell him that I am going to be healed. I speak with authority to him! Let us review a few scriptures on this search, so you can see how this works.

Matthew 8:5-10—This scripture is about the Centurion that did not feel worthy of having Jesus come to his house to heal his daughter, but knew that Jesus could heal her! So, he told Jesus to speak, and it would be done. I would read that verse to Satan and say to him that if the Centurion, who probably was not even a Christian, but had heard of the miracles of Jesus could ask and receive for his daughter, then I as a child of God, is worthy to receive my healing! My faith will make me whole.

Mark 9:23—All things are possible to him who believes

Luke 8:50—Fear not: believe only, and you should be made whole.

Psalm 147:3—He heals the brokenhearted and bindeth up their wounds. (that means I can be healed, Satan)!

Mark 10:52—Go thy way; thy faith has made thee whole. Satan, the scripture does not say anything about whether he was worthy or perfect, he asked, and he received. He was made whole!

Do you see how this works? There is no reason for you not to be a "scripture researcher" at once. The word of God is our key to battling Satan, who loves to use our minds against us! Use your phone, your computer, or iPad to help you fight successfully on the battlefield of your mind!

BE AWARE:

When you begin scripture and word searches on the internet, note that "Wikipedia" entries always show up. For new Christians, DO NOT READ any Wikipedia entries. There are entered by individuals, and they are not verified by any theologians. Some of the Christian entries are not accurate. I have found misquotes, typos, and lots of misinterpretations of the scriptures.

The second are to stay away from on the internet is sermons on other ministry websites, etc. Many confused people are posting sermons and sermon outlines on their ministry websites. There are also weekly blogs on websites that are not Biblically correct. If you know a minister or have researched his ministry purpose and standards, you may read their materials. However, you will ALWAYS need to go back to your Bible and ensure that the information is correct. Do not accept something because someone has it on their website. Not all preachers are spirit-filled. Some are wolves in sheep's clothing, doing the bidding of their master, Satan, to deceive the elect of Christ! Christian books are the same way. Be careful of what you read! Research everything you hear, see, or read about God against the Bible!

Once you have mastered your "research skills," and you have read through the Bible at least 25 times, you will be able to read something and immediately know if it is scriptural or not. You can lay that book, movie, or website print-outs to the side or put them in the garbage can. If you are going to share with others that the information is wrong, you need to conduct research and find the scriptures that support your theory that the sermon is wrong and then find the scriptures that prove the correct version! However, until you reach that level of spiritual maturity, do not confuse yourself by listening to false teachers and preachers.

Remember

When you got your new cell phone, you spent hours learning how to use it....give God the same amount of attention as you get accustomed to using his word, your most awesome tool...the Bible!

Chapter Five:

LEVIATHAN SPIRIT

This section was taken from my book, "Why am I not Living a Victorious Life?" If you want more information on this topic and how to live a victorious life, then contact us for a copy of this book. The Kindle Version is available through Amazon.com. The comments made in this chapter in message boxes like this one will indicate what new content was added to assist the reader with why this topic is relevant for this book.

The Leviathan spirit is a stubborn demon that is based in pride and carries with it jealousy, self-righteousness, and many other spirits. This spirit can transfer from one person to another person. These transfers of spirits only "oppress" you initially. If you do not get deliverance, over-time, they will possess you. These spirits transfer through the phone, by touch, or just by being in the presence of a possessed person. This spirit loves to mock as it attacks true Christians. It hates and tries to destroy anyone who has a genuine relationship with Christ. If you desire to do God's will, then this spirit will seek to destroy you. It passionately hates anyone who is obedient to the will of God or his purpose for their lives!

If your ministry has been under attack by individuals falsely accusing you or fabricating fake evidence against you, then you need to study this chapter and learn all the tricks of this spirit. This demon twist facts and lies. It will deceptively twist things that will deceive other church members and other pastors in your fellowship. Once you learn how to recognize this spirit, you can bind it. However, to recognize it, you need to have a clear definition of this spirit and study the behavior characteristics it employs!

This spirit has one goal—twist and deceives everyone that will listen to it. The purpose for its deception and twisting facts or the truth is based on the need to "control" everything, everyone, and your life! This spirit desires to destroy every individual and church that it cannot control.

89

DEFINITION:

Leviathan is translated from the Hebrew word "livyathan--which means twisted or coiled." (KingJamesBibleDictionary.com, 2020). There are references in the Bible that references this spirit to be like a crocodile or a crooked snake.

SCRIPTURE REFERENCES FOR LEVIATHAN:

Numerous scriptures in the Bible deal with the Leviathan spirit and how it has influenced people during Bible times. These scriptures are too extensive for me to list and explain each one in this book. All of these scriptures have been discussed in detail in the "Keys to Victorious Living Series." A majority of them are covered in book two, *The Spiritual Warrior.* I have listed the key scriptures for you below. You can look each one up and read it later.

Job 3:8
Job 41:15-Job 41:1-34
Psalm 74:14
Psalm 104:26
Isaiah 27:1

CHARACTERISTICS OF THE LEVIATHAN SPIRIT:

The Leviathan demon manifests itself in many ways. An essential characteristic is based upon the very definition of the word Leviathan which means "twister." **This spirit's number one characteristic is how it twists things that others say in its presence**. This spirit is an influencer in our churches, just like there are social influencers on our social media accounts. These influencers share information, ideas, topics, and products with the intent of changing their follower's perspective on those topics. The Leviathan spirit does the same thing in our churches. Instead of a positive or promotional sharing on social media, it is a harmful and damaging sharing against whoever had the true anointing of God on their lives.

The Leviathan spirit uses people it possesses to come against the real move of God. It despises the gift of discernment and will try to destroy the reputation of anyone God has given any of the spiritual gifts.

This spirit's second major characteristic is "deception." The Leviathan spirit loves to twist things using one fact of truth and twisting around that truth many false statements. Then present that information in a fashion that results in the deception of the person hearing the news. If this spirit can lead you to draw a wrong conclusion from the conversation, then it knows that it can count on you to spread that information as it was the truth. Within your circle of friends and colleagues, you can influence them to believe what the Leviathan spirit caused you to think. Not only do you become deceived, but you lead at least 20 to 50 other individuals to believe a false doctrine or truth without realizing the trap you have entered.

When I was working on my degree at the university, I had two professors so oppressed by this spirit that they were spiraling out of control. I watched in amazement as I would present course work and how they would react or become defensive. Especially, if my course work for that assignment touched on any of the works of the flesh or related topics on sin.

We had a couple of international students in one class that had limited English skills. How they were accepted into a doctoral program at an American Christian University was mind-blowing. They came from very wealthy families, and our entire class assumed that money bought their admission, not grades or command of the English language. These two professors were so tormented by spirits that they could not even look the ones of us that were true Christians in the eye. Direct eye-to-eye contact was out of the question for me. On the other hand, these two international students were still struggling with letting go of the idol worship that was so common in their countries. They held onto the cultural rituals based on those religions—resulting in a kindred spirit to side with these professors.

Every student in our class recognized how much favoritism was shown to the two international students. They were given "As" on papers and praised openly in the class for course work that was not even at an undergraduate level, might less doctoral level. At the same time, the students filled with the Holy Ghost would receive scores of below 60 on all tests and letter grades of "C" and "D" on all papers.

I met with both professors separately and in private to discuss what I was witnessing. I tried to approach the topic with the love and respect that was due to their positions. The private meetings did not work. So, myself and three other students move to the level of involving the Dean for that division of the school into the conversation.

The four of us sat in shock as we met with these two professors, the dean, and two other faculty members to review these professors' actions. There was ample proof of discrimination and favoritism. Even the two professors present agreed that the letter grades were too low on the course work, the four of us had submitted. Yet, when the meeting came to a close, they fell under the spell of the spirits controlling these two professors. Those two professors gave closing remarks at the meeting, and we could see the facial expressions of the university leadership change before our eyes. These two professors claimed that nothing had happened and that they had never engaged in discrimination. As these professors made eye-to-eye contact with the panel deciding their fate, it was evident that the spirits controlling them were capable of controlling this panel.

We finished that semester and were so glad to be out from under these two professors. The four of us swore we would never take a class offered by them again. We would work extra hard and bring up our low grades in those two classes. However, other students continued to complain about these two professors. Finally, the board of the directors realized that something was going in this division and began a secret investigation. It was determined that these two professors were "close-closet homosexuals" that were covering their alternate lifestyles from their churches and their wives. That was the reason those spirits on the two international students had so much control over them.

The Dean of this school had not been a Christian very long. He was new to the Christian walk, even though he had over 20 years of experience as a dean in a secular college. He did not understand spiritual warfare and was not filled with the Holy Ghost. It was easy for the spirits on these two professors to control him. We must put on the whole armor of God each day to protect our minds from these spirits!

The four of us never saw our grades corrected because we had graduated before the scandal came to light. However, we believe that our intercessory prayers over this situation brought the scandal to the forefront. Now, students can go through courses in that division and receive a quality Christian education. My purpose for sharing this story is to inform you how spirits can control leadership. It can happen in your churches just like that university. How this dean was no match for these two deceitful professors is how our associate pastors, teachers, and novice leadership teams get under the control of spirits in our churches today. We need the gift of discernment.

You must remember that you and I are no better than Joseph, who was falsely accused, or Jesus, who died for something he did not do! If the wrong done to you is never corrected here on Earth, know that you will be rewarded for keeping the faith and having a good attitude in Heaven. You will also be rewarded for patiently waiting on God to exonerate you. God will honor the fact that you chose not to retaliate against your accusers.

I would rather have God's favor and blessings on my life with his anointing on my ministry than to win the legal battle against my false accusers. This attitude or behavior is a true manifestation of the "fruits of the spirit" in your life. that is what God wants us to demonstrate—our love for our enemies and true forgiveness.

The Leviathan spirit's characteristics include actions and behaviors that can be classified as arrogant, haughty, proud, rebellious, stubborn, defiant, egotistical, scornful, self-exalting, puffed-up, anti-submissive, and covered in vanity and perfection.

Listed below are character traits that you will notice when you are in the presence of someone influenced by this spirit or possessed by it.

1. Pride, haughty spirits, boaster
2. Jealousy, envy
3. Controlling spirit
4. A twister of facts and truths
5. An individual with false humility
6. They appear to be very religious
7. Loves to start confusion and initiate stressful situations
8. Loves to control everything around them
9. They become upset if they cannot control everyone
10. Self-righteous, self-exalting, self-sufficient in a controlling manner
11. A person under the influence of this spirit will not see the truth when shown to them.
12. This spirit blinds the people it influences and dulls their spiritual senses so that they will not discern the truth of the situation.
13. People this spirit influences become confused and disoriented.
14. This spirit causes people to be for things they were against in the past.
15. It causes people to be against things they believed in, in the past.
16. It causes them to change their viewpoints on the scriptures.
17. They are challenging about non-scriptural things or facts.

18. They demonstrate behaviors opposite of the fruits of the spirit.
19. It prefers war, strife, conflicts, favoritism, sadness, self-pity, bondage, limited outreach, and destruction.
20. It resists humility, being under subjections, submissiveness, and real spiritual authority.

THE LEVIATHAN SPIRIT'S GOAL:

The Leviathan spirit desires to generate confusion and descensions in our churches and our lives. This spirit wants to create so much control over the church that it can influence who stays and who goes with regards to members. It wants to be the person who determines who can be a church worker while completely controlling that individual, the pastor, and all leadership staff.

The Leviathan spirit wants to influence the people in our inner circles and our churches' leadership teams to the point that they make decisions without regard to the church members' feelings or needs. The same holds true in schools, universities, and workplaces. This spirit wants to control all decision-making and promotions. If you watch closely, you will recognize who in leadership is being controlled by this spirit because they will always praise, promote, and select the person with the most influence over them. If you look closely, you will realize that their actions are always the "selfish-choice."

A PASTOR UNDER THE INFLUENCE OF LEVIATHAN:

A pastor influenced by the Leviathan spirit will experience this spirit controlling his or her actions, agendas, and decisions. The first noticeable characteristic that you will notice is ***pride***. When a preacher becomes haughty, proud, arrogant, and prideful, watch to see if they will accept correction or spiritual advice. If they will not, then they are being controlled by the Leviathan spirit. This spirit prevents a true move of God. It limits chances for the deliverance of the members who are possessed or controlled by this spirit. If you find that this spirit controls your pastor, then you need to find another church. If you "play-with" this spirit, you will come under its influence too.

It is challenging for a person to get deliverance from the Leviathan spirit and even harder for preachers. This spirit feeds on pride and arrogance. Once it gets rooted in a man or woman's heart, toxic behaviors begin to unfold in their lives. You need to know and be aware of the warning signs that the Leviathan spirit controls your pastor or church leaders.

1. They will have pride that loves to boast on their spiritual accomplishments, ministry accomplishments, etc. The preacher under Leviathan's control will praise his or her accomplishments more than they will honor the works of Jesus or the spirit in your church.

2. They will always brag about what they can do and will not table their pride to honor a more senior preacher or pastor. They do not show respect to other ministers with more experience. They appear threatened or afraid of these ministers, what they know, or what they can discern about them.

3. The preacher controlled by the Leviathan spirit will disregard wisdom and experience. You will notice that most of these preachers are young novices in ministry or self-proclaimed preachers and prophets that took their positions and titles and began promoting themselves before any training, education, or apprenticeships.

4. I heard one pastor brag that he went from the bar-room (night club) on one Saturday night to church on Sunday and gave his life to the Lord. Then he stated that he started preaching immediately. He began pastoring within one year of getting saved. He never trained under another minister or sought any formal education, not even correspondence courses, to learn about the Bible and church management. This pastor stated that he had never been to church and did not know anything about the Bible when he got saved. He frequently bragged that he did not need anyone to teach him anything about the Bible or attend school. He stated that God told him he would teach him the Bible.

5. Preachers under Leviathan's influence are oblivious to others' successes, benefits of other ministries, or the positive works of other ministries because of their pride in their ministries.

6. These preachers will always brag and exalt themselves because of the gifts that God has given to them. They will boast that no one has the revelations they have or have heard from God like them. These ministers are incapable of accepting or honoring other preachers unless they can control those individuals.

7. These preachers are always against worship. They do not promote worshipping God in their services. They have to start the service, control the service, and they are the only ones that can get the spirit flowing. These preachers do not show any signs or passionate desires for worship.

8. These preachers do not desire to have altar services or spend time in prayer. There are no callouses on their knees! There is no passion for pray in their churches or personal lives.

9. These preachers do not ever admit that they are at fault. However, they are continually pointing out everyone's flaws in their church, every church they attend, or every preacher that they watch on TV. No one else is good enough or even remotely in the same category as they are in their relationship with God.

10. Transparency is a curse word to them. Their pride will take over and verbally accost a person who even mentions or recommend transparency and integrity.

11. If you see this preacher at another church or revival, you will notice that they are never in anyone else's prayer line. They feel that they are better than everyone else and that no other minister has what they have in their relationship with God. So, they think it would be a waste of time for them to get anointed by another minister.

12. They do not understand the concept that preachers need to be ministered to just like the members. They do not feel that they ever need to recharge their spiritual batteries with help from others. They think that God supplies all of that to them directly. They also believe that they do not need to listen to other preacher's sermons or read their books.

96

13. They do not feel that they should help others, but that everybody should help them and give to them.

14. They have never established themselves under a senior minister or pastor for training. They have never been submissive to anyone else in ministry. If staying at a place required this, then they would jump up and leave. There is no longevity in their ministry in most cases.

15. They criticize everyone, demoting, degrading, and killing them with their tongue. They call the names of other ministers from their pulpit and verbally destroy those ministries in their sermons. We are not to be the judge of other ministries or continuously compare ourselves to others. God has a different purpose, focus, and outreach for every church or ministry. We are all to be about getting souls saved. The strategies and the "how's" may be different for each minister and church.

16. These ministers will get on TV and openly call other ministers by name, demanding that they repent and pray. (Most of the times, they are committing sins of greater moral turpitude themselves).

17. They criticize every new strategy, concept, ministerial tool, music ministry tool, etc., that is demonstrated or discussed on TV, making it the works of Satan, unless it was their idea.

18. If these ministers come up with an original idea or program, they will brag that their ideas are the "best thing since sliced bread" and should be in every church. Pride and arrogance are prominent.

As you can see, everything that the Leviathan-influenced preacher does is through pride. Every choice they make is for their good alone. If it does not benefit them or promote them, then it is wrong or evil. These preachers must be in control at all times, yet never wrong!

A SPIRITUAL WARRIOR MUST ALWAYS HAVE HIS ARMOR ON AND BE PREPARED TO GO TO BATTLE AT A MOMENT'S NOTICE!

FACTS ABOUT THE LEVIATHAN SPIRIT:

We have not been placed here on earth to be the judge, jury, and executioner of other pastors and their ministries. We are here to be soul-winners for Christ. We are to be focused on God, souls, and our churches, not ourselves. One common sign with all ministers affected by the spirit of Leviathan is a selfish-nature or self-centered attitude that controls everything around them.

A person who is bound by this spirit believes that the spirit talking to them is from God. They do not realize that it is the Leviathan spirit that is telling them information, showing them things, or leading them. I have seen this spirit say to the preacher confidential stuff about people in the audience so that they could prophesy to people and deceive them.

I have seen people who were bound by this spirit get up with a fake move of God and shout, dance, talk in a tongue, and outwardly demonstrate that they were under the influence of the Holy Spirit. If the pastor is spirit-filled and not under the control of the Leviathan spirit, then he or she will sit this person down. If the pastor is under the influence of this spirit, they will not recognize this spirit, but they will praise it, support it, or urge it to continue. You could say the Leviathan spirit disables a preacher's true gift of discernment and replaces it with a counterfeit version without them even be aware of this change.

The Leviathan spirit loves to bring false accusations against anyone who might recognize the spirit in them. This spirit loves to bring outrageous allegations against true men and women of God. It also likes to take one truthful fact and surround it with ten false statements, twisting the facts to deceive people into believing the false accusations. This spirit will devour another church member with more venom than a hungry lion and not feel bad about it at all.

When two or more people in a church are under the influence of this spirit, you will notice that they always stand together against individuals that are used by God. You will see that both individuals have the characteristics associated with this spirit, and their comradery is perfectly aligned. Kindred spirits always stick together. They form church cliques and try to get preachers, teachers, and church leaders that they cannot control out of the church. They will go to every effort, including trying to lie and prosecute people with criminal charges that are not guilty!

Any time a church begins to grow spiritually and the gifts of the spirit start to operate in that church or group, you can be confident that the Leviathan spirit will find someone to send to the church or will search for members in the church that it can work through. So, if you are in a church that is growing spiritually, you need to be fasting and praying for discernment. You need to be on the look-out for this hideous demonic spirit that is extremely powerful and righteous acting. This spirit has many heads that all love to cause confusion, distrust, and disloyalty. This spirit specializes in gossip and rumors! It loves doctrinal disputing and feeds off of the energy created in these situations.

Remember, this haughty, prideful spirit is powerful and destructive. Do not confront it ever by yourself! Never try to straighten out this spirit or dispute its lies. There is no way to win over or control the Leviathan spirit. The only thing you can do with it is cast it out of your church. This spirit will fuel rebellion in any weak Christians and cause them to rebel against the true word of God and your preaching on sin. This demon is the spirit that lies on preachers and sends them to prison for 20-years for sexual abuse and rape when it never happened! This spirit lies and twists the truth ruining many ministries in its path each year! Intercessory prayer and spiritual backup are necessary to fight this demon.

IS DELIVERANCE POSSIBLE?

Yes, deliverance is possible, but not probable. Less than 10% of people who are possessed and less than 40% of those oppressed by this spirit ever receive deliverance. One of the reasons for such low deliverance rates is because most pastors do not know how to recognize this spirit. If you do not recognize it, then how can you help someone to find deliverance? If you do not recognize that you are being influenced as a pastor by these spirits in your congregation, how can you preach the information they need to hear to help them find deliverance?

Pride is the root of this Leviathan spirit, and control over others is its power. While under its influence, it is impossible to see or recognize it. The pride that develops when this spirit possesses a person prevents them from accepting correction or reproof. If a person cannot take correction and are not willing to change, how will you get them to change? See the dilemma here with this spirit? Now you understand why it is almost impossible for a preacher who is bound by this spirit to get deliverance.

If a person is only influenced or oppressed by the Leviathan spirit, deliverance is possible if you can get them to break fellowship with the host demon. If you can get them to change jobs, churches, or quit hanging around with the person who is possessed that keeps influencing them, then a deliverance can be obtained. In most cases, people are affected by family members or close associates that breaking free from is almost impossible. The only way to get away from Leviathan's influence is to separate yourself from them, which includes not talking to them on the phone!

I have seen this spirit work in churches and families so much over the past 20 years of ministry. I saw one pastor ask for forgiveness and repent, but he did not separate himself from the largest tithe payer in his church (which is where he acquired the demon in the first place). After about six months, this pastor was repossessed by the Leviathan demon, and it brought seven more with it.

I saw one pastor's wife walk away from all of her family, give up her two best friends, and put everything in her life on hold to get deliverance. I am sure that would not have happened if it had not been for her daughter. She loved that daughter so much that she finally listened to the daughter's pleas to separate herself. Once she realized what the Leviathan demon was doing to her and her husband's ministry, she changed. Today, she is working to help pastor's wives across America, helping them to avoid falling into this trap. Her desire to make everyone happy was the fault that this spirit used to influence and control her. She wanted all of the members to love and support her husband. She did not want anyone ever to be mad at them. The first thing you must realize in ministry is that you cannot make 100% of the people happy 100% of the time. It is not possible, so do not try. The only way to please everybody is to be two-faced, which results in compromises, deceit, and manipulations. These three will bring the Leviathan spirit in just as quick as pride. I have seen this so many times over the years. Do not let this spirit deceive you!

HOW IS DELIVERANCE OBTAINED:

Deliverance is discussed in detail with all the steps and strategies outlined in *"The Keys to Victorious Living Series"* Book 11, _The Spiritual Warrior._ The critical steps utilized in obtaining deliverance from this spirit are listed. The process is a 12-step process that is not easy to accomplish. I will list the 12 steps for you, but there is not enough space in this book to describe them in detail. Know that this process is proven effective!

1. Recognition that you have a problem
2. A desire to change and break the tie
3. Acceptance of correction and reproof
4. Submission to a senior pastor or minister trained in helping people get deliverance

5. Accepting an accountability partner to help you through the process
6. Transparency in all aspects of their life and ministry
7. Prayer, lots of prayers
8. Daily Bible reading every morning and every night
9. Fasting as much as possible
10. Taking communion after deliverance and an extended fast
11. Studying and learning about the Leviathan spirit and how to recognize any signs that it might be trying to attach itself again
12. Humility! Humility! Humility!

HOW DO YOU KEEP DELIVERANCE?

In the following books from the "***Keys to Victorious Living Series***," you will learn how to obtain and maintain deliverance from spirits along with tools to use to help you recognize or discern when these spirits are in operation in your church, home, workplace, or life. The "Spiritual Warrior" and the "Prayer Warrior" provide you will all of the steps and techniques to get deliverance from these spirits. They are a must-read, even if you do not think that these spirits are controlling your life. You need to know what to do when you eventually encounter them. You WILL encounter them in these last days!

1) Book # 11: *The Spiritual Warrior*
2) Book # 12: *The Spiritual Warrior Journal*
3) Book # 13: *The Prayer Warrior Devotional*
4) Book # 14: *The Prayer Warrior Prayer Journal*

Humbly accepting an accountability partner and staying in God's word daily, with lots of prayers. It is a one-day at a time process! You will learn more in book two. Reading, praying, and fasting are the three initial steps. Remember, humble yourself and pray! God will lead you through this process. Then we will discuss in more detail in book two, *The Spiritual Warrior*, how to prepare and protect yourself against this spirit.

Humility in all aspects of our lives and ministries is essential for God's blessings and anointing. As Jesus was teaching the disciples and his followers about prayer, he also gave them the keys to being blessed as he told them, "Blessed are the poor in spirit: for theirs is the kingdom of heaven" (Matthew 5:3, KJV, 2020). He then explained that they also needed "to hunger and thirst after righteousness" (Matthew 5:6, KJV, 2020). Remember that one of the pieces of our spiritual armor is the breastplate of righteousness? Jesus mentions it here in this verse, too.

No matter how much God has blessed and multiplied your ministry or business, you need to remain humble before him and accept God's instructions, reproof, and any words of wisdom he sends you. At no point in our lives should we become so confident in our abilities that we feel that we do not need to receive counsel. A key to being rapture ready is seeking God with humility and listening to his voice when it speaks. None of us are perfect and never will be, but we are forgiven and righteous before God through the blood of Jesus Christ!

I realize that I have shared in several sections of this book warnings about not being deceived in these last days. Now, I want to give you a promise to stand on...stay humble and seek God's will for your life...you will not be deceived! Yes, if you lay aside your arrogant, self-centered nature (the Adam nature we all have) and humbly seek God with an open heart, he will lead you to the truth. However, to be led to this truth, you must be daily reading God's word (the Bible). If we "hunger and thirst after righteousness" (Matthew 5:6, KJV, 2020), God will open your eyes to the truth of his word, or the truth of the matter you are dealing with in your everyday life.

Jesus also preached, "Repent: for the kingdom of heaven is at hand" (Matthew 4:17, KJV, 2020). This should be our message each week in our churches. We all need to be reminded that we must confess our sins, seek God's will, bear the crosses or burdens he has assigned to us, and humbly seek God. We are guaranteed that if we seek God will humility that he will answer us. "Behold, I stand at the door and knock: if any man hears my voice, and open the door, I will come into him and will sup with him, and he with me" (Revelation 3:20, KJV, 2020). We must remember that Jesus is the only way to Heaven. His blood is the only way we can go before our Holy God. We can only receive God's righteousness through the blood of Jesus. So, we must approach him with humility and a teachable heart.

In Jesus' ministry here on earth over 2000 years ago, we find that he told them in John 7:47-48 that they needed to not only present humbly, but that they needed to put on this breastplate of righteousness, the girdle of truth, and take up the shield of faith so that they would not be deceived. Jesus did not want his disciples to become like the Pharisees. Even though deception will be Satan's greatest tool during these last days, we do not have to fear being deceived as long as we stay humble before God and daily in God's word seeking him. We must remember that the only thing that can destroy us...is us! If we do not stay in God's word, we will be deceived. The prophet Hosea said it best, "my people are destroyed for lack of knowledge" (Hosea 4:6, KJV, 2020).

Chapter Six:

THE SPIRIT OF JEZEBEL

This section was taken from my book, "Why am I not Living a Victorious Life?" If you want more information on this topic and how to live a victorious life, then contact us for a copy of this book. The Kindle Version is available through Amazon.com. The comments made in this chapter in message boxes like this one will indicate what new content was added to assist the reader with why this topic is relevant for this book.

To understand this demonic spirit and the stronghold that it has in most churches today, I need to share with you the definition of this spirit. It is imperative to know its purpose and the characteristics that it presents with, plus the symptoms that a person will have in their life if this spirit influences them. If you think that this spirit is not in the Bible, I will introduce you to people who have allowed this spirit to destroy their lives in the Old and New Testaments. Then we will talk about how to have a victory from this spirit and how to recognize it so that the spirit of Jezebel will never deceive you in the future. This spirit is one of the greatest hindrances to victorious living in the church of America today.

JEZEBEL SPIRIT DEFINED:

The spirit of Jezebel is an enchanting spirit that amazes individuals, charms them, and allures them into their circle of friends, church, or group. A person who is possessed with the spirit of Jezebel can malign (speak untruths) with such finesse and charm that most people will not recognize the spirit or its lies. This spirit is a master deceiver who specializes in making false representations and spreading malicious lies. It can enchant while it preaches to the point that most Christians will not even notice the lies that are being taught.

This spirit can attract and lure, especially young people, into their churches and groups, by telling them what they want to hear or giving them the license, they need to sin without regret!

PURPOSE OR MISSION OF THE JEZEBEL SPIRIT:

The spirit of Jezebel is a demonic spirit that loves to mislead Christians and get them involved in sexual immorality, idolatry, and other sins that promote the gratification of their flesh. This spirit wants to get you involved in the satisfaction of all of your sexual desires. It wants you to encourage selfishness, self-centeredness, and self-gratification in your life and others through the spirit of pride. It desires to destroy your testimony, ministry, and physical body. The primary purpose of the Jezebel spirit is to cripple your ministry, rendering it crippled or stopped altogether. When a Jezebel spirit takes over a pastor or his wife, pride, arrogance, and haughtiness are usually the first two symptoms manifested. Following the spirit of pride, follows jealousy, and controlling spirits. The spirit of Jezebel often brings with it several other spirits, depending on the weaknesses of the individual that it is possessing.

We will discuss this spirit and how it interacts with other spirits later in this chapter. In the second main book of this series, *The Spiritual Warrior*, you will get a more in-depth look at this spirit's actions, tools that it uses, and the traps that it sets. We will also discuss how this spirit interacts with other spirits and how to block them from having control in your life or ministry.

HISTORY OF THE JEZEBEL SPIRIT:

Discussions of the spirit of Jezebel go as far back as the first four books of the Old Testament. It is a spirit that controls, manipulates, seduces, murders, and tricks people into immorality and idolatry. It is not a spirit that only affects women but men. I have seen just as many men possessed with this spirit as women in dealing with this demonic force. The spirit of Jezebel can influence you, oppress you, or possess you. Not everyone under its spell is possessed. However, it will lead to that if you continue to play with this spirit. It is very dangerous and should not be allowed to stop by for a visit in your mind. It makes its initial approach to most people through either pride or the lust of the flesh.

HOW THE SPIRIT OF JEZEBEL WORKS:

The spirit of Jezebel is an "executive or master" spirit in the realm of the supernatural. It is an in-control spirit that brings numerous spirits when it moves in to possess the individual. It always brings in anger, bitterness, lust, murder, deceitfulness, revenge, vengeance, adultery, and fornication. This spirit is the most cunning in Satan's toolbox. This spirit is brilliant and will deceive any Christian that is weak spiritually or ignorant of Satan's tactics. This spirit can single-handed destroy a church, pastor, ministry, company, coach, marriage, or an individual's life.

The spirit of Jezebel loves to work through the professing Christian. To the church members and church leaders who have not prayed for the gift of discernment, these individuals appear to be so loving, kind, and the perfect choice for critical positions in the church. Individuals with the Jezebel spirit possessing them love to appear righteous and holy! However, if you stay around them and pray, God will reveal to you their lack of the fruits of the spirit in their lives.

Jesus, in his teachings and Paul in his letters, advises us not to take away from it. Both stated numerous times that altering God's word created an environment open to seducing and bewitching spirits to deceive us.

THE SPIRIT OF JEZEBEL DESTROYS CHURCHES:

A self-righteous religious spirit and the spirit of Jezebel love to destroy churches and the lives of ministers. It does not help that our state and federal government officials like to fuel the fires of immorality. They promote the works of the flesh before our young people and revel in flaunting the "benefits" of giving your flesh everything that it desires while ignoring Christian values, moral convictions, and standards of integrity.

The spirit of Jezebel is a spirit with a plan to manipulate and control churches in a way to extensively destroys them. The Jezebel spirit likes to join with the Leviathan, Moloch, Python, and other deceitful spirits to bring the destruction of pastors, ministers, and churches to their knees or destruction.

The spirit of Jezebel likes to use the spirit of seduction to woo people into immoral acts or behaviors that embrace idolatry, fortune-telling, and other practices that kill, still, and destroy the lives of church members and their impact in the community.

Any minister, teacher, or church leader that boldly stands up and declares the word of the Lord and preaches the truth of the gospel will stir up the Jezebel spirits in their midst. Jezebel is an evil controlling spirit that does not want to see the work of God move forward, nor souls saved. This spirit has only one goal… to stop the actual work of God at any cost and any way possible!

I was asked to minister one weekend at a small country church that had started growing. The pastor had been there for less than ten years. He had taken the church from five members to over 60 members. They had just built a new church and were beginning to be blessed. He was excited that God had sent him several families that were longing to "work" in the church. It also helped that these families had excellent jobs and would be extremely large tithe payers. We arrived at the church approximately 45-minutes before the time for Sunday School to start. We needed to set-up and get ready for the service. During this time, I had the opportunity to talk with the pastor. He was telling me all about his five top tithe payers. As he thanked God, I rejoiced with him. I love to hear of church growth on all levels.

As the Sunday morning service was called to order and the children were sent to the appropriate Sunday School classes, the Adult Sunday School teacher took her place. When she introduced herself, I recognized this as one of the names that the pastor had mentioned before service. About 35 minutes into the lesson, a lady in the back commented on one of the lesson points. I noticed that the teacher got irritable and began to fidget. She did not say anything, but I recognized that a spirit was working on her. Under my breath, I began to pray. I immediately asked the Holy Spirit to come into the service and bind any hindering spirits. I asked it to tie up the hands and bind the tongue of any individuals that would hinder the anointing in the service. I also asked the Lord to let any demons that were working behind the scenes unknown to this pastor to show themselves that day.

The worst thing that can happen to a young minister or a minister that is new to pastoral duties to be sabotaged by a religious spirit or the Jezebel spirit. I began interceding for this pastor with a heavy heart. I felt that it was critical. Approximately five minutes after I finished my prayer, another man on the right side of the church asked the teacher a question. It was lesson related and was an excellent question. There was nothing wrong with his question or the attitude in which he asked. However, this teacher completely lost it. The demon took full control of her. Her countenance changed; her voice got very loud, boisterous, abrupt, blunt, and gruff. The words that then flowed from this woman's mouth had the pastor sitting there wide-eyed, mouth open, and a look of shock on his face.

That was the last time this lady taught Sunday school in that church, and two weeks later, she and her husband left the church. They were angry at the pastor and proceeded to berate him in public every chance they got. The last that I heard from this Jezebel spirit possessed woman, and her husband was that they were suffering severe health issues. Both had suffered severe life-threatening heart attacks and needed open-heart surgery. Both were in critical condition. It does not pay to "play church" or to put your tongue on God's anointed.

As spirit-filled Christians, we have the right to ask for spirits to show their true colors and their malicious intent. Without the devil revealing himself or uncovering his actions by accident, most Christians do not discern evil spirits or destructive spirits in their midst. The pastor of this church claimed to have the gift of discernment, but he did not recognize this spirit in his mist. He had even promoted this spirit and put it in charge. This woman and her husband (both severely oppressed by the spirit of Jezebel) had deceived this pastor. They were continually volunteering and injecting themselves into work in the church. They freely gave money to help each problem that was mentioned by the pastor. They made this pastor feel that they were the God-sent miracle he had been praying about for the past couple of years!

JEZEBEL SPIRITS INFLUENCE PEOPLE:

There are several key indicators that this spirit is affecting a person or trying to influence them. *One of the most critical traps* for ministers, pastors, missionaries, and church leaders is that this spirit approaches them, wanting to "help or volunteer" their services. They get under the person that is in charge so that they can hide in plain sight to prevent detection longer. They will trick the pastor or church leader into taking their side when others in the church try to get the pastor to see the strife and confusion that they are generating in the membership. This Jezebel spirit will flip and play the victim. This spirit is always persecuted, but never wrong. This type of manipulation allows them to blame everyone else and block discernment of their true nature even longer.

I have witnessed the Jezebel spirit deceiving ministry leaders in the state, regional, and national offices in some of the largest evangelical organizations in the United States. Their free services, lavish donations, charismatic personalities, and false humility show their super-spiritual demonstrations to help them gain acceptance while working their "spells" on the unsuspecting ministers. I have also witnessed these same tactics utilized by other professors and instructors who were not qualified to be professors or department chairs. I have several physician friends who have shared their experiences with this spirit in hospital settings. They claim that the worst position for the Jezebel spirit to acquire is a nurse manager, supervisor, or nursing director. With the second-worst position being any department head in the organization. I could write a 1000+ page book on just the stories they have shared with me and the havoc that this spirit can generate regarding employee morale, productivity, quality of care or services, and future expansion projects.

Now imagine this spirit sitting beside you in church, trying to disrupt the service, distract the visiting sinner! As you read this detailed description, I am sure that your mind has immediately begun to remember a person or two you have encountered that fits this description. Now, you can start to see why Satan loves to use pride and the spirit of Jezebel first on churches.

The following signs or attitudes will be demonstrated by the person or pastor oppressed or possessed by the Jezebel spirit. A person does not have to show all of these characteristics but will have _at least two_ of them present and very noticeable. If you continue to watch this individual and ask God to show you the truth, you will see all present over time. Remember, this spirit is very deceptive. It is a master at hiding what it does not want you to see or notice!

1) <u>Selfish attitude or a selfish agenda</u>: This controlling spirit is motivated by an influential personal agenda that is always opposite to the true Biblical way to handle problems. However, this person does not care. They only want their way in all circumstances and decisions.

2) <u>This spirit causes fear, confusion, a desire for flight, destruction, and discouragement</u> everywhere that they go. This is true on every job they have, every church they attend, and every marriage they enter.

3) <u>They work and act like bullies</u>: These individuals will choose any form of manipulation, deception, bullying, and ego control to

convince the pastors, husbands, family members, and others in the church that they are the true leader of the church, not the real pastor. They self-appoint themselves as the "chosen one with the gift of discernment" so that they can convince everyone to lean on them.

4) <u>Deceptive and manipulative</u>: These individuals will use intrigue, flattery, stories, etc., to help them gain access to key people. They will even use hero-type acts and servant leadership acts to make the leaders trust them. When that fails, they will throw money at the situation. Some people provide, give, and do things to keep the church leadership or corporate staff from discerning who they are or what their plan is for the control of the church.

5) <u>Arrogant, take charge, undermine the people in authority, and other leadership individuals</u>: The person with the Jezebel spirit frequently use judgmental prophecies that are always covered up with flattery and touchy-feely words. These individuals always see the "improvements" needed and take them to the church leaders or the persons in authority. They often use sharp words without brotherly love to suppress others, including intentionally depressing people to get control over them or to get them to confident the "bully" and share the information that they need. This individual is proud, independent, and rebellious while accusing others of these same sins.

6) <u>Has a seriously religious spirit</u>: The person under the spirit of Jezebel will demonstrate a religious spirit that is a legalistic, scripture quoting, authoritarian. These individuals love to call themselves prophets and prophetess.

7) <u>Dysfunctional lives and families</u>: While claiming to be so spiritual, most of the time, their spouses and children do not even attend church. Their families are out of order, lofty, unhappy individuals, while the person with the Jezebel spirit shows none of the fruits of the spirit, no evidence of the true Holy Spirit in their lives.

People who are captured by the "allurement of religion" and the many forms it cloaks itself in as the spirit of Jezebel begins to take control of the church or group they are associating. Most Christians have no idea what it looks like or feels like to experience true freedom and liberty in the Lord Jesus Christ. So, deception by false faith, false miracles, and false preachers is easy. Entrapment by this spirit is possible because of its cunning and deceitful ways. You need to know the power of these spirits, how they work, and how to deal with them when you encounter them.

A PERSON UNDER INFLUENCE OF JEZEBEL SPIRIT SHOWS:

Through the years of ministry, I have witnessed the Jezebel spirit controlling church boards and church members using various strategies. The above list of seven characteristics is the most common. However, there are other, more subtle characteristics that we tend to write off as personality traits and ignore that they are indicators of a deeper spiritual problem in an individual's life.

People who have experienced rejection at some point in their childhood or young adult life, primarily due to physical and emotional abuse, are easy targets for the spirit of Jezebel. This spirit loves to take a person's fear of rejection and use that fear to cause them to try to control the church and its members. The spirit of Jezebel will even blind this traumatized person to hurt others to gain control. If this fear does not drive them to become control freaks, it will cause them to deceitfully promote themselves by exaggerating their abilities or past accomplishments to be accepted. These individuals will make commitments, pledges, and promises to impress others but grumble later that everyone expects them to do everything!

The individual who has the spirit of Jezebel controlling their lives through the fear of rejection will also be quick to accuse others, play the victim, blame everyone else, and play on the church leadership's compassion to block their discernment of them. At times, this person will demonstrate false humility, and manipulate other individuals privately, triggering them to feel isolated and insecure. As these individuals advance their spiritual attacks on the church, they go for the leadership. They want to publicly assassinate the pastor and senior leadership, making them look like imposters. All of this occurs to prevent the detection of the truth about themselves.

MINISTERIAL AND RELIGIOUS PRIDE

Ministerial pride is a big issue that we all see because of media coverage and Christian television programs. However, there is another form of pride that I call **religious pride** that affects the pew, not the pulpit. It centers around "appearing to be holy and spiritual." Many Christians think it makes them look good, honored, favored, and blessed if they can speak in tongues in a service. Some want to prophesy. Others want to continually receive recognition for their gifts, abilities, and activities that they are involved in at the church. They are not doing their deeds or giving their tithes and offerings with humility before God. They are seeking recognition of men like the Pharisee in Paul's day.

Religious pride is a spirit that causes an individual to become a self-seeking, self-gratifying, self-promoting, egotistical, pompous, proud, ruthless, self-centered, and always seeking praise from others and the limelight at church activities. This spirit will take over a church service if given a chance. This person's pride will be evident in all that they do. It may or may not be visible in their dress or appearance. I have encountered this spirit in individuals who dressed to appear extremely holy and humble. They had learned through the years that if their pride made them look too puffed-up, that they could not deceive others as easily. The most dangerous form of religious pride is the group of people who have become "seasoned or experienced religious pride demonstrators." They have perfected their deceptive skills.

I met a holiness minister and his wife in the late 1970s that were pastoring a southern country church. When you walked into the service immediately, you noticed several people were talented with music and could sing beautifully. So, my initial perception was that everyone seems to be holy and dedicated. The singing appeared anointed and led by individuals who wanted to serve God humbly. I did not see any demonstrations of a haughty or flaunting spirit. After about three songs, one of the men in the group began to testify. He started by thanking God for saving him and delivering him from sin. Then he quickly moved to compare himself with his brother, his sister, father, and another man he had grown up with (possibly in the community or high school). This initial demonstration of humility shattered as he began to rant in a praise testimony of how God had saved him, and he was not like these other people. He had never committed the sins that they were so tempted with each day. I noticed that the use of the pronoun "I" was in almost every sentence. It was not what God had done, but what he had done because he got saved. His testimony ended with this theme of what he had never done without sharing anything to glorify God or edify the church. A few specific points he shared remain seared in my brain.

"I have never drunk alcoholic beverages. I cannot imagine why anyone would desire to be out of control of their minds and body! I have never had sex with anyone but my wife. I never lust after anyone. That temptation never tries me. I do not understand why when people get saved that they keep on sinning. All I can say is that they never really got saved! Because when you get saved, you do not want to do these things anymore. See, God saved me as a boy. I did not have anyone to teach me better. My parents were not Christians. When my mother went to church, she went to the little Baptist Church across the road from our house. My momma did not teach me about God or what was a sin. But as a boy, I knew what was right because God taught me what I needed to know. If God did that for me, he would do it for others if they got saved as I did!"

Oh, this rant continued for over 20 minutes. I felt so embarrassed for any sinner people who were sitting in that service. This rant would prevent any sinners from responding to an altar call. How could they ever meet this level of perfection? This man's testimony shattered any hope that God accepts us as we are in our imperfect state and helps us become the men and women he desires!

What about the people sitting there that had slipped up that week and done something that they should not have done? Would they be free to come forward and get prayer? Or would they slip out the door still bound and give up on God? Our God is a God of mercy who loves you regardless of what you have done wrong. However, a religious spirit will never allow you to see that mercy. It wants to be the center of attention, the main attraction, and the one that everyone should desire to be like! This is a spirit of Jezebel that is controlling this person. If you stay around them for a couple of years or return in a few years to visit a church where a person like this attend, you will notice that this spirit gets stronger and stronger each time you visit.

Eventually, you will notice that this religious pride will turn to anger—these individuals begin prophesying doom on anyone who dares to come against them. I have heard ministers and minister's wives declare that God had killed people who came against them. Yet, these religious individuals would talk about other preachers from their pulpits without considering that person's testimony or ministry. They would degrade other ministers, and at times, I have even heard ministers with religious pride and the spirit of Jezebel state in anger prophesies of doom.

When anger begins to be demonstrated behind the pulpit against other churches and ministers consistently, run, run, run, and do not look back. Get away from these churches and ministers. No matter how anointed they have been in the past, and they are walking on dangerous ground. They are playing with a fire that will bring God's judgment on them. Our ministries and our churches are to be focused on getting people saved, delivered, and healed. We are to be a salvation station and a restoration center. It is not about us, but about what God can do! Do not lose your focus on the purpose of the gospel and what the role of the church is…to help the widows and orphans…not about promoting us or getting all that we can acquire!

About a year after I met the couple that could sing so beautifully but had the self-righteous, religious pride spirit, I ran into his wife in Walmart in a neighboring town. She was not aware that anyone around her knew who she was or where she lived. She was talking with a man that was not her husband. She was openly flirting with him and inappropriately touching him. As I stood there in shock, I heard her say to this man, "oh, come on, no one will know. You and I can go to club X, get a drink, then go around the corner to the Ramada Inn." This man replied, "I am so shocked. I thought you were Mr. X's wife and that you went to X Holiness Church." She replied, "I am, and I do. But don't you worry your little head. My husband and those people are so crazy, and if I wear my hair in a bun and my sleeves long, with my dress or skirts to the floor, they will never discern what I am doing! It is so easy to fool these people as long as you dress right and say the right things!"

This type of behavior is a common characteristic of the spirit of Jezebel as it transitions through the religious spirit to the point of possessing the individual. The demons that take up residence in the Christian that has played church and live hypocritical lives convince these individuals that they can eat at God's table, have his blessing, and play with any sins that they desire if they keep it hidden. They will justify their "hidden sins" as not hurting anyone else, so they are harmless. This spirit has not only helped them to deceive others at this stage, but it has also deceived them! They become captives in Satan's game. They can no longer control their urges but must succumb to the biddings of Satan. They are enslaved to him!

I got off that aisle and toward the front of the store as soon as possible. I did not even bother to look for the remaining items on my list. Whatever I could get en route to the register was all that I got. I did not want them to see me. I also did not want anyone else in Walmart to know that I knew that individual. I prayed sincerely for the pastor of this church that he would be given the gift of discernment. In these last days, the gift of discernment is the most important, and it is essential for you not to be deceived. Every Christian needs this gift, not just pastors and church leaders!

BEWITCHING SPIRITS

There are many types of bewitching spirits. The most common one is the Jezebel spirit. Please read the information below to determine the differences and how they work in our churches.

HOW PASTORS ARE "BEWITCHED:"

The spirit of Jezebel is known as the "bewitching spirit," as Paul described in Galatians. The Jezebel spirit loves to mislead, misconstrue the facts, deceive, and its favorite activity is to provide "false representation and untruths" as factual testimony against God's anointed. This spirit thrives and feeds on pride, unrepentant sins like **I Corinthians 10:14-22** states.

I Corinthians 10:14-22: Wherefore, my dearly beloved, flee from idolatry. I speak as to wise men; judge ye what I say. The cup of blessing which we bless, is it not the communion of the blood of Christ? The bread which we break is it not the communion of the body of Christ? For we being many are one bread, and one body: for we are all partakers of that one bread. Behold Israel after the flesh: are not they which eat of the sacrifice's partakers of the altar? What say I then? That the idol is anything or that which is offered in sacrifice to idols is anything? But I say that the things which the Gentiles sacrifice, they sacrifice to devils, and not to God: and I would not that ye should have fellowship with devils. Ye cannot drink the cup of the Lord and the cup of devils: ye cannot be partakers of the Lord's table and of the table of devils. Do we provoke the Lord to jealousy? are we stronger than he? (KJV, 2020).

If you are a pastor and you feel that the spirit of Jezebel has been operating in your church, I want you to ask yourself a few questions. When this spirit begins to attack you, trying to destroy your testimony, life, ministry, or stop your ministry, several things can happen. These questions will help you to determine if you have been under attack by this spirit.

1) Have I been experiencing an unusual amount of fear lately?
2) Am I always afraid of what will happen to me?
3) Has the desire to isolate myself increased recently?
4) Have I been experiencing unreasonable exhaustion and physical fatigue lately?
5) Have strange illnesses and diagnoses occurred in my life?
6) Have I had sexually perverse thoughts or dreams flooding my mind recently?
7) Have strange accidents been happening to me?
8) Have I become accident-prone in my personal life?

If you answered yes to two or more of the questions above, then the Jezebel spirit has been attacking you. The next step is to determine through whom this spirit is attacking and why. Make sure you begin praying and asking God to help you identify the source of these attacks. Once you have identified the source, take action to break the ties this spirit has on you. The only two steps you can take are first to separate yourself from the person(s) under the influence of the Jezebel spirit. Then through a spiritual warfare prayer, break any ties and set yourself free in Jesus' name! You must get away from the sphere of this spirits' influence. Then contact your most trusted prayer partners to help you battle this spirit.

If you are the pastor, you cannot leave your church without knowing that it is God's will for you to move on. However, if you are just a member of a church and you realize that your attack is from the Jezebel spirit attacking you through other members, the pastor, or church leadership, the best decision is to change churches. If this spirit is attacking you on your job, pray, and begin searching for a new job. If you do not break this spirit's influence and ties to you, it will destroy your marriage, life, and ministry. If you are a business owner, it will ruin or bankrupt your business. This spirit is an evil spirit that will require spiritual reinforcements for you to break-break-lose and stop! Dealing with the Jezebel spirit is a serious matter.

When the Jezebel spirit gets in your church, as the pastor, you cannot run away or change churches unless God directs you to. However, you can get your trusted spiritual counselors, mentors, other pastors, and your spouse to join with you fasting and praying for deliverance in your church.

If you do not take action to break this spirit's hold, you will begin to see ministerial pride and religious pride slip into your ministry. Many pastors today are under the influence of the Jezebel spirit. They have given fuel to these two types of pride without even realizing that they are in direct violation of God's commandments.

OTHER BEWITCHING SPIRITS:

Bewitching spirits come in many forms. They range from false teachers, preachers, false religions, teachers who urge us to be tolerant of sin, and other doctrines that do not claim that Jesus Christ is the son of God who gave his life for us. Paul and Jude admonished us to be aware of pride, unconfessed sins, and our attraction to the lust of the flesh and the desires of the eye. Pride, revenge, and jealousy appear to be the tools of choice that Satan likes to use on Christians that are in positions of power in a church or who could be a threat to his kingdom as spiritual prayer warriors. We also need to be aware of church and community atmospheres that promote legalism, rituals, and traditions of man that focuses on men and not God. We need to separate ourselves from these types of churches. God is the head of the church, not a man or a woman. The focus of each church service should be on God's word and what God can do in a life that is consecrated to him, not on what you can get from God, what you need to give to the church, and worship of the pastor or leaders. Worship, praise, adoration, and thanksgiving to God are what we should be doing from when we enter the church until we exit it each time.

For years, I have said that the true test of a pastor's honesty and humility is whether that pastor could be dropped off in the jungles of the Amazon without any TV cameras around and continue to love God, worship Him, and share the good news. The second test would be to place a pastor in a small country church with 50 to 60 senior citizens on fixed incomes that do not cover their bills, might less leave funds for them to lavish on the pastor. Would that pastor hold down a full-time job and pastor? Would he or she hold a part-time job and pastor if the district or organization was subsidizing his income? Most would not consider ministering where they are the focus and where their every desire was not fulfilled. If a pastor is of this mindset, he is a wolf in sheep's clothing and not a true shepherd.

The apostle Paul instructed Timothy not to depart from the teachings that he had given him on faith. He informed him to always be diligent in recognizing seducing spirits, demonic activity, lies, hypocrisy, and pray to recognize those speaking doctrines of devils and those with their conscience that had been compromised. *(See scripture below)*.

I Timothy 4:1-2: Now the Spirit speaketh expressly, that in the latter times some shall depart from the faith, giving heed to seducing spirits, and doctrines of devils; Speaking lies in hypocrisy; having their conscience seared with a hot iron; (KJV, 2020).

In this letter to Timothy, the apostle Paul clarifies that many will abandon the Christian walk and follow these deceiving spirits in the latter times. Many preachers will be deceived and begin to teach false doctrines or incorporate false beliefs into their teaching regimes. Any minister that begins to compromise God's word to please the pew or to receive offerings opens a gap in his or her spiritual hedge. As they start to embrace a compromised gospel, they become candidates for the bewitching spirit of Jezebel to possess them.

The "bewitching spirit concepts" that Satan tries to get in individuals' lives include hypocritical lies, preaching for self-gain, teaching for recognition, using the church as a social club or a lustful playground. For ministers who delete from their sermons the scriptures against sin for fear that they will offend someone attending, they open this door for Satan. One of the most crucial ways to get possessed of this spirit is for a minister to allow a clique or one individual to tell them who can be used in the services or hold offices in the church. For example, if the piano player informs the pastor that the Adult Sunday School teacher must be removed from his position or her and her husband are going to remove their tithes from the church and convinces him that he must make this decision, then this pastor has fallen prey to the bewitching spirit.

Another sign that the pastor has been bewitched includes him or her making changes in the church and its protocols. When men of God are misguided by this bewitching spirit, they make changes that will increase leisure, pleasure, self-gratification, and make themselves popular. They move the congregation into works, rituals, adding all types of rules and legalism. They begin to feel that they are superior to all local pastors and that their church has something that other churches cannot get or obtain.

It is extremely easy for a person who is honorable to be influenced by the lies of the spirit of Jezebel. Individuals who are oppressed or possessed by the spirit of Jezebel are usually charismatic individuals that want to appear to be holy, anointed, and favored by God. Because of this apparent move of God on them, it is easy for them to convince Christians that they are not fully endowed with the true gift of discernment of false truths. These individuals use vain words and vague promises to make people feel good or bad, if necessary, to control them.

The only way for the control of this spirit to be broken is for the spiritual leader of the church to yield to the Holy Spirit and reveal to him that they have been bewitched and led astray. This type of revelation must begin in the pulpit and go to the pew. Many pastors know the truth, but they do not want to accept it because they fear letting go of the "money people" in their church. I have had so many preachers tell me, "What am I going to do if I let God take charge, and my membership drops down to 25 people?" I always respond, "It is better to have 25 and a true move of God, with the freedom for the Holy Spirit to move in your church, than to have 325 people, and you are worried about every word in your sermon!"

Where our pastors need to be is in a place of humility. A place where they have died out to themselves and begun to focus on Jesus Christ alone! Do not be deceived into thinking that you can reason with the spirit of Jezebel or any other demonic spirits. If you try, you are walking into a spiritual trap in which you will not walk away without serious injury. The spirit of Jezebel must be brought down by supernatural means. The pastor must ensure that the membership has been taught the truth about the spirit of Jezebel and how it works in a church. The only way to bring down this spirit is to train the people it is trying to deceive, so their eyes are opened, and they recognize the spirit of Jezebel for its deceptive nature. The influence of the Jezebel spirit must be torn down and destroyed. This is done with spiritual warfare prayers. This comes when prayer and fasting are present—spiritual warfare by the pastor and members are essential in these circumstances.

Remember that you cannot preach it out of this person, counsel it out, or shame and scold them into submission. This spirit has such a grip on the persons that it oppresses or possesses that will not let go without a significant deliverance. My father always said that it took the type of prayer that "Rocked the gates of hell and sent the demons running, shaking, and fearing for their lives!" It takes intercessory prayer that is capable of breaking soul ties, strongholds, and other spirits. It takes a mountain-moving level of faith to undertake the prayer power needed to bring about this type of spiritual deliverance. You need not enter this warfare battle hoping to salvage the person as a member of your church.

The last piece of advice that I must give to you on recognizing the spirit of Jezebel has to do with possession by this spirit. If you are in a church where you feel that this spirit has been moved in and has begun to influence the pastor, start to watch for signs of spiritual impurity and immorality. Once this spirit takes possession of a pastor or any other man, they will have difficulty controlling their desires for women and will fall prey to adultery. I have seen pastors possessed with this spirit that had as many as five wives with three of them in the same church at the same time as members, while he continued as the pastor. The pastor in a media spotlight (like a TV preacher) may better control the adultery, but there will be an addiction to pornography or same-sex relations. Each time these people are caught, or it appears that they might get exposed, they become embarrassed and excessively repent.

SUMMARY OF THE BEWITCHING AND JEZEBEL SPIRITS:

There are a few other indicators that the spirit of Jezebel has moved into your church, work-place, home, or community. Even though these may not be used as often, they are still potent. I have encountered two women (sisters) in my ministry that were what I termed "possessed super-Jezebel demons." They had every indicator of the Jezebel spirit that I had learned or studied in their lives very active.

These other indicators include, but not limited to: their own agenda; wine until they get their way; grumble, grip, and blast others until they convince the majority to push them out of the church; control others; usually have a history of trauma or abuse in their lives as children, or young adult lives; they make commitments and make promises quickly, but never follow-through; always trying to impress others; steal ideas that others present, ma king it appear that it was their idea, design, or concept; use false humility; act entitled; they do not want to be accountable to anyone else; they do not want any checks and balances in the church; they search out the hurt and abused in the church and try to mentor or coach those individuals; falsely accuse people; have moments of insecurity, that are usually masked with false prophecies or false messages; they will initial witchcraft prayers, or other idolatry or witchcraft methods trying to get control; they try to use fear to get people to do what they want; they will target a spiritual leader, minister or teacher and push them until they isolate themselves; they try to

119

exhaust the people who could possibly discern them, so that they can remain undetected; they will pray prayers over people putting sicknesses on them; unusual accidents occur in their presence, especially to people who could possibly discern them; they operate in the circle of influence of the church leaders; if they cannot get a position in this circle of influence, they will target people in that circle, so that they can control the pastor, district, section, region, or national leaders.

You must realize that these spirits are not spirits that you can fight alone. You need reinforcements and prayer partners willing to fast with you. If you are reading this book and feel that as a pastor, you are so good that you can handle this spirit or any other demon spirit, you are in for a rude awakening...this spirit already has control over you. It uses pride and super-spiritual power the most on pastors and leaders. This spirit can attack you, influence you, and oppress you, and it will happen quicker than you can think or imagine. You must realize that any unopposed bewitching spirits spirit WILL destroy your ministry, church, marriage, and business or career if you are not careful. They destroy everyone, even pastors.

If you have realized that you are encountering this spirit after reading this chapter today, confide in your spouse or your most trusted spiritual prayer partner. Ask them to join with you and bind this spirit each day. I recommend that you design a spiritual warfare prayer that addresses your situation, the person(s) involved, and pray it morning and night. If you do not see any changes within one week, then start fasting meals. If there is no change after a week, begin fasting all day. Jesus told his disciples that some types of demons only come out "by prayer and fasting" (Mark 9:29). If you do not know how to write out a spiritual warfare prayer that will be effective in your situation, consult my book *The Spiritual Warrior*. It provides you with detailed instructions to pray effectively in warfare.

Mark 9:28-29: And when he was come into the house, his disciples asked him privately, why could not we cast him out? And he said unto them; this kind can come forth by nothing, but by prayer and fasting. (KJV, 2020).

Remember that each person who is influenced by a religious spirit or the spirit of Jezebel will eventually be possessed. I realize that I am sharing some of the more extreme cases I have witnessed in my ministry.

When individuals hang around with possessed people or individuals with these attitudes or character traits, these characteristics "attaches" to these spiritually weaker Christians. Also, individuals without the Holy Ghost are more susceptible to being influenced by spirits.

More times than I can count, I have seen spirit-filled Christians, and twice, Pastors play with these spirits trying to appease them. As these pastors tried to "control" these spirits, they were compromising so they could keep the tithes coming in and not lose the entire family in their churches. When you compromise and given into these spirits at times, even merely allowing them to keep positions in the church, this results in spirits possessing you. Playing with this spirit instead of standing on the word of God and preaching the uncompromised word of God is very dangerous!

Remember the story in I Kings chapters 18-21 about Elijah, the prophet, and his encounter with Queen Jezebel (wife to King Ahab)? In this scripture, we see where God had pronounced judgment onto the children of Israel through the Prophet Elijah saying that a draught was coming if they did not turn from their evil ways. This draught was a direct result of the children of Israel worshipping Baal (Moloch). After God answers by fire and the children of Israel agree to worship only the one true God, Elijah has all the prophets of Baal killed. This made Jezebel very angry, and she decided to kill Elijah. I want you to notice how the spirit of Jezebel and her choices affected Elijah. This is what this spirit does in our churches. As you read this story, if you are a minister, consider if this spirit has ever attacked in your church. If you are not a minister, have you seen this spirit in operation? Or maybe you have seen the circumstances listed below.

CHARACTERISTICS OF THE JEZEBEL SPIRIT:

1) The number one characteristic of the spirit of Jezebel is that it loves to <u>confuse</u>. This spirit was able to confuse Elijah. It had him convinced that he was the only prophet left and that no one, not even God, cared.

2) <u>The Jezebel spirit causes fear</u>. Elijah ran and hid for fear of his life. This powerful man of God who had just witnessed the remarkable miracle of fire coming down from heaven to consume his offering was afraid of one woman!

3) When the spirit of Jezebel invokes <u>fear, it will make you run like it made Elijah run.</u> This spirit does not want you to stand on the promises of God. This spirit can generate fear intense enough to make you cringe; it can kill your faith. Where there is no faith, there are no miracles! To combat the Jezebel spirit, you must stand your ground in faith, claiming God's promises instead of allowing fear to consume you.

4) <u>The spirit of Jezebel causes divisions.</u> It causes leaders, ministers, business owners, families, and anyone it attacks to divide up, usually over insignificant issues. It does not matter how it divides or why. It had a couple of goals planned: divide and conquer, destroy and take over; create fear and diminish the person's power; and cause confusion that permanently separates churches and families.

5) Finally, the Jezebel spirit loves to <u>create an environment filled with despair and despondency.</u> If this spirit can dash hopes, kills dreams, and give depressing prophecies, it will ensure that the people's vision is destroyed. The Bible says that ***"where there is no vision, the people perish" (Proverbs 29:18).***

With an increase in pornography and radical feminism, the area of influence of this spirit has mushroomed. With the rise in the number of abortions, alternate lifestyle acceptance, and quick-easy divorces, the destruction of the home in American has fallen prey to this spirit and its influence. This spirit is sucking the church into a new form of idolatry while it is spiritually lulling us to sleep. Satan does not care if you go to church or if you pray. He just does not want you to understand spiritual warfare, how to have an active prayer life, and answered prayers. If Satan can use the Jezebel spirit to keep you from living a victorious life, he has won! That is all that matters to him!

So many people deceitfully play with
religious pride and ministerial pride.
This is dangerous and can lead to
demonic possession.

Chapter Seven:

THE MOLOCH SPIRIT

This section was taken from my book, "Why am I not Living a Victorious Life?" If you want more information on this topic and how to live a victorious life, then contact us for a copy of this book. The Kindle Version is available through Amazon.com. The comments made in this chapter in message boxes like this one will indicate what new content was added to assist the reader with why this topic is relevant for this book.

In the Old Testament, the Amalekites worshipped a god by the name of Moloch. This god demanded the first-born child of each family to be sacrificed before him with much fertility. This god also rewarded any other parents who would sacrifice more children with fortunes. These were live sacrifices placed on the extended arms of the idols. The spirit of Moloch is a fierce, passionate, and destructive spirit that loves to destroy churches by starting spiritual fires that cannot be contained and destroying the lives of the children of the church leadership. The practitioners who worshipped this god demonstrated their loyalty in Bible-times by allowing their child to be burned alive on this alter to Moloch.

It is unlawful to sacrifice your children to any gods or any religious practices in the 21st Century. Moloch has found a new, more convenient way for young people to offer their children in sacrifice to him. It is called abortion! Most people in the Bible described the Moloch spirit by the rituals or characteristics of this Amalekites' god. However, it was sometimes called Baal in the Old Testament. The names are interchanged extensively throughout the scriptures.

This spirit of Moloch requires the loyalty of the people it controls. This god or demon secures this loyalty by convincing Christians that it is okay to "murder" other people or the church leadership with their tongues. If it cannot get you to abort your child, this spirit will convince you that you can emotionally abuse your child without consequences. This spirit does not care if you use physical, psychological, and emotional abuse or blackmail to control your children. He wants you to plant seeds in their minds that he can utilize at a future date to destroy them by ruining their lives with criminal behaviors or destroying their physical bodies with suicide. Satan does not care how he gets them; he wants your children to be his for eternity!

HISTORY OF THE MOLOCH SPIRIT:

Baal was known as the god of fertility with the title of Prince of the Earth. He was also known as the god of rain and dew. In most Greek literature, you will see the interchange of the words Baal and Moloch. You will see this throughout the Old Testament too. In discussing this spirit of Moloch, I want to share another story from the Book of Kings in the Old Testament. The culture surrounding the worship of Baal or Moloch is barbaric.

The Greek god, Moloch, was a god that required the sacrifice of children to worship him. The purpose of requiring individuals to sacrifice their children was to atone for their sins. The children of Israel offered their first-born children in a live sacrifice to Moloch.

Before you judge the children of Israel for being prey to such a simple lie as future prosperity, consider why most abortions are requested by the mother here in America. Many young ladies have an abortion in exchange for a better career path, the ability to complete school or college, financial security, convenience, and oh yes, the big one…reputation. If I abort the results of my sins, no one will know what I was doing! Many Christian homes have children who have had abortions because the parents could not afford to have the people in their church understand what their daughter had been doing.

In the 21st Century, we cannot offer live sacrifices on an altar without being arrested and punished for the crime of murder. However, this god has found a couple of new ways that we can worship him. **The first method of sacrifice is abortion**. Offering our unborn to him generates compliance. Most people supporting abortion or having abortions do not realize that they are appeasing this demonic god. There is also another way to satisfy this god that I see so many Christians involved. **This second method of pleasing this spirit is the emotional abuse of your children**. This abuse is as devastating to the life and future of a child as sacrificing them before an idol.

Our spiritual focus centers around us when sin is present in our lives. Our focus should be on God's will and our obedience. This new focus makes self the priority. The scripture (Exodus 20) says that we are to have no other gods before God the Father. People oppressed by this spirit are focused on themselves. Their personal focus is so intent that they substitute God and their relationship with him for themselves. To know if this spirit has affected you, simply ask yourself if God's will is still a priority in your life? If you want your way in all things, desire everything for yourself, then you have been oppressed by this spirit. It causes you to ignore God's will or procrastinate on implementing God's will in your life until a time that is more convenient for you.

This second method may not sound as critical to you at first. However, bear with me as I explain what this is doing to the next generation (Generation Millennials and Generation C). When we continuously destroy individuals' mental abilities by implementing "slave mentality" into their lives, we destroy their ability to function and succeed. In other words, we are killing their futures. The by-product of this type of mental slavery results in young people who shoot up their schools. After they become adults, these individuals return to work after a lunch break and shoot their colleagues and bosses.

Recently, I was at a Christmas dinner with a family in our church. There was so much peace and happiness in the home as we all sat around the dining room table talking. This family had gathered around the matriarch of this family to shower her with gifts and love. The beauty of watching these grandchildren honor this 80-year-old woman was breathtaking. Then the front door to the home opened, and a wild, whirlwind spirit came storming through the door.

This matriarch's daughter had arrived with her husband, two daughters, and their grandchildren in tow. The loud, angry voices that entered the door shouting at each other shatter the peace in this home in just seconds. I looked at this family's matriarch, and I notice the sad look that came over her face. Then she looked at me and said, "that is my daughter X; she is the associate pastor at X Holiness Church in X, Alabama. I do not know what has happened to her since she started attending there. It appears that some type of spirit has gotten on my daughter. She is so stressed that she just screams at everyone she sees."

I had never been to this church, but I had met the pastor a few weeks prior. We were at the funeral of another local pastor. This pastor's voice was loud, rude, and angry. All of his comments were negative about other ministers and churches. He was judgmental of all of the television ministers. He consistently commented that none of the churches except his had the real move of God operating in them.

I did not share my assessment of this pastor with this lady. Instead, I was in too much shock at what I was watching that I could not say a word. This preacher lady was chasing her 9-year-old granddaughter around the kitchen table and into the living room with her hand raised to slap her, shouting, "X, you little devil you! X, X, can you hear me calling you? Stop, you little devil! I am going to beat the _____-_____ out of you, you little devil!"

Without warning, this lady stopped in front of me. I guess she recognized the look of shock on my face. "Oh, preacher, do not be so shocked. I am sure you do the same behind closed doors! You have no right to judge me. I am not a hypocrite; I just say what I think in public and not hide behind my priestly robes or collar! That child is a devil. Satan has possessed her just to torment me. It is her momma's fault!"

I replied to her, "I do not understand how a person who claims to be a spirit-filled, tongue talking, evangelical can curse like a sailor and verbally abuse a child! I do not know what God you serve or where your Holy Ghost comes from, but the God I serve and the Holy Ghost that speaks through me will not live in an unclean temple. Your tongues are not from the same heavenly sources as mine!"

With the conclusion of her rant to me, she picked up where she left off, chasing that child, calling her a devil. When she caught up with the child, she slapped her hard across the face, then shook her violently with both hands. Before I knew what was going on, my spouse had gotten up, run to this woman, pulled the child away from her, and in a very stern voice said, "Go pick on someone your size! It takes a devil to know a devil! You have two seconds to stop, or I will call 911. When I dial that number, I will ask for the police and social services."

Later, I explained to my spouse that I insisted that we leave immediately because it would not do any good to call law enforcement on this lady. The son-in-law (father of the child being slapped) was an FBI Agent, the daughter (mother of the child) was a registered nurse. They had probably been abusing those children emotionally for years. They had the

126

perfect jobs to cover up the crimes. I told my spouse, "If you call 911, who will they believe, you or the FBI agent?" So, we got in our car and left.

I have shared this story so that you can see that no matter the laws in place, people oppressed or possessed by the Moloch spirit do not care. They will defy the law and the Bible to handle things the way they desire. The Moloch spirit is a very demanding, controlling, and abusive spirit.

Child abuse, suppressing children's dreams, and verbally destroying a child's life with negative words and curses is another way of offering your children to Moloch. If we as Christians allow Satan to use us, he will take our words and make the next generation hate church!

Satan does not care how he keeps the future generations out of the church. However, if he can use the Christians and pastors to accomplish this goal, he kills two birds with one stone. He gets the next generation and destroys the church of today. I hate to sound like doom and gloom, but there is no way a church allowing ministers to act in this fashion while holding offices in the church can grow. There is no way a preacher cursing and verbally abusing a child can go in the Rapture. This behavior is one of the works of the flesh. Refer back to the chapter where each of the works of the flesh is explained.

If you disagree with me on this topic, do not stop reading. Even though I have defined this abuse as idolatry and a demonstration of demonic behavior, do not let this point keep you from reading the rest of this book. There is not a scripture that states that this behavior is idolatry. However, it does say that a Christian is expected to have humility, peace, love, longsuffering, meekness, kindness, etc. Did you see any of the fruits of the spirit in this lady's life? If the fruits of the spirit are not present, then the works of the flesh are present. Galatians, the 5th chapter, clearly states that the works of the flesh "are an abomination and shall not enter heaven!"

With all this drama, we quickly found an excuse to leave. I never prayed with that family as they had requested. We always pray with everyone before I leave their home. I never went back to that home again until they called me to come to pray that the matriarch was dying.

You may disagree with me, but I believe that this mother and grandmother were offering this child on the altar of Moloch supernaturally. In twenty years, this child will be a child-abuser herself or worse the employee that snaps and goes back to work the next day with an AK-47 and fills the employees and walls with bullets!

In the Bible, the children of Israel were drawn to the idol worship of Baal. Under Ahab and Jezebel's reign, they were encouraged to forget about the covenant's restrictive laws. They wanted everyone to do what felt right to them and be blessed. That sounds like today's media viewpoint! Elijah challenged the 450 prophets of Baal and the 400 prophets of Asherah on Mount Carmel to have their god answer by fire. Both sides agreed, along with all the children of Israel, present that they would serve whichever God answered by fire.

There are various scriptures in the old testament that deal with the offering of children to Moloch. When you have time, read Leviticus **20:2** and **Jeremiah 32:35.**

HOW IS THE SPIRIT OF MOLOCH IMPACTING THE CHURCH OF AMERICA?

The spirit of Moloch is getting pastors so caught up in what is popular, what entertains best, and what activities will reach the biggest audience. Instead of evaluating our churches by the numbers saved or changed, we judge based upon average attendance! The new god that is controlling churches in America is MONEY! The larger audience usually results in more money in the offerings.

While writing this book, I watched one televangelist had a fundraiser during the pandemic. Instead of encouraging people and asking how he could help others, he was concerned about the double-digit millions that he needed to operate during the projected two to four weeks that they would not have services. He set up a special website where people could pay their weekly tithes. The website did not have anywhere that the membership could ask for help or prayer.

This minister exceeded the amount of money he was trying to raise. His gimmick was that if they planted a seed, God would protect them from the Coronavirus! When the governor in his state decided to extend the "stay at home orders" till the end of the month, he had another fundraiser. This time, this televangelist asked for double the amount of money he collected in the first fundraiser. When the offerings did not rapidly flow in like the first one, he began to preach "doom" to the people who would not be giving.

I do not know your experience with God's mercy and judgment, but it does not work this way. God judges us by our hearts and whether we have the fruits of the spirit in our lives. God is concerned with our relationship with him, not what man thinks about us. God does not have to ask a preacher somewhere whether he should bless you or curse you.

The prosperity sermons and the "I've got to be bigger than any other ministry" are the mentality that is choking out God's true move in our churches. It takes over the church and makes the future generations sick to their stomach at the nonsense that flows from preacher's mouths.

The actions of a few lousy television ministries should not impact all of them. Not all are wrong or bad. Most preachers have a pure heart. However, the bad programs and preachers get so much recognition. This negative press causes the world to look at the church as some type of circus spectacle.

The purpose of today's church is to win the lost, spread the gospel, take care of the widows and orphans, and evangelize the world. Nowhere in our Biblical job description does God say that we are to entertain, take care of, feed, clothe, and make famous the church leadership, church workers, or build programs that entertain instead of preaching.

I visited a 24-year-old in jail last year. He attended an evangelical church in the town where he lived. I was aware of the large youth group at that church and the programs they had for them. There was something at the church every day of the week except Monday for the young people. When I began to witness to him and give him scriptures, I noticed that he had a strange look on his face. I asked if he understood what I was sharing. His reply startled me, "Oh, it is not that preacher. I just want to know if that is really in the Bible or just something you have memorized to quote. I went to church X for 15 years. I never heard anyone there say that you had to ask God to come into your heart. They never told us to read our Bible every day and pray."

I asked what did they teach. He replied, "Well, the youth ministers do not teach or preach to us. We were always doing activities, games, etc. For most services, we just stood around at the "coffee bar" in the church fellowship hall and talked. They fed us on Wednesday and Friday nights. There were numerous times that my buddies and I would leave as soon as we ate. Then come back just before church is dismissed in the sanctuary. Our parents never knew that we were not there the entire time. I saw more drugs and alcohol at those church events that I saw partying with my friends." I started to cry! What a tragedy! The church must wake up! We must get our

129

priorities in order. Entertaining is not the answer; the word of God is the answer!

The days of preaching not to offend are over! Most of the "new age" preachers conveniently do not preach on sin, just peace and prosperity! They want to make people feel good, enlightened, and blessed so that they will give generously to the organization. They want them to feel comfortable so that they will continue to come. The spirit of Moloch has ministers bragging on church size, bottom-lines, and other things, but not souls! This spirit also controls what the preacher does, says, or enforces!

SUMMARY

The primary way that the spirit of Moloch attacks many church members is through abortions. The children of Israel and the heathens in Canaan offered their first-born children to this god. In the worship of self, abortion provides the child sacrifice that this god craves and causes the mother to declare that she is more important than her child. This worship of self also pleases this god. Providing counseling to women who have had abortions, in our ministry, we have had to work with 100% of these women to get deliverance from the spirit of Moloch. When it inhabits women in your church, this spirit will destroy your church quicker than the Leviathan spirit.

Remember that the spirit of Moloch wants its worshipers to reject God and his authority. These individuals do not want anyone in the church, including the pastor, to have power over them or make rules that they must abide by or correct them. They are not capable of being submissive to their spouses, church leaders, or God. They promote self while claiming that it is in the interest of human rights or women's rights. They will encourage self-provocation at all costs, even if it defies God's will or plan. They will also promote themselves at the expense of their neighbors, family, and church family.

In the worship of self and their rights, this spirit creeps into our churches and begins to influence others. If you are a pastor, you need to determine if your church's problem and trouble makers have had abortions. If you find that a person had an abortion earlier in their lives, then I strongly encourage you to start counseling sessions with this woman and her husband. She must get deliverance from this evil spirit. Putting this person in leadership or as a teacher in your church will destroy it. These individuals need removal until deliverance can be obtained. This spirit has one motive; it is to obliterate your ministry and suppress your church. This spirit loves church confusion and church busts.

The idols built to this god were usually bronze or brass statutes with the head of a bull, the bulging belly of a man with fires built under this god's extended hands. I saw photos in college history textbooks of the idol Moloch. They all showed an idol with a bulging belly that was a firebox that works like some of the southern pot-bellied stoves. All books that I reviewed listed shrine prostitution as one of the benefits or perks of membership for the men at the temples in these foreign countries.

The children offered to these idols were laid in the idol's hand. Then they were burned alive, suffocating in the fires beneath this idol's hands. The people would chant to this god for blessings. Some of the idol's fire pits were large enough to offer men and women as live sacrifices. All sacrifices were to appease this god and secure the promised prosperity. More information on the spirit of Moloch will be available in my next book of this series, *The Spiritual Warrior*.

Chapter Eight:

DECEITFUL SPIRITS AND

FALSE PREACHERS

This section was taken from my book, "Why am I not Living a Victorious Life?" If you want more information on this topic and how to live a victorious life, then contact us for a copy of this book. The Kindle Version is available through Amazon.com. The comments made in this chapter in message boxes like this one will indicate what new content was added to assist the reader with why this topic is relevant for this book.

DEMONIC INFLUENCES

No one is immune to influences by demonic or evil spirits. But we have the greatest tool to protect us…the Bible, God's word, combined with prayer and fasting. Most protestant churches understand demonic spirits. However, the Catholic church is more advanced than most protestant churches regarding deliverance from demonic spirits or exorcisms. I want to remind you that you must be aware of Jesus' teachings to the disciples that "these come by fasting and prayer" only.

For up-to-date statistics on the hunger that the spirit of Moloch has and its control here in America, you can google the Center for Disease Control (CDC) and search their site for the statistic for abortions. There are over three-quarters of a million babies aborted each year in America. There have been more than 13 million abortions or child sacrifices before Moloch since the supreme court rendered "*Roe versus Wade.*"

Moloch represents the male version of this god. The female goddess to Moloch is Ashtoreth. These foreign gods all used sexual relationships between the temple goddesses and the worshippers as it taught that self should not be denied anything that it wanted, including unbridled sensuality. Leviticus in the Old Testament forbids these pagan worshipers. Then the apostle Paul, some 1400 plus years later, forbids these practices and worships in Romans 1:26-27; plus, he also condemned the lewd orgies and same-sex relationships.

Romans 1:26-27: For this cause, God gave them up unto vile affections: for even their women did change the natural use into that which I against nature: and likewise, also the men, leaving the natural use for the woman, burned in their lust one toward another; men with men working that which is unseemly, and receiving in themselves that recompense of their error which was meet. (KJV, 2020).

As the demonic influences have become more assertive in America, we have seen Roe versus Wade approved, and same-sex marriages becoming more common. Now, the legalization of the same-sex relationship as a family unit. The 21st Century has redefined the definition of the family unit and the definition of marriage to include what the first chapter of Romans condemns.

In making this statement, I am not in any way condoning "hate crimes" or discrimination against these individuals. They are first and foremost human beings that are United States citizens, and they should have all the rights that are entitled to a US citizen. However, my acceptance of them as a human being with rights, that deserves my respect does not mean that I have to promote their lifestyle choices or preach them into heaven! The Bible is clear in the New Testament (Galatians 5) that this is an abomination and will NOT enter heaven. I do not want anything to keep me out of Heaven, and I recommend that you make the same commitment to God. He will help you clean up the mess you have in your life and make the right choices for him!

DEMONIC INFLUENCES AND FALSE TEACHINGS:

Know that the spiritual gift of discernment is needed now, more than ever, to make it through to the rapture! But there is one key you need to understand about discernment. Discernment is NOT judging. I see so many Christians who claim the gift of discernment, and they use that gift as a license to judge, condemn, criticize, and defame other Christians and ministers. The gift of discernment is for your personal walk with God. If you are a minister, it is to help you and your church from being deceived. If we allow Satan to convince us that our gift of discernment is a license to judge and condemn others, then we are already deceived!

Rabbi Loren Jacobs (2012) explained that the "last days revivals" would also bring about the "end-time Apostasy" that would deceive many Christians. She defined the revival versus apostasy period as "The whole gamut of today's so-called revival scene, from Toronto to Pensacola, must be seriously faced! Videos of the services show people crawling on the floor, howling like wolves, barking like dogs, roaring like lions, going through bodily contortions impossible without the aid of some spiritual power, unable to speak or even remember their names when they try to give a testimony, and worse. Many of these baptized at Pensacola seem to lose consciousness or shake so violently that they must be carried out of the baptismal tank lest they drown. Others flail about so wildly as to require several men to handle them. Such manifestations were also found in past 'revivals' among the Shakers, the Mormons, and many other cults. That such things could now be widely accepted as evidence of the Holy Spirit only testifies to the extent of the delusion that is already permeating the messianic community!" (para. 17).

Rabbi Jacobs continues to explain that Jude 3 warns us of these types of events that will happen inside the church, not from outside influences. He says that these spirits will condemn. "Contend earnestly for the faith which was once for all delivered to the saints…for certain persons have crept in unnoticed" (Jude 3-4, JKV, 2020). The best way for Satan to deceive the church is to send false prophets into the church. If the attacks come from outside the church, they will recognize it immediately. However, if Satan can insert a person into the congregation or leadership staff that is charismatic, he can use that individual to deceive the pastor and congregation.

I attended a few nights of the Brownsville Revival in Pensacola, Florida. I was a licensed Assembly of God minister at that time. This church was in the fellowship of the Assemblies of God. The pastor and the evangelist running the revival was also licensed with the Assemblies of God. I felt like both ministers loved God and wanted to do what was right. However, in their hunger for souls (which was so obvious), they began to overlook events happening around them. Anytime revival breaks out, everyone flocks to that church or town. You get just as many "wild-fire seekers" as you do sincere Christians that join in the revival. This presents a major dilemma for pastors. Do you openly rebuke the fake demonstrations or ignore them and continue with your message or prayer line? Most pastors fear that many non-Christians would be turned off and not come forward in the process of openly rebuking one. So, they elect to continue with the service.

I teach that open rebuke and casting out of demons should not be done in a mixed congregation. There have been times when I have had to sit someone down that was disrupting a service. However, my most trusted members and I deal with the disruptive person or the demon-possessed person in private. I try to err on the side of caution with these cases. Every human deserves respect and dignity when possible. But each situation is unique, and there is not a "cookie-cutter protocol or algorithm" that I can give you that will work in all situations. You have to have the discernment of the spirits and the anointing of God to handle these situations.

I shared this review of the Brownsville Revival by Rabbi Jacobs so that you could understand through the eyes of a non-Pentecostal how some of the actions we take appear. When you look at things through their eyes, you see how foolish some of our charismatic demonstrations and church rituals appear to non-Christians. The nights that I attended I noticed a large number of demon-possessed individuals in the service. I felt that Satan had sent them for the purpose of disrupting the services and preventing people from coming forward to give their lives to Christ. Fake religious demonstrations are a turn off to the sinner person who is educated or has had a real experience with Christ in the past.

We cannot let the fear of being deceived keep us from enjoying worship and fellowship with other Christians. We just have to be on guard for who will hinder or disrupt the services. Ask God to give you the gift of discernment and direct you in each service you attend or officiate. Know that if you are humble and seeking God, he will lead you. You do not have to fear, but you must be alert at all times to false teachings, preachers, prophets, and false doctrines.

On February 28, 2020, a local minister in Anyuan, Philippines (I am not going to quote him directly or share his name because I do not believe in public rebukings or calling an individual out in a book or on TV unless I have spoken with them directly and can share their side of the story), wrote a message to his "followers" telling them that Jesus had already returned here to earth and was walking secretly amongst us as he was trying to get people to accept him and be ready for his return that was real soon. A friend brought me the newsletter she received.

There were so many facts listed that were accurate that it made the letter appear to be a true word from God. He quoted I Peter 4:17 in his letter, implying that God was coming to the preachers first and judging them. He was rebuking and correcting the preachers so they could change their ministries to redemption and holiness. He quotes some of the same events and statistics that I have pulled from various websites for this book. He was obviously aware of some of the natural disasters here in the United States. He talked about how all of these events and the persecution of Christians worldwide were signs of the end of times.

Although these statistical and natural disaster facts were true, the message of the letter was a false teaching. Jesus is not here on earth, walking amongst us trying to get preachers to accept him. Yes, I believe, because of the dream I had and the message from God, that he is dealing with pastors around the world. I believe that he has started with the preachers, teachers, and pastors like I Peter 4:17 implies, and he is calling us all back to Calvary. I believe that God is "stirring-up" pastors and ministers to preach about his Jesus' soon return and the church being rapture ready! But in our search for truth and directions on how to be ready for his return, we must not become deceived by false doctrines, demonic influences, and lying spirits. Double-check everything with the Bible. Fast and pray if you are not sure about your research. The Holy Spirit will lead you.

This doctrine that Jesus has already returned to the earth is not a new wave of teachings that have resulted because of COVID-19. On July 24, 2019, Xiao Fei posted on www.holyspiritspeaks.org that Jesus had already come back to earth and that he was secretly walking around testing people. Fei said in his website post that when Jesus had finished testing people and showing people around the world his works and miracles that he would finish his coming by appearing in the clouds with the Saints riding on a horse coming down from heaven to earth. He stated that if we were saved, demonstrating holiness, and living righteous lives, we would be caught up in the clouds with him and go with him to Jerusalem to set up his kingdom. This minister left out about the rapture of the church, the dead in Christ being raised, and the 7-years in heaven for the marriage supper of the lamb. He jumped directly to the Millennial Reign. My friends, you must study the books of Daniel, Isaiah, Hosea, Matthew 24, II Thessalonians, Titus, and Revelation. You must know the word of God (The Bible), or you will be deceived in these last days!

During August 2019, I went back to this www.holyspiritspeaks.org website to see if the message from 2018 was still there. It was, plus several others had been added. On May 14, 2019, there was a message from a LiMin and one on June 23, 2019, from a Zhon Jing.

Zhon Jing shared the story of the five wise virgins and the five foolish virgins to prove the points that he was making. Then he made this recommendation, "If we hear someone say that the Lord has already returned, that he has uttered new words and id doing the work of judging and purifying mankind, we can't waste any time in looking into it. As long as we can confirm that it is God's work and words, we must accept and submit to it. That way, we will be able to welcome the return of the Lord and attend the feast with him" (Jing, 2019, para. 13). Then he excitedly proclaimed, "Thanks be to the Lord! Now I finally know that the key to welcoming the Lord's second coming is in being a wise virgin and being careful to hear God's voice. As long as I confirm that words are uttered by God, I must rush to accept this—that's the only way to welcome his return" (para. 14).

As I have stated already, Satan deceives us with the use of God's word, twisted, or with facts. As you can see in these two quotes, there are true facts present, but false statements entwined. Yes, we need to be like the wise virgins. This parable Jesus taught gives us insight into what is required to make it to Heaven. However, his comments that as long as we can confirm something that someone says with scriptures, then it is from God is not true. Satan knows the Bible better than you or I will ever understand it. He will use quotes out of context, partial verses, and statements with only one or two words changed in them. For the person who never reads God's word, they will not recognize the omission of a word or two or the changing of a word. Jing's comment that if there is scripture to support a claim that we MUST accept it as being from God is not true. We have to pray over every word from God, prophecy, or words of wisdom shared. We cannot afford to be deceived in these last days!

Zhon-Jing and LiMin listed their research and how they had come to the same conclusion that Jesus was here on earth, walking amongst us now. They quoted Mark 8:15 and Matthew 12:24 to support this theory. Both quoted Luke 21:27 and Revelation 1:7 to support their theories of the New Jerusalem. These scriptures have been taken out of context and do not refer to the interpretations they had posted. It is imperative that you know the history of the Bible and the cultural circumstances for each chapter. It is worth every dollar you will pay to have a good concordance (I use Strong's and Thompson Chain) for my research. I also have a Dake's Bible that I refer to for statistical information and research at times. Because I have traveled extensively, I have history books from around the world, which helps me understand the cultures, ethnic practices, and history that would have been present during the times the scriptures were written.

Even cheap Bibles without many resources will tell you the approximate time that each of the books of the Bible was written and who is believed to be the book's author. These facts can help you to research the historical events and the culture of that time. It is essential to understand why something was written. It helps you to make it relevant for today. Do not let a minister tell you that you do not need to study and research topics or look up Greek and Hebrew words. Please do not accept a pastor that tells you he does not have to study because the Holy Spirit, Gabriel, Michael, or Jesus give him the sermons he must deliver.

DEMONIC INFLUENCES THROUGH ANTI-CHRISTS:

Know that in Paul's day, he told the people of Asian Minor in his letters and his instructions to Timothy that antichrists were walking amongst them trying to deceive them and make themselves like God. If Paul felt that there were antichrists in those days, then there are antichrists around the world spreading a counterfeit gospel. We are all aware of the antichrist that will be identified as the "beast in Revelation." He will deceive the world and establish his kingdom, claiming to be the messiah, the redeemer. He will work wonders and miracles, but he will not be of our heavenly Father, God. He will be an antichrist. Of the people you meet today, if they tell you that they do not believe in God, we call them an atheist. If they tell you they believe in God, but they teach a false doctrine, we call them a false prophet. However, some false prophets are just confused because that is what they have been taught their entire lives. When they learn the truth, the Holy Spirit deals with them and changes them. For the ones you are false prophets that God has "turned over to a reprobate mind to believe a lie and be damned," those individuals are an antichrist, not a false or confused prophet! (Romans 1:27-29, KJV). See the full scripture on previous pages.

I John 4: 1-4: *Beloved, believe not every spirit, but try the spirits whether they are of God: because many false prophets are gone out into the world. Hereby know ye the Spirit of God: every spirit that confesseth that Jesus Christ is come in the flesh is of God: and every spirit that confesseth not that Jesus Christ is come in the flesh is not of*

God: and this is that spirit of antichrist, whereof ye have heard that it should come; and even now already is it in the world. (KJV, 2020).

I John 2:21-22: Who is a liar but he that denieth that Jesus in the Christ? He is antichrist, that denieth the Father and the Son. Whosoever denieth the Son, the same hath not the Father: he that acknowledgeth the Son hath the Father also. (KJV, 2020).

II Peter 2:1- 10: But there were false prophets also among the people, even as there shall be false teachers among you, who privily shall bring in damnable heresies, even denying the Lord that bought them, and bring upon themselves swift destruction. And many shall follow their pernicious ways; by reason of whom, the way of truth shall be evil spoken of. And many shall follow their pernicious ways; by reason of whom, the way of truth shall be evil spoken of. And through covetousness shall they with feigned words make merchandise of you: whose judgment now of a long time lingereth not, and their damnation slumbereth not. For if God spared not the angels that sinned, but cast them down to hell, and delivered them into chains of darkness, to be reserved unto judgment; and spared not the old world; but saved Noah the eighth person, a preacher of righteousness, bringing in the flood upon the world of the ungodly; and turning the cities of Sodom and Gomorrah into ashes condemned them with an overthrow, making them an ensample unto those that after should live ungodly; and delivered just Lot, vexed with the filthy conversation of the wicked; for that righteous man dwelling among them, in seeing and hearing, vexed his righteous soul from day to day with their unlawful deeds;) The Lord knoweth how to deliver the godly out of temptations, and to reserve the unjust unto the day of judgment to be punished: But chiefly them that walk after the flesh in the lust of uncleanness, and despise government. Presumptuous are they, self-willed, they are not afraid to speak evil of dignities. (KJV, 2020).

Without spiritual discernment, you and I will be deceived in these last days. The counterfeits that Satan is putting in the pulpits have rocked the church to sleep. They have spoken, "name it and claim it," until the people do not even know the word of God any longer. They have become deceived due to their search for an answer that they like or desire. To help you understand how these false preachers and teachers are deceiving churches across America, let us review what Peter taught on this topic of false preachers and teachers in II Peter.

In the Word from God listed in chapter one, God mentioned that there would be consequences for the false preachers, teachers, and prophets. Although there are numerous occasions in the Old Testament where God tells us about false prophets (example: Balaam), and we are shown the consequences that fell on the children of Israel when they chose to listen to the prophets of Baal instead of the word from God, the scripture in II Peter gives the most concise and clear instructions on what we are to do with false teachings, how to recognize false prophets, etc. First, let us review what God said he was going to do to the false preachers, teachers, and prophets in the message:

a) Call them to repentance; if they turn to me (God), I will treat them as righteous pastors.
b) If they refuse to turn to me, I will remove them from their pulpits.
c) "Why have my children turned their backs on me?"

To fall into the hands of an angry God is not a place that I ever want to be in as a minister. I want God's blessing and favor. But for the men and women who are demonstrating false teachings and misleading the church members, as Peter wrote about in II Peter the second chapter, it would be better for them that they had never been born.

You may be asking yourself how I will recognize these false preachers and teachers if Satan's counterfeits are as good as you have mentioned in previous chapters. This is a valid question. The best answer to this question is also found in II Peter. The apostle Peter may have denied Christ three times, but he repented of his sins and turned his entire life around for Christ. Peter was a powerful man of God, who won very many people to the Lord during his days of ministry.

Sometime around 60 A.D., the apostle Peter wrote a couple of letters to the Christians that suffered persecution for their faith in Jesus Christ. As Peter was writing to them, he offered words of encouragement, but he also stressed the points of living a pure life sanctified before God. Peter shared principles with this early church that most of us refer to today as "Core Principles" or standards of integrity.

Even though Peter tells these young Christians that they will be tested, some killed for their beliefs, and others persecuted, they also share with them that they will be saved, given a heavenly home, and blessed here on earth. It sounds almost like a contradiction. Well, it is not. God's word promises us that we will be tested but that our salvation can be secured, even through our periods of testing. At times, we are tested to get the rough edges off of us or remove things that will hinder us in the future. Other times, we are tried so that God can deliver us, and he can win lost souls as we give our testimony of deliverance. (These teachings of Peter will be discussed in detail in a later chapter).

Then Peter begins to explain salvation, cleansing of our sin, and why it is vital for us not to have sin in our lives. Once he completes this sermon, he shifts to the topic of false teachers and preachers who are deceiving the church. He explains what is going to happen and the judgments of God. The most remarkable part of this letter from Peter is his recollection of an Old Testament story about Balaam. The story of Balaam is a perfect example of the false prophets that are standing behind pulpits today and gracing our television screens with their "name it, claim it, get-rich schemes!" Not all televangelists are false prophets. Not all sermons on God's blessings are wrong or schemes. It is scriptural to be blessed and favored. But to secure these blessings, you must first repent of your sins and turn from your wicked ways as Peter admonishes these young Christians.

I knew a man who was a mid-level politician in state government. He was a man who would give you the shirt off his back if he liked you. He could be compassionate and tenderhearted. However, a dark side would connive and wheel or deal to get what he wanted. Most of his political arrangements heavily favored himself. At times I would get the opportunity to witness to him. His favorite remark to me was, "Oh preacher, you know that you and your father have always been the apple of God's eye. You both have been favored and blessed so much; everyone has to know that God has a favorite! Why can't you get some of those blessings shifted my way?" No matter how many times I witnessed to him and shared with him God's promises and how he could have them in his life, he would always present an excuse for not committing.

One day he showed up at my office with a broad smile on his face. "You are not going to believe what I learned a couple of weeks ago. I was listening to this preacher on Trinity Broadcasting Network. He said that God had called him to be a prophet to help the children of God get out of debt! He shared about planting seeds and reaping a harvest. I sat mesmerized in front of the TV. He spoke with such authority; I know it was God that I was home at that moment to hear his sermon." This man went on to tell me more specifics of the sermon and the preacher's name. I listened without commenting. Then his eyes widened and began to glow as he said, "Now, preacher, here is the best part. He said that if I would plant $ X.00 in his ministry every week for a year that God would open the doors of heaven, and I would be blessed. He said that I would be rich and that God would give me peace, happiness, and give me favor."

I explained to him that all of those promises and scriptures were in the Bible and true. However, there is a condition for reaping the blessing from sowing seeds. It is salvation! For about an hour, we peacefully argued about how sin in your life would prevent the blessings of God. Regardless of how much money you gave to this minister or any ministry. But I never convinced him that the guarantee that this televangelist was issuing was a scam to get people to give money. The promises of God are real, and you can experience them, but not while lying, cheating on your wife, scamming the state government, and getting involved in "shady deals!"

Finally, I told this guy, "X, I will not debate this with you anymore. We both see this differently, and we both have scriptures to support our sides. Let us agree to disagree on this topic. I will put my judgments of this televangelist's scam on a shelf and pray and ask God to show you the truth about this matter. In the meantime, I want you to be safe. Do not invest in this man's ministry any more money than you can afford to lose. This is a gamble you are taking. One year from today, I want you to come to see me. Bring your mortgages, bank statements, and anything else you have acquired from this planting exercise like house and land deeds, vehicle titles, 401K balances, savings balances, etc. I want you to prove to me that I am wrong." We shook hands, agreed, and promised not to address this topic for 365 days! We both put an appointment on our calendars for 366 days later.

On the 366th day, this man walked into my office with a banker's box running over with papers. There was a somber look on his face. "Preacher, I should have listened to you. I gave $10,000 per month to this ministry for 12 months. He said that if you gave that amount that God would give you a 1000-fold blessing. So, I gave it! One thousand-fold of 1.2 million dollars should have been a lot of money. This one year of seed planting should have been my last year to have worked in my life! But it did not happen, so I called this preacher yesterday and told him that he was wrong. I told him how you warned me, but I did not listen. I asked him for my money back. He said he guaranteed it to work. To me, that means he owes me my money back. He told me that was not how it worked. He did not know why it did not work for me. He said he was told to do that, and it worked for him, so he was not preaching it to everyone, and it worked for most. Sometimes, it does not work, and I do not know why. Maybe this is your time of testing of your faith. I told him that I did not accept that!"

"Oh, Preacher, what am I going to do? I am out $1.2 million, my wife has left me, my three children will not even speak to me, the governor fired me last week, and I have 13 lawsuits filed against me!" It was my time to show my shock. I replied, "Well, X, I am sorry to hear this, but I thought you were bringing me proof that it worked. If it did not work, then what is in the box?" He dropped his head and began to cry, "Oh, this box is all that is left of my life…a box of past-due notices, lawsuits served on me these past two weeks, overdraft notices from the bank, and the divorce papers my wife served me this morning! Can you pray over them, so God will make this all go away? God always answers your prayers. I should have planted that money in this ministry instead of X's ministry!"

I got up, walked over to this man, put my arms around him, and said, "I am so sorry to hear that all of this has happened to you. I will not say 'I told you so' because you do not need to hear that now. But I will share with you a way out of this mess you are in if you will listen. But first, I need to clarify one thing for you. It may sound harsh, but you know I have always been honest with you. Even if you had planted your money in this ministry, then the same things would have happened to you. You cannot buy your way into Heaven. You cannot scam your way into riches without consequences! The only way out of this for you is to give your heart and life entirely to Jesus Christ, lay this mess at his feet, and ask him to help you make amends, restitution, and put the pieces back together."

Sadly, like the young rich ruler in the parable Jesus told, he left my office with his head hung low. He did not want to commit to a life of integrity. He thought that was too much. Last year as I stood by his hospital bed as he was dying, he looked at me and said words that I will never forget, "Preacher, you were right. It took losing everything just to make me angry at God. It took God taking my health to turn me back to him. I now know that all I needed was God in charge of my life, but Ole X here had to be in control of everything! I have nothing; I am on Medicaid; I have lived in a nursing home for months now. My family will not talk to me. When I die, I doubt that my children will come to my funeral. I have asked them to come to see me here, but they think I am trying to scam them! Preacher, I am dying, and no one believes me but you! What can I do? I have to go to Heaven. I need that agreement you have with God. Somehow, he always comes through for you. What is the secret?

I had the opportunity to share God's love, grace, and mercy. He said he had been praying. He said he had already asked God to come into his heart. I had to let go of this man, wondering if it all was really under the blood. I want to believe that everything was right, as he said. But so many times he told us stories, so many scams he ran, it was so hard to determine when he was honest and when he was not. I do not like the feeling of not knowing for sure.

But I can guarantee you one thing today. You cannot buy your way into Heaven; you cannot scam, wheel, or deal an agreement with God. You cannot blackmail God or play the "poor me, sympathy" card with him either. The only thing that will get you in Heaven is to be saved, washed in the blood of Jesus, born again, with a new heart! Sin is not going to enter Heaven, regardless of your reasons to justify it. If it is listed in the works of the flesh (Chapter Four), it is not going to Heaven. Regardless of who you are, how much money you have, or if you have been preaching for 40 years, if sin is in your life, you will not make it in the rapture! Salvation and dedication are the prerequisites to getting into Heaven and having the blessings and favor of God in your life.

I shared this story about the politician so you could understand what it takes to be blessed by God, what it takes to make all of the principles that I will share in this book work for you. Now I need to shift focus and share with you the first point in this message from God. Remember that this televangelist was the one telling everyone to plant seeds and get a 1000-fold return? Let us discuss the first sign that lets you know that a preacher, teacher, missionary, or prophet is a false teacher, as Peter mentioned in II Peter 2.

GROWING DELUSIONS THAT WE ARE SEEING:

1) False signs and wonders performed by false prophets
2) Christians being deceived because of miracles performed by false prophets
3) Replacement of sound doctrine that is Bible-based with personal experiences and proclamations of deliverances they experienced
4) Rejection of Bible teachings about end-time events, apostasy, and deception
5) Rejection of the idea of revivals because of the fake revivals and emotionalism that has gotten so much attention

The New Testament provides us with numerous scriptures to warn us of these things that will occur in the end-times that we must be aware of…which supports this message or word from God for the church!

Acts 20:29-30: For I know this, that after my departing shall grievous wolves enter in among you, not sparing the flock. Also, of your own selves shall men arise, speaking perverse things, to draw away disciples after them. (KJV, 2020).

II Timothy 3:1-9: This know also that in the last days perilous times shall come. For men shall be lovers of their own selves, covetous, boasters, proud, blasphemers, disobedient to parents, unthankful, unholy, without natural affection, trucebreakers, false accusers, incontinent, fierce, despisers of those that are good, traitors, heady, high-minded, lovers of pleasures more than lovers of God; having a form of godliness, but denying the power thereof: from such turn away. For of this sort are they which creep into houses, and lead captive silly women laden with sins, led away with divers' lusts, ever learning, and never able to come to the knowledge of the truth. Now, as Jannes and Jambres withstood Moses, so do these also resist the truth: men of corrupt minds, reprobate concerning the faith. But they shall proceed no further: for their folly shall be manifest unto all men, as theirs also was. (KJV, 2020).

II Thessalonians 2:3-12: Let no man deceive you by any means: for that day shall not come, except there comes a falling away first, and that man of sin be revealed, the son of perdition; who opposeth and exalteth himself above all that is called God, or that is worshipped; so that he as God sitteth in the temple of God, shewing himself that he is God. Remember ye not, that, when I was yet with you, I told you these things? And now ye know what withholdeth that he might be revealed in his time. For the mystery of iniquity doth already work: only he who now letteth will let until he be taken out of the way. And then shall

146

that Wicked be revealed, whom the Lord shall consume with the spirit of his mouth, and shall destroy with the brightness of his coming: Even him, whose coming is after the working of Satan with all power and signs and lying wonders, and with all deceivableness of unrighteousness in them that perish; because they received not the love of the truth, that they might be saved. And for this cause, God shall send them strong delusion, that they should believe a lie: That they all might be damned who believed not the truth but had pleasure in unrighteousness. (KJV, 2020).

I Timothy 4:1-2: Now the Spirit speaketh expressly, that in the latter times some shall depart from the faith, giving heed to seducing spirits, and doctrines of devils; Speaking lies in hypocrisy; having their conscience seared with a hot iron; (KJV, 2020).

The New Testament provides us with explicit instructions on how to handles these types of situations, individuals, and false teachers. However, we must remember that the most important component of dealing with deception and false teachers is to have the gift of discernment. You cannot lead a church without this gift. As members of your church, you should be encouraging all of them to seek God for the gift of discernment. This gift is not for ministers only—it for anyone who will honestly and humbly seek God.

Perry Stone (2013) shares some intriguing concepts in his book, *The Judas Goat,* that will help us recognize the false prophets and teachers. If you have not read this book, I recommend that you secure a copy from Amazon.com. It is a difficult book to read in sections, and you may get lost in some of the details. This is not a book to read on public transportation where you may receive many interruptions. This is a book that you have to read in quiet solitude. Interruptions will prevent you from understanding the meaning. I do not recommend reading it when you only have a few minutes. To grasp the concepts thoroughly, you need to read the entire chapter in one sitting.

Perry Stone provides you with the history of the Judas Goat, the Old Testament concepts, and how they are relevant today. I do not want to share concepts that will give away the entire storyline, but I want to share some concepts that will hopefully intrigue you enough to read this book. Perry Stone defines the various types of Goats, and their significances in the church in the Old Testament, then he moves to the New Testament church and the church of today. I want to share a few concepts that support this message from God and the tools I have shared with you. (Know that I did not read this book until after God had given me these dreams).

"Fear of failure—One of the greatest hindrances to stepping out in faith" (Stone, 2013, p. 75); is the tool that Satan loves to use on new converts and new pastors. This fear will drive an inexperienced pastor to lean-on senior church members to help him, or her make the politically correct choices. These choices may or may not align with God's word or his will for that church. We must be careful of who we take instructions from today. There are so many hirelings out there that will take advantage of you or your church. Stone also lists "arrogance" as the leadership trait that identifies a "Judas Goat in the pulpit" (p. 75).

Then Stone lists some of the greatest dangers for ministers. See these concepts that I found throughout several of the chapters. The presence of these in a minister's life means he is a Judas Goat in the pulpit trying to destroy the church from the inside out.

1) Hearing and understanding the word differently from what it really says (p. 31).
2) Disobedience (pp. 41-46).
3) Ministers attacking ministers (pp. 47-50)
4) Spiritual manipulators (Stone says that spiritual manipulation in ministry is as dangerous as sin…Goat in pulpit…is a preacher concerned about money, prophesying blessings, and a word different from God's word—read Jeremiah 23:1-2).
5) Judgmental ministers (Psalms 1: 1; 51:11-12)
6) Live a life contrary to what the Bible says is required of a Christian while claiming to be operating in the gifts.
7) "a natural or spiritual gift may impress or bless the people, even if the anointing is absent" (p. 230).
8) "A minister living in unconfessed sin or a secret bondage…continues to manifest gifts, causing him or her to think that [their] actions are approved by God because of the crowds…offerings…membership is growing, and everybody loves [them]," (p. 231).

Throughout this book, Perry Stone encourages the reader to look for evidence of the sins of the flesh, the works of the flesh, the pride of life, and the pride of the eye in Church pastors. He states that this is a sign that they are a hireling and not a true shepherd. I was so glad that my pastor friend recommended me to read this book after I had shared my dreams with him. It makes it easier to share God's word or instructions with us when we realize that he has been dealing with other ministers and pastors along the same lines. This witness of the spirit encourages you to share. God gave Peter and Paul the exact instructions as he did John while he was on the isle of Patmos. He is still laying this on the hearts of ministers around the world. This indicates that it is essential for all Christians in these last days to have the gift of discernment and learn how to recognize false teachers and preachers. Now he wants you to help your friends and church family to understand these concepts. Our mission is to see as many lost souls saved as possible and to help as many Christians move from their lukewarm positions to a place where they are rapture ready and helping others to get prepared.

Chapter Nine:

ARE WE FACING THE SECOND COMING OF CHRIST?

There are many signs that the rapture is getting closer. Almost annually since 1949, ministers have been preaching that the second coming of Christ would be any day. As a result, so many have turned away from these Evangelical teachings, saying that they were just "hype" to scare people into the church to get their money. Many now claim that the "end of the world teachings" are all nonsense or propaganda to clean out people's pockets. However, considering the world events that have occurred since 2008, especially since 2016, are these end-time teachings and prophecies nonsense? NO! The rapture is closer than you may think!

In Revelation 22:12, John wrote, "And, behold, I come quickly." That passage was written over 2000 years ago. As ministers, we are aware of the passage that states that one day is as a thousand years and a thousand years as one day with the Lord. We may not know God's timetable, and we do not know the date of Christ's return. Only the Father knows the date. We are waiting to hear him say, "Son, go and get your bride…today is your wedding day!"

SIGNS OF THE LAST DAYS

Even though we do not know the day of his coming, we can still be aware, watching, and waiting, because of the signs that he said he would give us before the end of time. We know that evil will be in control as it was in the days of Noah, Sodom, and Gomorrah. If you look closely and compare the state of affairs worldwide, especially in the United States, you will see that evil is operating like it was in these Old Testament places that John and Paul mention. The warning signs are present. Our time is limited. We need to be getting our families and friends ready to go in the rapture.

Mark 13:5-12: *And Jesus answering them began to say, take heed lest any man deceives you: For many shall come in my name, saying, I am Christ; and shall deceive many. And when ye shall hear of wars and rumours of wars, be ye not troubled: for such things must needs be; but the end shall not be yet. For nation shall rise against nation, and kingdom against kingdom: and there shall be earthquakes in divers' places, and there shall be famines and troubles: these are the beginnings of sorrows. But take heed to yourselves: for they shall deliver you up to councils; and in the synagogues, ye shall be beaten: and ye shall be brought before rulers and kings for my sake, for a testimony against them. And the gospel must first be published among all nations. But when they shall lead you, and deliver you up, take no thought beforehand what ye shall speak, neither do ye premeditate: but whatsoever shall be given you in that hour, that speak ye: for it is not ye that speaks, but the Holy Ghost. Now the brother shall betray the brother to death, and the father the son; and children shall rise up against their parents, and shall cause them to be put to death. (KJV, 2020).*

These signs that Jesus was teaching the disciples about did not mean the end was present, but that they were pointing to the end getting close. This has been a misconception in so many "Revelation Studies" or books written. John, while exiled on the isle of Patmos, was shown many things by God. God gave these visions to John to share with the church of that day. However, those things are still relevant to us today. We are still waiting on the return of Jesus Christ to take his bride to Heaven.

Think of the signs that we have seen since 2000. They have been numerous. I will not list all of them, but let us recap a few keys, world-known events. In September 2001, we saw the bombing of the NYC Twin Towers and many deaths from the alleged Al-Qaeda terrorist attacks. In September of 2019, there were bushfires in Australia that lasted for months. Almost annually, there have been mudslides and fires in California. Desert locust invaded east Africa in 2019, causing a food shortage in several African countries. Venice, Italy, was flooded in November 2019. A blizzard hit Newfoundland, Canada, at the beginning of this year (2020). Other countries like the Kuril Islands, Turkey, the Caribbean, Cuba, and rare places in the United States have seen earthquakes between 2016 to 2019.

With confidence, we can declare that we are seeing signs of wars and rumors of wars, with calamities abound occurring since the beginning of the 21st Century. Car bombings, civil unrest in the Middle East, missiles sent in anger, hijackings, bombings, and other terrorist-style events initiated in anger as feuds between Middle Eastern countries are fanned like the flames of an unquenchable fire!

I feel that it would be safe to say that the generations we are living now will see the second coming of the Lord in the sky to call his children home (Rapture of the church). As we watch the world events leading up to a one-world dictatorship, one-currency, a paperless money society, and lives controlled and mandated by government agencies (loss of our freedoms), we will see the beginning of the setup of the Mark of the Beast.

As a pre-tribulation rapture believer, I pray that my interpretations are right. I do not want to be here when things get bad. However, over the years, as I have watched the church drift so far from God and sleep through the "wake-up calls" like 9-11-2001, I fear that God may extend the church's time on earth longer. I believe that God will allow the church to remain here further into the One World Leadership setup, trying to wake them up! I still believe that we will be raptured out before the Beast is in control, but I fully believe that we will know who the Anti-Christ will be by the time he pulls us out of here. God is merciful…he will tarry and deal with the church as long as he can…then the church will wake up to a God that is our Judge, not our savior!

In May 1948, Israel was restored as a nation. The Jews began to return to their homeland to establish a government. Most theologians believe that this is a fulfillment of the fig tree parable of Matthew 24 and Luke 21. Another sign that we are seeing completed includes the gospel being preached to all nations, as Matthew 24:14 describes. As satellite television, cable television, and internet news access have become prominent in most countries, access to Christian preaching has spread. Even in countries where non-Islamic religions are not allowed, people hear about the gospel message and the saving grace of Jesus Christ. Numerous Muslims, Hindus, Buddhists, and other eastern religions are losing members at an alarming rate as they give their lives and hearts to Jesus Christ. These are two definite signs that we cannot deny.

I am frequently asked how we will know when the gospel has made it to every nation and translated into every tongue. We may not have a way of tracking these finite details. Still, all you have to do is listen to Daystar, Son Life Broadcasting, and Trinity Broadcasting Networks to see how the gospel is being sent to hundreds of nations in their native tongues. With Bibles and study materials to accompany these Bibles, the word of God is reaching every corner of the world. We are about to see the fulfillment of this sign. Every man will soon be heard of the gospel of Jesus Christ!

As we get closer to the set-up of the "mark of the beast," we will see false Christ and false prophets come forth claiming to be Jesus returned to earth. They will perform miracles and deceive many. Even though we have not seen this from a global perspective, we are all aware of the Jim Jones cult and the mass suicide they all followed him to because they believed that he was Jesus or that he spoke through him. We have heard of various groups and cults worldwide, including the claim made years ago in South Korea that a man was Jesus Christ. He deceived many as he worked miracles and healed people.

A sign that we have seen with intensity since 1998 has been the emergence of heresies in religion and government. When the Obama administration went into the Office of the President of the United States, a lying spirit was released upon America like no other demonic spirit that I have ever encountered. Many people have been deceived by the propaganda provided through the national network news stations, television programming, and other "brainwashing political" events. Compounded with the lying spirit that has tried to take of the church world, we can say that for 20 years now, we have been seeing this spirit of heresies deceiving many in the Christian church, even long-time pastors. (Matthew 24:4-5).

A popular Christian group based in the Philippines has websites on the world-wide-web where they brag about current information on the return of Christ and the end of days. When you begin to read what they are writing and the scriptures they are quoting, you initially think they have received the gospel and become true converts. However, if you will continue reading, you will come across comments that they make that Jesus Christ has already returned and taken some. They will tell you that we are living in the tribulation period waiting for the "anti-Christ or mark of the beast" to set up completely. This site will tell you that President Obama was the fore-runner of the Anti-Christ and that Donald Trump is the person who will set up the one-world dictatorship, currencies, and one-world banking system. They even predict that by 2025, we will be in World War III, with Christ returning by 2028 to set up his kingdom here on earth. They give the signs for when we can know that Christ is returning. I watched a couple of videos that they have made (pretty decent quality), showing Christ riding back on white horses with his heavenly bride (the Christians both dead and raptured), coming back to give us peace, and set up the Millennial reign.

Somehow in their misconceptions, they felt that the rapture occurred between 2004 and 2005. They teach that this generation will see the mark of the beast set up, and the New Jerusalem comes down. A video circulating on Facebook shows clips from the videos on their website, with a popular gospel hymn playing in the background. These facts and concepts are way off! The rapture HAS NOT taken place at the time I am writing this book in early 2020. It may have occurred by the time you read this book, but what this group of Filipinos is sharing is false information. It is a false religion that they are teaching. What has shocked me has been the number of US Christians claiming to be Holy Ghost-filled who have shared this video on their Facebook pages and with their friends on the messenger app. I am telling you that we must review everything, compare it to the word of God, and not to share it unless every fact and concept is valid.

We are called to be "living witnesses" in the book of Acts (KJV, 2020). That is the purpose God has chosen for each of us. He wants us to live in a way that our lives are a witness, even if we do not open our mouths to say a word. If we share information that is not true or entirely inaccurate, we may cause a new convert to Christ to become confused. So, we must watch our steps, actions, and words. If not, we could cause new converts to walk away, thinking that all religions are just fake facades to deceive people and take their money.

A United States-based ministry chose a ministry a name that is a play on words of a ministry name utilized by one of the Assemblies of God's outreach programs. This name similarity has deceived people into thinking that this "false religion" is part of the Assemblies of God (Springfield, MO). This ministries' website has been misleading new converts, especially new Charismatic Christian converts. Their website quotes scriptures and makes it appear that we began the tribulation period in 2014. It states that we are currently entering into the last two years of the seven-year tribulation period.

This website brags that we have been in the last-day revival for the past 25 years and that we are in the "falling away of the Christians from the faith" phase of Revelation. Their reasoning for this declaration is that Christ has already returned to earth and has been here walking around secretly for several years, checking to see who will reject him and who will accept him.

On this website's home page, a banner and video claim we need to be watching the sky each day, looking for Jesus. That Jesus is here on earth now, but he will be ascending into heaven just any day to get the Christians who are already in heaven, and his army, so they can return back to earth in the clouds on white horses. They have even posted a video on social networking sites that shows all of this happening. They have warnings on the website to not reject anyone who shows up saying they are Jesus or that they have seen Jesus because this will be your test to determine if you are ready to join him in the clouds! Please do not be deceived! Jesus has not returned yet to earth. Before Jesus comes back in the "clouds of glory" riding on a white horse, there will be a rapture of the church, a seven-year tribulation period here on earth as we are in Heaven for the marriage supper of the Lamb. Then Jesus will come back to earth with all the Christians dead and raptured to live here on earth in the New Jerusalem for a 1000-year Millennial Reign. This website has the event out of order and their facts twisted. We must study the Bible for ourselves and ask the Holy Spirit to instruct us in all wisdom and knowledge! If we do not study God's word, we will be deceived!

You must research and compare to the Bible everything that you hear preached in these last days. You need to pray and ask God for the discernment of the spirits that are around you. In these last days, we know that there will be many false prophets, false teachers, and deceivers who will preach what the people desire to hear instead of God's word. I strongly encourage you to read and re-read I Peter, II Peter, Jude, Matthew 24, James, and Titus. You need to know what to expect and how to identify these false teachers and preachers on sight!

For years I have seen pastors and close friends of mine "try the spirits" by checking to see if the ministers were real, lived what they preached, and if their prophecies came true. In the 1940s through the 1980s, that was one way of identifying false preachers and teachers that were effective. However, in these pre-tribulation times, Satan is aware that his days are numbered. He is putting up a huge fight, one that is larger than you can imagine. He plans to deceive as many people as possible. To accomplish this, Satan is performing miracles, planning events that are such an accurate counterfeit of the real evangelical movement that it is deceiving some of the best pastors. The scripture says that they will declare that they have healed in Jesus' name and cast out demons in his name, but he will still tell them that he does not know them and cast them into hell.

I witnessed a Baptist minister turned Holiness, who was filled with the Holy Ghost and was used in the gift of prophecy to become deceived and caught up in the business of "telling people what they wanted to hear!" He would find out from the pastor of the church critical things about people in the congregation. Then by watching their behavior and interactions with others, he could make calculated guesses of what they were going through. He learned tricks and techniques when he was on the mission field in India. Spirits attached themselves to him while he was there, "playing and scamming" to move his ministry to the next level. After his return to the United States, his wife developed a cocaine addiction. Then several years later, he joined her and began abusing alcohol and drugs.

A mutual friend called me and asked me to intervene because he felt that he was demon-possessed. Considering the mutual friend was an agnostic, I took the call seriously and headed to Tennessee immediately. I worked with him for over a week. I finally got him into rehab. I kept trying to get him to see where and how he went wrong. The compromises he made in his ministry for his wife, then later for his lust. I never got through. So, I prayed that God would send the right people across his path while in rehab. It worked for a few years, then he hit bottom again, the first trial/test he faced. Now, that minister is sitting in federal prison on serious drug trafficking charges. It is so sad that a minister pastoring a Baptist church of over 300 people could get filled with the Holy Ghost, lead an entire town to a beautiful walk with Christ, then fall so hard, so fast! It happens because none of us are above temptation. If we do not stay rooted and grounded in the word of God, we will lose our way. It is not if it will happen; it is when it will happen. We can never lose sight of Jesus Christ and the cross. We must remind ourselves daily that we must be rapture ready more than anything else in our lives!

I was visiting a church one Sunday night, and this minister was in charge of the service. After his short testimony/sermon, he opened the altar for a healing line. He asked all of the ministers to form a line in front of the altar. Then he had us stand across from each other (eight of us were present that night). He asked the people to slowly walk through the line and allow the eight of us to lay hands on them and pray.

I was shocked to see that the prayer line went across the front of the church, down the center aisle, across the back, and up the right aisle to the piano player. It appeared that approximately two-thirds of the congregation was in the prayer line. There were severe illnesses and bondage present in that congregation. As we walked past this minister, he asked each of us where we went to church and what gifts God has placed in our lives. After answering his question, I gave him a special request. My spouse was standing directly behind me and heard everything that was said. I told this minister that I wanted him to pray for the guy who had just sung. I knew him, and he needed a deliverance in his life. The evangelist nodded, ok.

About halfway through that prayer line, this evangelist came over and stood by me. He asked, "I want to make sure I have the right person that you wanted us to pray for tonight. Is it that guy?" and he pointed to the man I had referenced. I said yes. His next question shocked me. "What is his problem? What is going on in his life? How and what do I pray for concerning him?" For a person claiming to be a prophet, I was shocked that he had to ask me what was wrong with the guy. But I answered him with a brief synopsis of the problem.

When this evangelist walked away, my spouse and I looked at each other, raised our eyebrows, and made a face. But we did not say anything. Forty minutes later, this evangelist began to holler and jerk around, like he was being spoken to by God. Then all of a sudden, he called that young man out. Asked him, "Son, do you know me? Have you ever seen me before? Have I ever talked to you before? Well, I have a word from the Lord for you!" The young man said no to all his questions, then bowed his head reverently, waiting for the man to prophecy over him. To my shock, this evangelist regurgitates every word I had said to him in perfect order. This young man began to cry and say that he knew that was God because no one in that service knew what he was going through except us, and he knew that we had not told anyone.

I did not cause a confusion in the service by confronting this evangelist. I let the service end, and then I told this young man as we were leaving to go to our vehicle. "Mr. X, call me next week when you get a chance. There is something that I need to share with you!" When he called my office, I told him what happened and to watch if this minister ever came back to his church again. I advised him never to let this minister lay hands on him ever again.

I did not appreciate being used in someone's religious scams. We made sure that we separated ourselves from the pastor of that church we visited and the guest minister that was speaking there. Numerous immoral things were going on in that church that came out over the next few months. The pastor had four women in the church that he had had sexual relations with in addition to his wife, while he was the pastor. He had three former wives in that church. I do not know about you, but if I was a pastor's wife, and he had five ex-wives, of which three were still in the church, I would not go to that church. I would not have married him and been his 6th wife anyway! There has to be some level of accountability that is required of the pulpit!

Accountability, integrity, honesty, and moral standards are essential requirements to fill the pulpit. I do not understand how this portion of the gospel has gotten so convoluted! It is evident that we are in the last days, and there are lying spirits going out to deceive people, including the preachers and pastors. If you are in a church with this type of lifestyle being tolerated, do not leave, RUN, RUN, RUN! Do not look back!

In the late 1980s, a televangelist from the Arizona area began running tent revivals across Florida, Georgia, Alabama, and Texas. His radio and television ads preyed on the weak-minded and minorities. He would raise massive offerings in these tent revivals with his prayer lines and blessing promises. He prophesied to people, and then they would shower him with gifts and money because of the good words that he spoke over them. He would preach of the end-time and the events of the last days. He would at least once per month prophecy something that was going to happen before the tribulation period.

A lady in our church got his monthly newsletter. She was always bringing it to me to read. I would have cold chills go up my spine each time that I read those prophecies. My spirit did not bear witness with this man and his ministry at all. Each time I told this lady that she needed to walk away from this ministry, she would remind me that I could not judge. I kept telling her I am not judging this prophet, but my spirit does not bear witness, so be careful. Even if these prophecies come true, it does not mean that he is a true prophet of God. As the year passed, there was the second marriage, the second set of kids, and his complete denunciation of the first set of children. When his first wife died, he dropped his two kids off at his in-laws, left, and never looked back. A true man of God cannot abandon his family. A faithful minister will have, first and foremost in his life, a heart of love. How can you love people, be concerned about their problems when you cannot raise your children?

In the early 2000s, this man died. When he left this world, he had assets in the triple-digit millions. He owned a large church worth about 20 million (property value), homes, ranches, vehicles, and millions in the bank. Over 90 percent of his church demographic was African Americans, Nigerians, and Mexicans. According to his church records, no one that was a member had ever attended college. Most of his parishioners had not graduated from high school. I am not his judge, but something was not right in this ministry. I pray that he made things right with God before he left this world. Over 60 percent of the things that he prophesied had come true before his death. He has been dead for more than 12 years now, and his prediction success rate is approximately 80 percent.

Even Satan knows what is going to happen in the end times. Yes, Satan can read the Bible. He probably knows more about the scriptures than you and me. He was there when the worlds were formed. He witnessed first-hand things that you and I struggle to wrap our human minds around. Therefore, do not be deceived. Know that he can prophesy the future with accuracy! Look at more than works and miracles. Look for the fruits of the spirits; they must be present. Then look for the works of the flesh; they should not be present. The anointed of the Lord will always have a loving, merciful heart and a passion for souls. If this is not present…run!

I. <u>WILL THE PROJECTED EVENTS OF REVELATION OCCUR BEFORE THE END OF TIME?</u>

The Bible prophecies will all be fulfilled. Whether you and I see all of the prophecies will depend on when the Rapture takes place. If it occurs pre-tribulation, we will not see all of the prophecies listed in Revelation occur before we leave earth, but they will all occur before we return with Christ.

If the Rapture does not occur until mid-tribulation, we will see more of the prophecies appear. I do not know about you, but I am not concerned about seeing all of the things listed. I am concerned about going in the Rapture and helping get as many souls saved as possible. I do not desire to be here when the seals are opened and the plagues brought out on earth. I want to be raptured out of here before all of these signs occur. To be hung up on what will happen when or whether it will happen at all is not the issue that we should be concerned with—we should be concerned with being rapture ready ourselves!

II. <u>WILL DONALD TRUMP BE THE PRESIDENT THAT HELPS HOLD OFF THE RAPTURE OF THE CHURCH FOR FOUR MORE YEARS? WILL HE BE THE PRESIDENT THAT CRUSHES THE CABAL AND SETS UP THE ONE-WORLD GOVERNMENT?</u>

God is the only person who knows the answer to these two questions. I will explain to you as best as I can what I think God wants out of us. I am not campaigning for or promoting a political candidate. However, I advise you to compare against the works of the flesh what strategies a candidate is running. For example: If a candidate is pro-choice and believes that abortion is a woman's choice and should be protected, then that candidate is engaged in a lifestyle choice that is indicative of several of the works of the flesh. (Idolatry, immoral behavior, murder, sexual impurity, lasciviousness, and others). Do not vote for that individual. If the only two candidate choices both support abortion, then you will have to pray and ask God to show you the lesser of the two evils. There will never be a perfect political candidate. The only perfect candidate would be Jesus, and he will not be a choice in our upcoming elections.

As a conservative evangelical, I admit that I voted for Trump during his first campaign, and I will be voting for him this second time. In my assessment, he has less of the works of the flesh in his life than the other candidate choices. He is pro-Israel, pro-life, pro-Veterans, pro-elderly, pro-education, and a brilliant businessman. He has made both good and bad choices. If you or I were in the White House, we would have done the same thing. No one is perfect. But at least he is trying to make good choices!

My final advice on this topic is to watch, pray, study, research topics, be informed, and make sound Biblical choices. Do not blindly follow any man, not even the President of the United States of America! Christ is the only one that we should be looking to for our answers. Focus on making sure you are ready to leave earth…that is the most critical task on your job description. Winning souls is the only other spiritual task that should take precedence in your life.

BOOK SUMMARY

We need to be informed Christians in this 21st Century. We can no longer afford the luxury of going to church and absorbing everything that we see and hear without comparing the events, actions, and words to the word of God (The Bible). We cannot follow a man anymore. I remember the days when pastors were men of integrity, and you could take what they said to the bank. You could risk everything in your life on what was prophesied over you.

Today, in American, we have too many pastors who are after fame and fortune, not God's will. Too many televangelists are focused on "empire building" instead of "soul-saving." We must know the people who are ministering to us. We must be good stewards of where we put our money.

There are times that I will listen to a minister because of a point or topic that they are discussing. Even though I listen to them and take the good things, ignoring the things contrary to God's word, I do not ever financially support these ministers. Even a false prophet can speak the truth occasionally.

I do not recommend that new Christians engage in Christian TV binge-watching because it can confuse them. If you are a new Christian, do not waste your time watching secular TV programs that promote the works of the flesh. Read your Bible or a Christian book. If you binge-watch preachers, you will get confused. Before you try listening to a large group of preachers, you need to figure out what you believe and why you believe it. If you know what the Bible says about a topic, you will recognize false or confused teaching or preaching on TV.

The same thing can occur when reading books by different authors. As an experienced minister, I read books by all faiths, denominations, and Christian writers. I read them as research. I compare every book with the Bible. This helps me have the information that I need to share with my church members and new converts to keep them from being deceived. I do NOT call preachers names from my pulpit. I do not encourage that either. I do not want to defame a preacher who may be wrong on a topic today; because God may show him tomorrow, and he repents. That may be the person God wants to use to help you next month to get through a difficult

163

time. We are all human. We all make mistakes. To err is human; to be longsuffering and forgiving is Christ!

Instead of wasting your time on frivolous games, movies, and "fake news," spend that time reading your Bible and praying. Once you are established in God's word and read through the Bible at least 20 to 25 times, you can start watching TV preachers as long as you set down the points, topics, and thoughts they share (to research later). Then go to your Bible. You will need to explore, examine, and research thoroughly those topics for yourself. If they have preached according to the word of God, stand on it, and share it with others. If not, throw those notes in the garbage!

SUMMARY OF I PETER:

Let us review I Peter (written probably around 64-65 AD) and study the concept that Peter provided, "Living Victoriously amidst suffering and persecutions." During this time period, Nero had burned most of Rome. Because of the wide-spread devastation and the homelessness of the Romans, Nero's bitterness and resentment toward the Christians began to increase. He went as far as to band the Christians from the city. In I Peter 1, he taught them that suffering increased their faith, helping them to because more holy than words could say. However, he instructed them to remain holy and to love one another.

In I Peter 2, he reminded them that they were chosen and needed to submit to the authority of Jesus Christ, their companion and friend, following his example in all that we do. Peter admonished them to accept Jesus as their companion and show respect to all people in authority. Living Godly lives in harmony with others was the main point of I Peter 3 as he instructed them to be considerate of their spouses and respectful to them. If we do this, we will have a clear conscience even when we are suffering unjustly.

I Peter 4 tells us that the end is near and that suffering will increase, but we are to love deeply regardless of our persecutions. We are to serve others with our gifts. If we follow these commandments, we are promised that we will be blessed when we are insulted by man. I Peter 5 provides instructions to church leaders and pastors on how to be a "Good Shepherd," who is humble, resisting evil, standing firm in the faith, and giving all anxiety to God. This sounds like a good, solid management plan. God's word has the answer for every dilemma that we face or difficult circumstance that we find ourselves in…we only have to read and study his word to know what to do in these last days to be victorious, successful, and rapture ready!

SUMMARY OF II PETER:

The epistle of II Peter was written around 67 to 68 AD. Peter focuses on false teachers and our need to always be on guard for these destructive doctrines, and these false teachers infiltrate the church as believers. Peter tells us that we can recognize these individuals because they will introduce heresies to the membership. This means that they will inject destructive heresies and immoral behavior into the congregation as they engage in these activities and encourage others to do so, too.

II Peter 1 reminds us that our salvation can be sure and confident with forgiveness for all of our sins. Peter tells them that they can trust his teachings because he was an eyewitness to the crucifixion, death, burial, and resurrection of Jesus Christ. II Peter 2 warns us to beware of false teachers that cause divisions in the church. He says that they will present disguising themselves in grace while indulging in sin. If unchecked, they will secretly introduce destructive behaviors, immorality, and depravity into the church. They deceive many in the church with their promises of freedom, blessings, and victory when they are actually slaves in bondage to their sins.

II Peter 3 is about trustworthiness. Peter talks about the Lord's returning, how scoffers will create controversy in the church, and that persecution of the church will increase as we approach the rapture. Peter describes the intense persecutions, the final days, and reminds the church to live godly lives holy and on guard always! Peter states in II Peter 1:10 that godly living is the evidence of our salvation! Think about that…it is your first key to the discernment of false teachers….if their gospel is true, they will not be immoral, entangled in sins of all types, nor trying to twist the scriptures to mean what they want it to say!

We must be diligent, increasing in faith in God's word, demonstrating the fruits of the spirit, none of the works of the flesh, living lives of self-control, godliness, and seeking God continually. If we follow this plan adding in faith, virtue, knowledge, temperance, patience, and love, we will not be deceived! We will not fail! But we will make it to Heaven!

IS THE CORONAVIRUS PANDEMIC A SIGN OF THIS WORD FROM THE LORD?

God did not speak to me that the Coronavirus was sent as one of the warnings to the church. However, the fact that the Coronavirus arrived in America in late January (as most scientists concur), it does look like that this pandemic may have been allowed to draw the eyes of the church back to what is essential. Will this pandemic change the focus of the church for the future? For the true men and women of God pastoring, yes, it will change their focus. It should also change their strategies. The church's focus should NOT be on assets and more assets, but on souls, souls, souls, and more souls! Even though I cannot say that it is a sign of this word from God, I can confirm that it is a sign of the end-times which we are living.

You must know the word of God, and you need to analyze everything that you see and hear. Compare all sermons, songs, words, and Christian movies to the Bible. If it does not line up, you need to walk away, turn off the TV, or put the book in the garbage!

FINAL RECAP OF THIS MESSAGE FROM GOD

This message's primary purpose is to stir up men's and women's hearts worldwide and help them see their need for a closer relationship with God, the Father, and His Son, Jesus Christ! God desires for us to be so close to him that we can feel him breathe on us! God wants to be an integral part of our everyday lives and help us to live successful, victorious lives that are an example to the world of his amazing grace!

The second purpose of this message was to stir up ministers' and pastors' hearts worldwide, helping them realize that entertainment is not the church's goal; it is souls! Prosperity schemes are not the commodity that we should be selling! Prosperity is something that God desires for each of us. However, he said that he would like for us to "prosper as our souls prosper!"

III John 1:2: *Beloved, I wish above all things that thou mayest prosper and be in health, even as thy soul prospereth. (KJV, 2020).*

God does not want us to live in poverty. He wants to give us gifts and bless us. He wants us to be walking examples to the world of his love, grace, mercy, longsuffering, and blessings. But God does not want us to be hung up on prosperity and what we can get or achieve for ourselves. God wants us to be humble before him, desiring what he wants in our lives. God wants to bless us to give to others less fortunate and spread the good news of Jesus Christ to the entire world. Our blessings can be enjoyed, but they should not be our idols!

God does not desire for churches to be considered with numbers, assets, bragging rights, and being the biggest, most desired after or the 'flagship' church in our organizations. God wants his churches to be concerned with getting people saved, disciplining them, and meeting the church's needs and the needs of people in our communities. God wants us involved in domestic and foreign missions. God wants us to desire to reach every person for God that is possible.

In this message, God expresses his desire for everyone to be soul winners and for the pastors to stop seeking fame, fortunes, and assets and search for ways to help people learn how to live victorious lives and be rapture ready at all times. The pastors' message includes preaching salvation

167

and deliverance but focuses on the pastors helping their members learn God's word and not be deceived in these last days. God wants each Christian to train their children to walk lives of integrity and honesty, not lives of fleshly desires, with the works of the flesh controlling them. God wants us to be Christ-like, demonstrating the fruits of the spirit every day to everyone we are around.

This message has a robust corrective tone as it teaches us about the spirits in the spirit world that can impact our daily lives and churches, impeding the victory and blessings that God has planned for us. This strong tone is then used as he challenges pastors to teach on these spirits and disciple their members to learn about Christ and walk victoriously as spiritual warriors.

Toward the end of this message, God challenges the church members to know their pastors and seek a church where God's real move is allowed. If their pastors are not compromising what they preach to appease tithe payers and controlling families in the church, then that church is ok. However, if the pastor is compromising the gospel for money, they need to find a different church. God's closing thoughts in this message remind us that he will give us a "probationary period" to get our lives right and our churches in order, then he will begin to deal with the church leadership and the members. God wants a bride that is dedicated to him and soul-winning!

As a Christian, Christ compared us to the grapevine that needs pruning in the vineyard so that it can produce MUCH fruit. God is 'pruning us' with this message and challenging us to allow the Holy Spirit to cut off us the things that do not please God. God's words are not soft, gentle, or fluffy in this message. They are matter-of-a-fact and stern instructions like a parent would give to a wayward teenager who is selfish, self-centered, and rebellious. God wants the bride (the church) for his Son, Jesus, to be ready for this wedding (the marriage supper of the lamb), groomed, adorned, and prepared to be presentable on that day. God wants us to be victorious and prosperous here on earth, using our blessings and prosperity to forward the gospel of God's love and mercy to everyone we meet.

God gives instructions in this message for us to seek a church where the pastor has listened to God's voice and has implemented the things God wants for the church. After this period of allowing time to get the church and pastors ready, God will begin to deal with the process of cleaning out the churches and pulpits, like he cleaned the temple at Jerusalem. God's wrath is real. It can be avoided. It is not God's desire for us. Today he is our loving Savior and our defense attorney to the Father as he intercedes for us each day. But a tomorrow soon, he will be our Judge. He will not allow the 'abominations' that he had identified for us in the New Testament to enter into Heaven. If we want to be rapture ready, we must be doing our best to live by his commandments and follow the statutes listed for his bride.

God is aware that we are human and not perfect. He even made a way for us to be saved and redeemed when we fail or make mistakes. He has given us 'grace.' We have only to ask for forgiveness when we realize that we fall, or the Holy Spirit convicts our hearts that what we have just completed or done was not right. We must remember, forgiveness is one SIMPLE prayer away! When we no longer see the need to pray over our mistakes, we are on our way into a downward spiral.

God also promises us in this message that there will be individuals that he will deal with strongly during this probationary period. In their hearts, these are individuals who love God or have parents and grandparents interceding for them. God will grant them a "death-bed repentance" or a period of suffering where they will get things right with God.   Through the years, I have seen numerous people that could not walk away from an addiction or vice that had them bound. In their hearts, they wanted to live right. In their hearts, they prayed for God to help them. Then when they were diagnosed with a terminal disease, they began to pray. They would make God lots of promises as they tried to bargain for more years to be added to their lives. God did not grant the additional years, but he was longsuffering and merciful enough to allow them the time it took for them to get their hearts and minds right. Many evangelical ministers call this a "destruction of the flesh for the saving of the soul."

I Corinthians 5:5: *To deliver such a one unto Satan for the destruction of the flesh, that the spirit may be saved in the day of the Lord Jesus.* (KJV, 2020).

This message from God shows us his mercy, grace, love, hope, forgiveness, and his ultimate desire for our deliverance. God is a loving God that wants to hold us in his hands and protect us. God wants to be the one protecting us. Our choices and rebellion cause us to become a child in the hands of an angry God instead of a loving God. The option is ours to make. I want to close this book with one last plea to you to give God a chance to prune you. We need God to trim off the dead parts and cut back the branches that are not producing fruit. When God trims off the rough edges and applies the healing salve of the Holy Spirit to our lives, helping us "to love our neighbors as ourselves" and to forgive others, we can receive God's mercy,

169

love, and forgiveness. The choice is ours. We are the only ones that can study and learn to recognize Satan and his attacks. We are the only ones that can implement needed changes in our lives. God challenges us in this message and book, but ultimately the decision is ours. Today, I pray that you will not ignore this message, but you will give your whole heart to God and learn to put on your spiritual armor daily as you learn to walk victoriously in Christ!

Then pray over everything in your life, from your children to your career. Pray diligently about the church you are in and whether you should stay or change. Follow the advice in this book and get to know your pastor, Sunday school teachers, and church leaders. Protect your family from Satan's influences and the spirit world. Begin teaching the discipleship topics to your children each day. Help them to select personal standards and convictions that will help them to grow through Christ. Your children are NEVER too young to get saved or to learn about what God wants in them. Remember, mothers, it is not about being a beauty queen or the most popular girl at school; God wants you to train your daughters to be moral, ethical, pure, virtuous women like the Proverbs 31 woman.

Fathers, God desires for your sons to be husbands, like the example Jesus set. Men of integrity, honor, honesty, gentleness, loving (like Joseph), attentive, merciful, and supporters of their families. "Train your children in the way that they should go, and they will never depart!"

Proverbs 22:6: Train up a child in the way he should go: and when he is old, he will not depart from it. (KJV, 2020).

Finally, my last two points are as follows. The first one is a) I want to remind you to make sure that you make every effort to study the works of the flesh in-depth and get them out of your life. This may require assistance and a prayer partner. Do not be ashamed to ask for help. You will be amazed at the changes that will begin in your life, home, career, and marriage. Even friends, work, and dating relationships will change. Family members you have been estranged from will begin to change as they see the Holy Spirit at work in your life!

The second one is b) Search for a church where the pastor preaches on sin, promotes the fruits of the spirit, preaches against the works of the flesh, and requires church leaders and teachers to live, practice, and demonstrate Christian character. Look for a church where discipleship training is frequently offered, and the church is not embarrassed by their "we believe" list but promotes the development of personal standards and convictions. Make sure this church preaches and teaches that there is only *one way to heaven, through the blood of Jesus Christ, who died for our sins!* That there is a **Heaven and a Hell**. That there was a **Virgin Birth, Death, Burial, and Resurrection of Jesus Christ, the Rapture, Marriage Supper of the Lamb, and the Millennial Reign.** Most doctrinal issues are not significant or worth arguing about, but these key components are crucial. It will be necessary for your children to be taught these concepts, not to be swayed to accept the world's standards or the liberal lifestyles so opened promoted at our colleges and universities.

I pray that this book has helped you. I pray that this message from God will burn in your hearts and minds. I pray that God will help you implement the needed changes in your life, home, family, and church that are required to enjoy the blessings this message promises so that you will not suffer the destruction that is coming!

Keep your faith strong in God. Do not let the circumstances of the COVID-19 pandemic, natural disasters, lost jobs, difficulties, or any other political dramas cause you to ever doubt God. Know that God has got you through all of the trials of this year and this pandemic. God will keep you in the palm of his hand, as long as you desire to stay. But he will not hold you, prisoner. It must be your desire to be like him and used by him. God will allow you to jump ship or jump out of his hand anytime you desire. Just know that your jump may bring things you never wanted.

I will leave one closing thought with you that I have heard down through the years. I do not know who coined this phrase or made it popular in the evangelical community, but it holds true for anyone considering walking away from this Christian Life.

Sin will take you to a place you do not want to go to and Sin will cost you more than you wanted to pay; while it keeps you longer than you had planned to stay!
---author unknown

Do not throw this message away. Do not convince yourself that you have plenty of time to comply. Do not deceive yourself into thinking that you are young, and this message only applies to those who are old and about to die. Do not allow yourself to rationalize and explain away this message. Act today. Promise God that you will serve him with your whole heart!

Joshua 24:15: And if it seems evil unto you to serve the LORD, choose you this day whom ye will serve; whether the gods which your fathers served that were on the other side of the flood or the gods of the Amorites, in whose land ye dwell: but as for me and my house, we will serve the LORD. (KJV, 2020).

II Chronicles 7:14: If my people, which are called by my name, shall humble themselves, and pray, and seek my face, and turn from their wicked ways; then will I hear from heaven, and will forgive their sin, and will heal their land. (KJV, 2020).

Repent today, turn to God, give him complete and total control of your life, schedule, agenda, career, marriage, and ministry. Sit back and watch God bless and anoint you as you offer up your praise to him! Ask God to lead you, teach you, and guide you daily! Ask him to cover you and protect you as he enlarges your territory. God will give you favor with the people who can catapult your ministry to the next level…if you trust him!

The <u>intelligent</u> act on *knowledge*. The <u>wise</u> act on *wisdom, experience, and understanding.* <u>Successful people</u> use *knowledge, wisdom, experience, and understanding* together at all times. <u>A fool</u> has *wisdom without intelligence* or *intelligence without wisdom.*

<u>Which are you</u>? *Intelligent, Wise, Foolish, or Successful*!

CLOSING THOUGHTS

1) Satan will use dreams, visions, and miracles by false prophets, preachers, and teachers to deceive you. Make sure everything you are told aligns with the Bible on all points!

2) You must remove the works of the flesh from your life and separate yourself from people who cater to them.

3) Separate yourself from witchcraft, sorcery, bitterness, revenge, and individuals with a lack of faith.

4) Know that God will not accept a lying spirit. It will not enter Heaven.

5) Deceitfulness is the greatest hindrance to victorious living in most Christian's lives.

6) Satan is a master con-man who can produce excellent counterfeits. You must know the word of God to recognize them.

7) Satan will try to convince you that you are justified (in your case/ circumstances) for allowing bitterness, pride, arrogance, and lust into your life.

8) You must avoid all self-deception, self0exhaltations, exaggerations, and bearing of false witness against others if you want to live a victorious life and walk with the protection of God's spiritual armor!

SUCCESS IS FOUND WHEN YOU TEACH WHAT YOU NEED TO LEARN!

APPENDIX

Included in this section are the following resources:

How and Why this Book was Written
Supportive Scriptures by Topic
Outline
About the Author
Contact
References

CHARLIE O'NEAL

Appendix:

HOW AND WHY THIS BOOK
WAS WRITTEN

If you wonder why you need to read a message that God gave to a southern Alabama minister, read this section. I explain why God gave this message to me and how he wanted me to share it with the world. The first few chapters of this book explain the background information and history that you need to understand. Sometimes God gives a message to an individual or a church that is also relevant to other Christians and churches. After I finished this manuscript and was waiting for the editorial comments and proposed changes from the editor, I began hearing other preachers on TV sharing what God had given to them this past summer. It was amazing how many had messages similar to the dream that I had been given. Since the pandemic began, preachers have mailed out newsletters and posted messages on their websites pleading for people to turn back to the cross. It appears that so many churches have been engulfed in entertainment and forgotten about our real mission for souls. I felt that these messages were God's way of witnessing the dream through more than three people or ministers the things he gave to me.

This message that God gave me in a dream on December 3, 2019, was so powerful. I woke up from this dream with the Holy Spirit on me, shaking me in the bed. I got up and immediately wrote down everything that I could remember of this message. Then I began praying for God to help me deliver it precisely like it was given to me in the dream.

During the next several nights that followed, I had dreams from God, showing me how to explain this book's topics. In a couple of the dreams, I was preaching this message in churches. With each dream, I wrote down what I saw in my dreams. The first dream, on December 3rd, was a word from God to the church. As the first dream began, the Lord appeared and began to give this word (the message in chapter one) to share with their church. I wrote it down word for word.

My initial response to sharing this word from God was to discuss the dreams and message with our church and a few select pastors where I was scheduled to minister during 2020. When these pastors heard of this message, they urged me to write this message in a book or booklet and include a sermon outline for pastors. They felt that this message needed to be preached from every pulpit in America and around the world.

So, I began to pray and ask God if this was his intended purpose for this word. God witnessed to me and through three other ministers that came to me with a word of wisdom from God. They had no idea that I was praying to know whether to publish this book or not. However, God showed them that he had given me a message that needed to go out urgently world-wide. God spoke to me that this book was to be simply called *A Word from God for the Church*. In February 2020, after much fasting and praying, the outline of this book was finalized.

Calls began to come in about this message that I was preaching and sharing in some churches in the Northwest Florida and South Alabama areas. One lady called and spoke with one of the women helping edit this book. She told her, "WOW, this sermon Charlie preached is awesome. Please tell Charlie this is what all of our churches need! I have never heard anyone preach on these topics, especially with the depth that Charlie has spoken. I know, as a preacher and teacher, I would love to have this word in writing with a sermon outline, so I could share it with the churches that I minister in, plus my family. This message needs to be preached in every church in America. American pastors' eyes need to be opened to the tricks that Satan is using in their ministries. They need to understand how Satan is trying to destroy their churches. We need a revival in America! We need this book in the hands of every Christian around the world!"

Composing a book was not an issue for me, considering the books God had given me over the years. However, I was in the middle of writing a book series on *The Keys to Victorious Living*. I had already secured publishing for that book through Trinity Broadcasting Network and had a deadline. I did not feel that I had time to stop and work on this book. The contracts from TBN/Trilogy were lying on my desk when I had this dream. I did not know what to do, so I began fasting and praying. After God gave me this message, he let me know that if I shared it WITHOUT changing or diluting the content and providing all profits to the Heritage House Foundation, he would anoint this book and the victorious living series. God's anointing was what I wanted, so I had my answer. I want to be able to reach people around the world. I began blocking out extra hours each day to work on this book. Writing two books simultaneously and keeping the content separate was a more challenging task than I had imagined.

After receiving these instructions about the book and profits, I began searching for a publisher that would be willing to decrease their charges for publication so that the profits going to Heritage House Foundation would be higher. The Lord led me to HFT Publishing. They agreed to publish all books and handle the accounting, marketing, etc., then send all profits from the sales to Heritage House Foundation on my behalf. This offer freed up more of my time to work on writing the series.

The Lord had said I needed to remain anonymous and not receive any glory or profits. HFT Publishing agreed to handle this for me and keep my identity concealed. This will allow the ministry to promote the books, use the profits, and not have to worry about trying to protect my identity. I felt that this was a publication/marketing decision that made sense, and I changed publishers at the last minute. Several individuals thought I was crazy, but God began blessing and sending people to volunteer their services to get this book out!

The message in the dream was so powerful that I got out of bed at 2 AM on December 3rd (after waking up from this dream), I began to write. The power of God's anointing came on me, helping me to recall every word spoken in the dream. Then the next week, I began researching the topics mentioned in this word from God. After collecting copious amounts of notes over three weeks, Charlie began sharing with the church what God was saying. With each sermon or sharing of this message, people had questions. It became apparent that some of the first book's information (*Why am I not Living a Victorious Life?*) needed to be shared with this message. If you have already read this book, you will recognize a repeat of some information in several chapters. However, repeating this information is needed to help any individuals reading this book that has not read any of my other books.

As I began preaching about this word from God in the local churches, it was astonishing to me how little the people knew about the fruits of the spirit, the works of the flesh, spiritual warfare, and how to put on the whole armor of God, which is needed in these last days. The Holy Spirit stirred-up in me a message and a powerful desire for revival and winning souls. I had always focused on soul-winning and discipleship, but God began to reveal how Satan had stolen this desire for Christians to be "fishers of men" from the 21st Century Church. We need to return to the focus and the commission that God gave to us to share the good news of the gospel of Jesus Christ! We need to be more concerned with getting people to the cross of Calvary and repentance more than anything else. Feel-good, prosperity teaching, and preaching will not get souls to Heaven. Only the saving grace of the blood of Jesus Christ will accomplish this task. Yes, God wants us to be blessed **as our souls prosper spiritually**. If your heart is right, your soul will be filled with the purpose and desires of God; and the blessings will automatically follow!

Whether you are reading the eBook in the Summer of 2020 or the paperback edition years later, know that this word from God will be appropriate for correction, reproof, and growth in your life and ministry whenever you are reading this book. This message is not limited to just 2020 to 2023, although you will see things that occur during this time frame that aligns with this message and the book of Revelation.

As the editors began reviewing this manuscript, they felt the urgency of getting this message worldwide. They decided to release it in eBook format in the US and ten other countries at the same time the paperback book would be released in America.

God promises that if we seek him with all of our hearts that he will answer, he will forgive us and heal our land! God will anoint the delivery of his word. He loves man and desires a relationship with everyone. However, he will not force it. We have free will, which has to be our choice. But God has a plan to reach the world in these last days with messages, writings, songs, and sermons that will move our lives into alignment with his word and our relationship to the next level with him!

The Lord also warned me that while I was sharing this word, to make sure it was shared as he spoke it to me and not allow the editing process to change or weaken the message, especially regarding the controversial issues. God also witnessed to share information, stories from the Bible, and stories from Charlie's ministry that would help all readers to fully understand why it is essential for them to lead a victorious Christian life. It is crucial to understand spiritual warfare and its impact in helping us to be rapture ready!

During the initial weeks of the "stay-at-home" mandate of the Coronavirus (COVID-19) pandemic in March 2020, while fasting, praying, and writing, the Lord let me see that Satan was planning to weaken the church during this time frame. Many churches have been built on entertainment and emotions without the discipleship training in the word that is needed. As God dealt with Charlie on these topics, he witnessed that it was essential for the readers to know...

1) Satan will weaken the faith of the churches and their members during this pandemic if not warned.
2) Many will begin to compromise in their convictions as they layout of the church.
3) Many will be tempted to get other things in first place in their lives during this pandemic.
4) TV will take the place of most prayer lives.
5) Many "false teachers and preachers" will make this pandemic about "name it, claim it, plant a seed so you can make it" messages, instead of what God wants out of you while you cannot attend church.
6) Many preachers will use this pandemic as a platform for "seed-planting" and "selling" schemes.
7) Because of this "falling away," we will lose the next two to three generations worldwide if the church does not wake up and take action.
8) Our churches' current leadership needs to begin to preach the word and help their churches refocus if they want to be ready to leave here.

9) Satan wants the existing church to be like the church
    of Laodicea, not the on-fire Azusa Street church!

God's word is not for sale, so I felt that my ministry should not profit from distributing this crucial message. The entire world needs to hear this message. God wanted it shared with everyone and for him to get the glory, not anyone else. God told me in the dream that if I would publish this word where no glory, fame, or TV interviews would highlight my ministry or career, that he would anoint this book. God promised to anoint this book to make a lasting impact on Christianity and ignite revival in churches and pastors worldwide in these last days!

The profits will go to the Heritage House Foundation. They help ministers and missionaries get this gospel message to everyone, ignite revival, and see souls saved! This foundation also helps retired ministers and missionaries with housing, medications, etc.

We have prayed over this paperback manuscript and the eBook version, asking God to send the Holy Ghost with each book. We ask the Holy Spirit to "arrest the hearts" of the people who need to change so that they will turn to God and begin a new life, covered in the blood of Jesus Christ! We want the people who read this book to be saved, redeemed, delivered, and healed! The rapture is too near not to share God's word with everyone. We do not have time to waste on trivial pursuits, cliques, petty differences, and unforgiveness. We must get ourselves ready, sanctified, and under subjection to the word of God so that we can help our families and friends be rapture ready!

This book is written for ministers and church members. We believe that "the knowledge of God's word" is not a key given only to preachers and church leaders, but it is a key that should be shared with everyone, so they can grow and learn about spiritual warfare.

The only way to successfully navigate through the days ahead of the church is to be aware of Satan's tactics, snares, and traps. You need to know what to look for to avoid these pitfalls that Satan will set for you. If you understand the principles of what God wants in your lives, then you can navigate the minefields of your minds that Satan uses against everyone!

As you read *A Word from God for the Church*, keep an open mind and heart. Do not judge the content or layout of this book. Do not put this book aside until you have read all chapters and the conclusion. This book will help you to open your heart to God's will for your life and ministry. It will help you to "forgive and love like you have never been hurt." (Franklin, 2018). It will help you to develop a spiritual battle plan for your life, family, and church. It will help you grow spiritually, increase in power, and see miracles occur in your lives.

Read this book, then fast, and pray. This book is not written to judge people, churches, or pastors, but it is written to help them realize how Satan has rocked the church to sleep with programs, entertainment, and money, while souls are dying and going to hell.

As you read, we pray that God will show you what he wants out of your life, family, ministry, and church. God has a "plan for you to prosper and be in good health" (Jeremiah 29:11-14, KJV, 2020). Know that a "whole heart dedication" is necessary for God to reveal his will for your life and ministry. God will not allow you to enjoy the benefits of his will if you are not dedicated to him. Each day you need to give God and the Holy Spirit complete control of your agenda and plans, and you pray and put on the whole armor of God daily (Ephesians 6:11-17). Daily spiritual warfare is needed at times to survive Satan's attacks. Please write to me at the HFT Publishing address or send me an email. We want to hear from you, rejoice with you and pray for you!

HERE IS MY PRAYER OVER YOU:

Dear Heavenly Father,

In the name of your Son, Jesus Christ, we pray that this book speaks to the hearts of every reader. We ask that the Holy Spirit direct each person on the lifestyle changes needed to be rapture ready. We invite you, God, to please change the hearts of each reader, giving him or her your new, pure heart, wisdom, discernment, understanding, and an incredible peace as they read this book. Lord, we ask that you bless each person abundantly above all that they could ever think or imagine as they consecrate their lives to you and begin to study your word. We ask you to protect them, keep them safe during this world-wide pandemic. We ask for a prayer covering over them, protecting them through the blood of Jesus Christ. If anyone reading this book has COVID-19, we ask you to heal them and use their healing as a testimony for you in these last days. We ask you to anoint the words of this book that it will take root in every reader's life, making a lasting change in them that Satan will never be able to influence or change! Give each reader victory through the name of your son, Jesus Christ. Give each one a desire to see souls saved and a desire to read and study your word! We pray that you, your family, church, and careers/businesses are favored and blessed in Jesus' name!

With love, prayers, and blessing,

Charlie O'Neal

Appendix:

IS THIS DREAM AND MESSAGE SCRIPTURAL?

As I wrote the words that God gave me in the dream, I knew in my spirit that they were scriptural. However, I was more focused on writing it down exactly as it was given to me than on what was said or how the scriptures supported each comment. As soon as I had the message from God written down, I began researching every line, phrase, and term. As I began to explore topic by topic, I found that there were scriptures in the Bible that I had read thousands of times and thought I knew what they meant. However, these scriptures began to come alive to me with new assurances.

In the pages to follow, I will give you the research that I found on God's "actions" in this message. There is a list of supportive scriptures covering each of the topics in this message in the appendix. There is also an outline of the message that God gave me. This outline will help anyone who desires to preach this book to their congregation or design Sunday school lessons or Bible study group lessons from these topics.

The topics covered in the sermon outline includes 1) a jealous God; 2) a loving Father; 3) blessing, honor, and favor God gives to us; 4) Gifts, healing, anointing, and inspiration; 5) being joint-heirs with Christ; 6) the church is compared to the bride of Christ; and other topics or comments mentioned in this message. I will not be covering all of these topics in the chapter most appropriate for that topic.

With each issue that I discuss in this chapter, I will be answering the questions that God asked in this message. 1) Why have my children turned their backs on me? 2) Why are they no longer under a burden for lost souls? 3) Why have they decided to play church? 4) Why are they allowing deceitful

185

spirits, the spirits of Python, Leviathan, Jezebel, and Moloch, to enter into my holy sanctuaries? 5) Why are the pastors more concerned with entertainment, numbers, offerings, programs, and fame than they are winning souls?

To help you understand what God wants, expects and promises to do for each of us as we move toward the "tribulation period" and the "coming of Christ." I will review the 15 major points of this word from God to help you know these concepts and issues. Hopefully, this will help you to organize your thoughts and help you to remember this word.

I. ISSUES NO LONGER ALLOWED IN THE PULPIT OR THE CHURCH:

In this message or word from God, he outlined several things that he would not be tolerated from the pulpits any longer. We should discuss these items in detail, including the definition of words that God chose to use in this message.

a) HYPOCRISY:

Hypocrisy is defined by Google (2020) as "the practice of claiming to have moral standards or beliefs to which one's behavior does not conform; pretense. Ex: Someone who says they care about the environment but are constantly littering."

Matthew 23:28: Even so ye also outwardly appear righteous unto men, but within ye are full of hypocrisy and iniquity. (JKV, 2020).

---

b) DECEITFULNESS:

According to Dictionary.com (2020), when used as an adjective, deceitfulness means "given to deceiving." It also states that "a deceitful person cannot keep friends for long" because they "deceive, mislead" them. It states that deceitfulness also includes "fraudulent or deceitful actions."

If we look at how the Bible interprets the term deceitfulness, we notice that it describes a deceitful person as a dishonest person or someone who willfully perverts the truth with the intent to deceive. Other words that are synonymous with deceit are scam, fraud, con, deception, swindle, cheat, etc. A deceitful person will lead you to think that they are talking about product "a" when they are talking about product "b." They want you to believe the wrong facts. Then you will confidently share the incorrect information with others thinking you are sharing the truth. God says in his word that he hates "lying lips." To lie, you have to be dishonest or deceitful at heart. Why else would you lie except to deceive?

Proverbs 12:22: Lying lips are an abomination to the LORD: but they that deal truly are his delight. (KJV, 2020).

Hebrews 3:12-13: Take heed, brethren, lest there be in any of you an evil heart of unbelief, in departing from the living God. But exhort one another daily, while it is called today; lest any of you be hardened through the deceitfulness of sin. (JKV, 2020).

---

c) PLAYHOUSE RELIGION:

There is no better way to describe "playhouse religion" than to use the Laodicean church's description in the book of Revelation. The apostles John and Paul give specific instructions in the books of the Bible they wrote about "playing church" or demonstrating apostasy. Both cover in detail the negative results that can happen in your life if you play church. Read the scripture below (Revelation 3:14-22).

Revelation 3:14-22: And unto the angel of the church of the Laodiceans write; These things saith the Amen, the faithful and true witness, the beginning of the creation of God; <u>I know thy works, that thou art neither cold nor hot:</u> I would thou wert cold or hot. So then because thou art lukewarm, and neither cold nor hot, I will spue thee out of my mouth. <u>Because thou sayest, I am rich, and increased with goods, and have need of nothing; and knowest not that thou art wretched, and miserable, and poor, and blind, and naked:</u> I counsel thee to buy of me gold tried in the fire, that thou mayest be rich; and white raiment, that thou mayest be clothed, and *that* the shame of thy nakedness does not appear; and anoint thine eyes with eyesalve, that thou mayest see. <u>As many as I love, I rebuke and chasten: be zealous therefore, and repent. Behold, I stand at the door and knock: if any man hears my voice and opens the door, I will come into him and will sup with him, and he with me.</u> To him that overcometh will I grant to sit with me in my throne, even as I also overcame, and am set down with my Father in his throne. He that hath an ear let him hear what the Spirit saith unto the churches. (KJV, 2020, *emphasis* added).

d) CONDITION OF YOUR HEART AND SOUL:

God knows the intent of our hearts, regardless of what we say. "*I know thy works, that thou art neither cold nor hot: I would thou wert cold or hot*" (Revelation 3:15, KJV, 2020). God knows when we are cold (playing church or acting religious), and he knows when we are hot (on fire and dedicated). We cannot fool God like we can fool each other!

John describes perfectly the current condition of so many churches today. "*thou sayest, I am rich, and increased with goods, and have need of nothing; and knowest not that thou art wretched, and miserable, and poor, and blind, and naked"* (Revelation 3:17, KJV, 2020). With our knowledge, technology, and logical reasoning skills, it is so easy for us to feel that we know better than God what we want or need in our lives. But our money, knowledge, and skills are nothing without Jesus! Today, many churches are running on their knowledge, expertise, and capital, not on what God expects of the word defines for the church.

We have to know that God loves us like we love our children. Because we love them, we desire to correct them. We do not want our children to be shunned, condemned, or lose in life because they do not know how to act or present themselves. It is the same with God. He does not desire for us to suffer but to be blessed. *"As many as I love, I rebuke and chasten: be zealous therefore, and repent. Behold, I stand at the door and knock: if any man hears my voice and opens the door, I will come into him and will sup with him, and he with me"* (Revelation 3:19-20).

It is our choice whether to have a relationship with Jesus or not. He desires to commune with us…give him a chance. Give him control of your life for six months. Give God a probationary period as you would receive on your job. Let God prove himself to you. I assure you that by the time you have reached the end of this probationary period if you have earnestly searched for God's will for your life, you will be amazed at what you will have found! God will do the impossible in your life, home, and ministry. He has a purpose for you!

II. GOD PROMISES THAT FOR THE PASTORS WHO LOVE HIM AND ARE RIGHTEOUS, THAT HE WILL:

a) OPEN THEIR EYES AND GIVE THEM A PERFECT VISION TO SEE WHAT IS HAPPENING:

This promise means that if you will diligently seek him, fast, and pray, he will make his perfect will for your life known to you. He will also show you what he expects from you and what he desires

189

regarding soul-winning in these last days. God is searching daily for prayer warriors and spiritual warriors. Join God's army today!

b) <u>ANOINT THEM WITH POWER TO PREACH THE BIBLE</u>:

God will anoint anyone willing to commit. To qualify, you need to be forgiven, not perfect! God does not require a master's degree or Ph.D. God wants a person who loves his word and his will to study and pray daily.

God will not anoint someone who does not prepare. You cannot show up at church one hour before the service and kneel or stand at the altar and say, "God give me the word for today! Let my finger fall on the verse right now!" The anointing does not work this way. You have to read, pray, fast, study, and meditate on the Bible. Once you put the word of God in you, God will fill your mouth!

c) <u>HELP THEM TO REBUILD THE ALTARS IN MY CHURCHES AND CALL THE PEOPLE BACK TO THE CROSS</u>:

God wants the pastors to rebuild the altars, preach on integrity, mercy, grace, and forgiveness. He wants an altar call given at the end of every sermon, regardless of the text. The members should always feel comfortable asking for prayer and assistance spiritually without fear of ridicule or gossip. Spiritual battles are won on our knees at the altar. God does not want us on the gossip circuit or at the coffee bar smarting off discord.

God wants the pastors to preach on sin and lead the church back to the cross, so they can lead lives that demonstrate the fruits of the spirit. God wants his church to desire to see souls saved and loves to work for God. He does not want to see the works of the flesh active in our lives.

d) <u>PREACH LIKE JEREMIAH WITH BOLDNESS, HUMILITY, AND A CONTRITE SPIRIT:</u>

If you fast and pray, the Holy Ghost will anoint you. With this anointing comes boldness. However, the Holy Ghost will not dwell in a person who is not humble. It is not your place to judge and decide who can and who cannot be used by God. If you are in a church that will not accept change and does not want to hear God's word but prefers to be entertained, God desires to send you to a different group of people or churches. Pray over this issue and ask God to show you where you need to go to church.

Remember, God has got you! He will honor, favor, and promote the men and women who are willing to stand for the truth of the gospel. God will help you make the needed changes in your church. He will send you people to work with you and help you if you are sincere.

e) <u>GOD WILL HELP YOU TO LEAD YOUR CHURCHES TO A VICTORIOUS LIFESTYLE:</u>

God does not expect us to get everything in our lives and our church right by ourselves. If you humbly come before God, he will prepare you and help you to lead your church to a victorious life. He will help you to prepare them for revival. Ephesians 6 explains the armor of God and the importance of daily putting on the whole armor. This allows us to be more than conquerors for Christ!

f) <u>GOD WILL HELP THE PASTORS TO LEAD THEIR CONGREGATIONS TOWARD LIVES OF INTEGRITY:</u>

God always helps the repentant pastors and Christians. Living a life of integrity in the 21st Century is a task that requires supernatural assistance. You cannot do it by yourself. So, pray, and God has promised that he will help you. He will give you the Holy

191

Spirit to lead and guide you through the steps of integrity and help you to maintain a lifestyle of integrity as an example for your church.

If you dedicate your life and ministry to God, he will help you. He has promised that he will help us to walk a lifestyle of integrity. God is fully aware that we cannot fight this battle by ourselves. Commit today and watch him fulfill this promise to help you. God is looking for men and women who will be ministers of integrity and soul-winners.

III. WHO IS A PASTOR THAT IS DECEIVED AND UNDER THE CONTROL OF SPIRITS?

1) A pastor concerned only with numbers, dollars, programs, fame, and recognition

2) A pastor that is more concerned with entertainment than preaching the word of God

3) A pastor who omits preaching on specific topics for fear of offending individual members

4) A pastor who makes decisions, then after talking with specific members, always changes his mind to what those members desire

5) A pastor that is always stressed out, distracted, tired, and emotionally frazzled or distressed all the time

IV. WHY ARE THE PASTORS MORE CONCERNED WITH FAME, NUMBERS, FORTUNES, ENTERTAINMENT OF THEIR MEMBERS, PROGRAMS, AND OFFERINGS, THAN THE WINNING OF SOULS?

When pastors are more concerned about their needs than they are souls, something is wrong. Ministers who are self-centered or selfish will always be focused on what they need, what will make them look better, or things for the church that will give them bragging rights. Their focus, especially fund-raising endeavors, will never focus on the homeless, helpless, or tools and materials for the church that will result in soul-winning. The only exception to being involved in the help of others is when it gets them TV time. Most of the "counterfeit pastors" need personal recognition and hero worship to become involved in anything that does not benefit them.

V.   A PERSON WHO LEADS THE BRIDE OF CHRIST AWAY FROM DEDICATION:

A minister that never preaches on sin if they think that it will offend someone. This minister is only concerned about preaching and teaching what will make everyone feel good and give offerings. A faithful and anointed pastor will preach on sin, even if he knows that a member is involved in that behavior and might stop attending. A faithful minister will want you to be rapture ready. He will not spare your feelings at the expense of your soul!

a) A person who accepts everything, everyone, and does what the majority wants instead of following God's laws or commandments.

b) A person who ignores the fact that we are required to preach against the works of the flesh.

c) A person who refuses to listen to the Holy Spirit and does not preach on abortions, deceitfulness, sin, or repentance; but compromises for personal gain, church growth, fame, and fortune

193

d)   A person who lets jealousy, greed, ego, and self-centeredness rule in their lives as they boast. They may even be arrogant, prideful, haughty, and disobedient.

e)   A person who stands in the pulpit not prepared to deliver God's word and does not have a burden for lost souls

f)   A person who has an unteachable spirit, with some of the works of the flesh present in their lives

g)   These individuals never have all of the fruits of the spirit working in their lives at the same time

h)   A person who does not want to accept authority, instruction, church or organizational management, and leadership recommendations, or obey governmental regulations.

i)   A person who feels that they have to be in control and that God cannot use any other church in town or use any other preacher other than them!

> **God is our provider, our keeper, our deliverer! Without him, we are nothing. But we can do ALL things through Christ!**

VI. WHAT IS ICHABOD?

The word Ichabod has been misused in the Evangelical and Charismatic circles over the past two decades. God did not give us this word in the Bible for us to go on "prophecies of doom" campaigns. This word has a true purpose in the Christian church, and it represents a severe condition that needs to be dealt with scripturally. To understand the intent and uses, let us look at the history of this word and the ways it was used in the Bible.

In the Old Testament, the name Ichabod was given to the chief priest, Eli's grandson. Eli had two sons Phinehas and Hophni. Both sons were killed in battle, Phinehas' wife gave birth to a son. She called this child Ichabod. Eli's two sons took the "ark of the covenant" into battle. They both had sin in their lives and were not worthy to even touch the ark, might less take it into battle. These actions cost them their lives and the children of Israel, the war against the Philistines.

The name Ichabod, according to the Bible, means "no glory." Remember how Phinehas' wife declared that she was naming this son Ichabod because God's *"glory had departed"* from Israel? (I Samuel 4:21).

---

1 Samuel 4:21-22: And she named the child Ichabod, saying, the glory is departed from Israel: because the ark of God was taken, and because of her father-in-law and her husband. And she said, the glory is departed from Israel: for the ark of God is taken. (KJV, 2020).

According to Google (2020), Ichabod means "without glory." This definition implies that the "glory," which is the favor and blessings of God, is not present in a church, group of people, home, or business. Many people prophesy doom and declare Ichabod has been written over the door of the church; therefore, that church is cursed and will never come forth or do anything for God. That is a partial truth. Let us talk about using the term Ichabod in that fashion.

To say that a church has been labeled "Ichabod" means to say that God no longer allows his love, grace, mercy, blessings, and favor to reside over that church. To know if that is indeed the case, look at the church's history and current state. For example, God is no longer blessing a church if that church has a long history of confusion and church splits. If the church builds up with each new pastor arriving to see it fall because of specific individuals or the church's management, then yes, Ichabod has been written over that church. God is no longer blessing that church.

Can a pastor and his leadership style cause God to remove his favor and blessings? Yes. Can the removal of that pastor bring back the glory?

Yes, if the remaining portion of the church leadership is also not corrupt. Most churches that select a corrupt pastor do so because people on the deacon board or selection committee are looking for people with the same "kindred" spirit that they possess. The removal of the pastor will not resolve the problem. Replacement of the church's entire leadership team and a complete change of all governing bodies etc., would be needed.

For example, there was an Assembly of God church here in a small town in south Alabama that, for over 35 years, had nothing but church trouble, splits, and criminal activity occurring within the church. They went through a pastor every 15 to 18 months. Finally, the Alabama District Office of the Assemblies of God in Montgomery, Alabama, had enough and pulled the sign down from this sovereign church. After a few years, various leaders in the church began to die. First was the chairman of the deacon board, then the Sunday School superintendent, etc. With each death, church members would rise-up and try to get a new pastor and change the situation. Nothing worked. Finally, the last founding member died. They had gone for over four years without a pastor, so the previous 20 members decided to close the church and sell the building.

A Baptist minister heard that the building was for sale. Considering it was a beautiful property with a fellowship hall and parsonage (rare for that area), he got funding and purchased the building. His first step was to destroy all old records and files for the church, clean it out, and invite several Baptist ministers he trusted to come to help him anoint the building. They prayed over the building, bound any evil spirits, and asked God to anoint the church, bless it, and be present always. God heard his prayer. The church began to grow and has done better than anyone ever imagined possible in this small town.

Yes, Ichabod was written over the door. It was a church without God's favor and blessings. Now, it has been reclaimed for God, and he has returned his glory, allowing blessings and favor on that church. However, there was a complete change of leadership and organization within that church. Too often, I have seen preachers take a church to pastor, thinking that they could be the one God uses to change the church and bring it back. You cannot get a church with faulty leadership back to fellowship with God and blessings. You can only accomplish this return to glory if you remove all leadership positions, teachers, secretaries, board members, choir, praise and worship teams, etc., and start over with all new leadership and workers.

The term Ichabod should not be used as a prophecy of doom, stating that the people in the church will die like Eli and his sons. Ichabod declared over a church is a warning to all who would come there, not to waste their time. Without a complete leadership and governing board change, their works in that church cannot be blessed. No one likes to work all week and not get paid. We should not desire to attend a church and work in it without God's blessings and favor. We should strive to work in a ministry that wants to see and is seeing souls saved, delivered, and healed.

If you are a minister and run a revival or minister at a church and God witnesses to you that Ichabod is written over that church, graciously complete your duties there and leave. Do not go everywhere telling people that God showed you Ichabod was written over that church. God revealed that to you to guide and direct you, not to defame that community's church. Begin praying for the church member that God will open their eyes and witness that they need to leave. Given time, God will clean out that church. God does not require you to do it for him or initiate the process!

Can a person have Ichabod written over their lives? Yes. I have met a few pastors over the years who did not have the blessings and favor of God in their ministries because they allowed demonic spirits to control them, or they were letting these spirits make the decisions for their churches. An individual who causes a church to lose its favor and blessing from God will also have the same demonstration of Ichabod in their personal lives. They will not be enjoying the benefits and favor of God.

What actions are taken in a church that will cause God to write Ichabod over the door?   Sin, disobedience, spiritual idolatry, greed, selfishness, self-centeredness, the works of the flesh, especially the sins of the flesh, the lust of the eye, and the pride of life. A pastor or leadership team that is arrogant, egotistical, and judgmental cause a church to lose favor with God.   If they promote or engaging in immorality, abortions, and deceitfulness, it will bring the wrath of God down on a church. God will remove all of the "glory of God" and his anointing from a church quicker for immorality and lack of humility than any other actions.

If a minister has "Ichabod" written over his or her life and ministry, you can read the story of the priest Eli and his two wicked sons found in **I Samuel 4:19-21** to see what you can expect to witness in that person's life or ministry. God caused Ichabod to be written over the story of Eli and his son's life. All of the good they accomplished is forgotten because of the bad that brought them to their end. Here are 20 characteristics that you can expect to see in the person's life, church, or ministry where Ichabod has been declared. The pastor of an Ichabod church may present with the following characteristics.

1) They live in attack mode
2) They are judgmental of all other ministers
3) Their church is the only church
4) They are the only real prophets of God

5) They engage in sexual immorality like Eli's sons

6) They always brag about their gifts, their prophecies, their ability to prophecy doom on someone, and it happens.

7) They brag about how God kills anyone that comes against them

8) An Ichabod preacher will not have a heart of love and mercy like the heart of God.

9) If you talk to these ministers for at least 30 minutes, you will notice a root of bitterness in their lives.

10) They have "war stories" to tell about how people attack them, cursed them, and God judged those people. They celebrate or brag about these events. There is no remorse and no evidence of sadness at a lost soul!

11) They fear man more than God. He is afraid of what man thinks of him more than he worries about being in God's will.

12) They will deliver prophecies of doom and celebrating other minister's demise.

13) If they have not reached the doom level's prophecies, you will still see a minister who is "spineless" and change their standards as necessary to keep everyone happy. These are the ministers who change their sermons to keep the members and their money coming!

14) You will see posts on social media where they "whine" or complain when people do not accept their prophecies or their beliefs.

15) You will notice that all decisions they make benefit them.

16) All choice they make will please their boards, governing authorities, licensing boards, and local politicians. They are basically "yes men" or "politically-correct" pastors.

17) They will join the group of popular opinion to prevent ridicule. There is an Old Testament story about the prophets that did just this to appease Israel's Kings. You can read about it in the book of I Kings the 22nd chapter.

18) Jeremiah 6:13-14 describes how these false teachers and preachers will prophecy what the people want to hear.

19) Jeremiah 23:21 describes how these false prophet's prophecy when God has not spoken to them.

20) These ministers are not concerned about the church membership (the Sheep). They are not good shepherds, as Jesus taught. They are the hirelings that are not concerned about the church's safety and security (sheep-fold). Refer to the parable that Jesus shared in the Gospels.

As you can see, _this list of 20 characteristics of an Ichabod minister_ is extensive. You may not see all 20 characteristics in a minster. However, if you see more than three characteristics in a pastor, move to another church. If you are attending a revival at a church and see three or more of these characteristics in the visiting minister, do not go back to that revival. If you notice five or more in the church pastor you are visiting, do not ever go back to that church while he is the pastor, even if your best friend runs a revival there.

If you are attending a church where five or more of these characteristics are noted in the pastor, associate pastor, board, or leadership team, find another church as soon as possible! God has a church for you and your family where you can enjoy the power of God, his anointing, favor, and blessings! Seek God earnestly, and he will show you where to go to church!

VII. WHY ARE PASTORS ALLOWING DECEITFUL SPIRITS, THE SPIRIT OF PYTHON, LEVIATHAN, JEZEBEL, AND MOLOCH TO BE IN THEIR CHURCHES?

When pastors allow spirits in their churches, it is usually through ignorance. You cannot control what spirits attend your church, but you can control which spirits take offices, hold positions, teach, preach, sing, play musical instruments, etc. A person working as a marriage counselor needs to be an individual with a stable marriage founded on God's word, not a counselor who is struggling with adultery or fornication. The children's church pastor does not need to be an individual with a history of child abuse, child pornography, or a history of rape and incest. It is easy to see why these individuals fighting these spirits should not be in an office. But it is just as essential to secure church leaders who are not fighting jealousy, envy, or revenge. Anyone taking a position in the church should not have the works of the flesh active in their lives. Even the deacon board or board of director positions should require integrity and cleanliness of their members.

If a pastor looks over his brother-in-law's temper to keep his wife happy, then that spirit will bring other spirits with it. As you compromise for one person, then the process of compromising or overlooking sin becomes easier and more comfortable. One day you will wake up and wonder how you became so desensitized to sin that you did not recognize the "alternate lifestyle, pro-choice" choir director that you just appointed to his or her position!

When God's judgment comes to your church as he witnessed in this message would arrive, God will not pass over if sin is present. Moses had the children of Israel place the sacrificial lamb's blood over the top of the door and on the side post of the door of their homes. When the death angel passed over each house in Egypt, he knew to pass by and not stop at the houses with the blood over the door. It is like the hymn that we sing "When I see the blood, I will pass over you!" That is what we need when judgment comes to the houses of God over the next few years. We need the death angel and the angels of destruction to pass over our homes and churches. That will only happen if the blood is applied. However, if spirits are inhabiting our homes, lives, and churches, the blood will not be applied. So, judgment is coming.

In this word, God said that he would start with the pulpits, then go to the pews. God said that he would allow the destruction of the flesh to save the soul (**I Corinthians 5:5**). This physical destruction or death-bed repentance will allow some individuals to be helped to get rapture ready. The Bible warns us of pestilence, wars, and rumors of wars and political conflicts in the last days (**Matthew 24:5-6**). These events are real and already happening! We must be rapture ready! Nothing else matters, but knowing that our hearts, homes, lives, children, families, and church are covered with the blood of Jesus Christ!

I Corinthians 5:5: To deliver such a one unto Satan for the destruction of the flesh, that the spirit may be saved in the day of the Lord Jesus. (KJV, 2020).

Matthew 24:5-6: For many shall come in my name, saying, I am Christ; and shall deceive many. And ye shall hear of wars and rumours of wars: see that ye be not troubled: for all *these things* must come to pass, but the end is not yet. (KJV, 2020).

You can also read the entire chapter of Matthew 24, Mark 13:1-20, and Luke 21:5-24 to get a better understanding of what Jesus was teaching about our future, what is to come, and what we need to do to be rapture ready. The Bible is full of numerous accounts of instructions to the churches that allow spirits to control them. There are also several scriptures in books other than Revelation that describes what it will take to be rapture ready. As you read through your Bible from Genesis to Revelation this year, ask the Holy Spirit to reveal to you the knowledge of God's word. You will be amazed at what you learn!

VIII. <u>WHAT DOES IT MEAN TO BE RAPTURE READY?</u>

Being rapture ready means that you have all sin covered under the blood of Jesus Christ and that you are trying to live right. A person rapture ready has a teachable spirit. They are humble and approach God with a contrite spirit when they pray. There is a "false humility" that is demonstrated by some Christians. Do not be deceived by that display of emotions. The easiest way to determine the difference between false humility and true humility is that a truly humble person does not go around telling people that he or she is humble. You see the humility in their actions and attitudes.

A person who desires to be rapture ready will want all of the fruits of the spirit present in their lives. Humility, a contrite heart, and a merciful spirit are the first three behaviors or attitudes that you should notice in them. You should see that they do not talk about people, judge, or cut other individuals, churches, and organizations. They will look for the good in everyone. Yet, they will have the strength or, as southerners say, "backbone" to stand for truth without compromising, yet demonstrating love at the same time. When you meet someone like this, you have encountered a person with standards, integrity, and a heart that is Christ-like and rapture ready!

<u>Definition of Integrity:</u> According to Google (2020), integrity is defined as "the quality of being honest and having strong moral principles; moral uprightness." Google also lists integrity as "the state of being whole and undivided."

Proverbs 11:1-6: A false balance is an abomination to the LORD: but a just weight is his delight. When pride cometh, then cometh shame: but with the lowly is wisdom. The integrity of the upright shall guide them: but the perverseness of transgressors shall destroy them—riches profit not in the day of wrath: but righteousness delivereth from death. The righteousness of the perfect shall direct his way: but the wicked shall fall by his own wickedness. The righteousness of the upright shall deliver them: but transgressors shall be taken in their own naughtiness. (KJV, 2020).

The Bible mentions various actions, attitudes, and behaviors throughout the Old and New Testament that are considered unpleasing to God. However, one chapter in the New Testament summarizes God's stories, recommendations, and words throughout the Bible. This section is found in Galatians, the fifth chapter. It is known to most ministers as the "list of abominations." It is one of the most misinterpreted sections of the Bible. It has been used as the "condemnation hammer" that the radical holiness group of churches uses to justify them criticizing and judging people.

The Apostle Paul lists the "works of the flesh" as an abomination, indicating that they SHALL NOT enter heaven. Paul was precise in his letter to the Galatian church about what would enter Heaven and what would not. (See the scripture below; study the works of the flesh and the fruits of the spirit thoroughly in the next two chapters).

Paul did not write the letter to the Galatians to issue a license to the Christian churches to become judge and jury, executing judgments and sentences on its members. With the heaviness of heart, I admit that the holiness, evangelical organizations that I was raised in have reverted to this type of non-Christian behavior. Over the years, their actions have caused many people to turn from church, refusing never to return. I fear the end result for these preachers and individuals who have judged others so harshly. We will discuss later in this book what will happen to people who continue to judge others.

In this chapter, I do not want to focus on the people who judge others. I want to focus on what we can do as 21st Century Christians and churches to ensure that there is a "bride" for Christ to return and secure. I want to go to Heaven more than anything else on this earth. I hope you feel the same and accept Paul's instructions to the Galatian church as such. Our job description is the list of the fruits of the spirit, and the "never to-do list" is the works of the flesh. Honesty, integrity, and purity are required of all, not just ministers!

Below is the scripture from Galatians. In the next two chapters, you will receive more detailed information on the fruits of the spirit and the works of the flesh. Once you have mastered the definitions of the terms Paul used, you will know your responsibilities as a Christian and what it will take for you to go to heaven, whether you go by way of the grave or in the rapture of the church!

Galatians 5:18-26: But if ye be led of the Spirit, ye are not under the law. Now the works of the flesh are manifest, which are these; Adultery, fornication, uncleanness, lasciviousness, idolatry, witchcraft, hatred, variance, emulations, wrath, strife, seditions, heresies, envyings, murders, drunkenness, revellings, and such like: of the which I tell you before, as I have also told you in time past, that they which do such things shall not inherit the kingdom of God. But the fruit of the Spirit is love, joy, peace, longsuffering, gentleness, goodness, faith, meekness, temperance: against such; there is no law. And they that are Christ's have crucified the flesh with the affections and lusts. If we live in the Spirit, let us also walk in the Spirit. Let us not be desirous of vain glory, provoking one another, envying one another. (KJV, 2020).

IX. WHAT IS A "LAST-DAY REVIVAL?"

The word revival is defined in religious circles as a weekend or week-long event where everyone assembles at a specified time at their church each day to hear a guest speaker share God's word. Most churches fast and pray before the revival week, asking God to send sinners to these meetings. Some churches advertise the revivals on the local radio programs, television stations and put-up posters around town to make people at other churches aware of the revival.

The major problem facing the 21st Century is that revival attendance is limited because of people's jobs, work hours, children's homework, and other activities that their children are involved in, like sports and extra-curricular activities. The second issue that has caused so many churches to stop planning revivals is the lack of attendance by non-Christians and non-members. People are so busy with their lives and families that they have difficulty attending the annual revival at their church, might less attend a revival at a neighboring church. Most non-Christians will tell you that there is no need for them to participate in a revival. If they desire to hear a sermon, they will turn on a Christian television channel like the Trinity Broadcasting Network (TBN) or Daystar Network. Of which, both offer excellent programming and dynamic speakers. However, hearing the word is not enough. We need to be "doers" of the word and helping others. If we attend church and work in that church, we can help other people learn how to live a victorious life!

If this is the average American's mindset, why are we expecting a "latter-day or end-time revival?" As with most understandings that occur in the English language, this misconception surrounds the inaccurate definition of the word "revival." The best way to give you an accurate interpretation of this word is to look at its synonyms. At times, I find that synonyms provide a more precise definition than even the world accepted definitions of Merriam-Webster Dictionaries or Dictionary.com. The top synonyms that Microsoft Word provides for the word revival are 1) stimulation, 2) renewal, 3) revitalization, 4) restoration, and reinforcement.

These synonyms probably set your mind in orbit like it did mine when I looked them up last year. Revival is not specifically about a week-long meeting or collaboration between churches in a planned event. Revival is something that starts with us…yes; each one of us can have revival in our spiritual lives that will make an end-time impact! Understand me; I still believe in revivals. I have attended revivals that were phenomenal. But I have also participated in some that were a waste of my time. Pastors, do not stop planning revivals or youth camps. Pastors, I want to discuss how you can have revival in your ministry every week and promote revival in your church members' lives.

1) Preach the word to your church. Teach them to seek the fruits of the spirit to be active in their lives. When you get the fruits of the spirit active in your lives, you will begin to have blessings and favor.

The changes that occur in your lives will attract other people to you. The greatest revivals that we will see in these last days will be the 1:1 witnessing and coaching.

2) Help your church members to seek the purpose that God has for their lives. When we get into God's will, we experience success. Things work better for us when we are fulfilling God's will for our lives. Once again, this result will attract others to you, including other Christians struggling and sinners.

3) Offer discipleship courses, classes, study materials, recorded sermons on MP3 downloads, CDs, and DVDs to your church members to help them grow spiritually and have a "revival" in their lives.

4) Once you have helped your members get their lives aligned with the Bible, find their purpose, and enabled them to become disciplined in their personal lives, you will see revival in them. When revival occurs, there will be a greater desire for God's word and increased evangelism automatically. There is no way to be immersed in God's word without impacting your life and how you talk with others.

5) As revival breaks out in the lives of your members, you will see revival in the church. People will be attracted to come would have never attended your church. They will want to check out the pastor who helps their church reach a new level in their relationship with Jesus.

6) Sinners will also be attracted to come to your church when they see miracles occurring in the lives of your members. Sinner people today are not interested in what you say or what you preach; they want to see results! Why should they come to hear you preach if they are more blessed than the members of your church?

7) Revival is stimulated when renewal and revitalization of your church members occurs. When the word of God helps your members to see restorations in their lives, they become encouraged to read, pray, fast, and witness more. When they become more involved spiritually, they become your reinforcements. Active prayer warriors in your church help you to see more extraordinary miracles. Plus, there will be renewals and restorations that begin to take place in other

members. All of this attracts sinners. See how this works? Revival is not a meeting; it is a lifestyle change!

8) Revival is coming to churches across America in 2020 that read this book and begin to seek to know God's will and purpose for their lives. As they become "rapture ready," revival occurs in their lives, overflowing to others. Revival may not be in the form of past events at your church...but revival occurs anywhere there is a strong move of God, with Holy Ghost power!

X.   THEREFORE, THE TERM "LAST DAYS" REVIVAL MEANS:

Yes, there will be a revival in the last days. This revival may not be configured, marketed, and performed in the past methods, as discussed above. I realize there will be some traditional revivals. There is a possibility that another "Brownsville Style" revival could occur. However, with the work limitations and current limitations on public gatherings that we are currently facing due to COVID-19, a week-long revival may not be physically or legally possible. But revival can come as we have already discussed, one person at a time, impacting their circle of influence.

Whether this last-day revival comes to your church or your town depends on you and your church members. God will not force any pastor or church to experience revival. You must desire revival. Your desire to see souls saved must be significant enough that you fast, pray, cry, and travail before the Lord. Spiritual warfare is a critical component in seeing a revival. If you have not read the first book of the series *"The Keys to Victorious Living"* that I began researching and writing in 2017, then I highly recommend that you look for the first book in that series, *"Why am I not Living a Victorious Life?"* You need the skills of spiritual warfare operational in your life and your church to see revival.

Has the last-day revival already started? Yes, I believe that it has already begun. I think that God has been dealing with ministers and Christians around the world. Can we see the results of this revival yet? Partially. I have been asked by several individuals the following questions. I thought the Azusa street revival was the "last days" revival. Did it not begin then, and is it continuing on today? I do not have an answer to this question. All I can explain is yes; there was a mighty revival in the Evangelical arena that began on Azusa street in California in the 20th Century. I believe that God used that revival to get the holiness and evangelical communities united and focused so that the gospel of Jesus Christ could be spread worldwide.

The second set of questions that I have been asked deal with the Brownsville revival in Pensacola in the late 1990s. Was this the beginning of the end of the last-days revival? Once again, I cannot explicitly declare that to be true. However, I met the pastor of that church and the evangelist who was running the Brownsville Revival. I believe that God used those men and that church to "stir-up" pastors across America and get them focused on soul-winning again. Soul winning has been the lost purpose of the American church for the past forty years. Even though the Brownsville Revival results were phenomenal and more fabulous than anyone expected, the revival faded away as quickly as it appeared. Why?

When revival comes, we get excited and spiritually invested in the progress and outcomes. It becomes an emotional roller-coaster ride. Many people jump on the roller coaster and enjoy the excitement of the journey, but never change. For revival to come and stay, there must be lifestyle changes that occur. Christianity cannot generate a revival itself. Christians love the emotionalism of the Charismatic movement and the Evangelicals. They love the way that revival makes them feel. But being ready to go in the rapture takes more than an emotion.

A physical church-sponsored week-long revival event requires a lot of preparations beforehand to accomplish. Revival requires dedication and commitment. All of the Evangelist's work and preaching are for naught if someone does not take responsibility for the new converts' discipleship. The church pastor must have a battle plan/war strategy ready for implementation once the revival is over, or Satan will have the new converts back in his clutches in less than sixty days.

Pastors must understand that revival is a lifestyle change for him, the membership, and definitely for the new converts. It is possible to have a church in constant revival with the right ministerial team. Revival does not have to be a three to five day or an event once per year. The desire for revival, the heart for revival, and the prayer life travailing for revival must be maintained all the time to see a revival that lasts.

So, yes, I feel that the last-days revival has tried to start several times in America. Even events like September 11, 2001, brought America to its knees and had people seeking God's face, but did it last? No! Why? There were no lifestyle changes, no mentoring of the new converts, and no one preparing them to maintain revival. Will this COVID-19 pandemic bring revival? Yes, to some areas of the United States. To other regions, it will bring chaos, riots, and destruction! Why? Because the pastors, evangelists, and ministers of America have failed the church of the 21st Century. They have been more concerned with numbers, events, programs, fund-raising, and other activities than in soul-winning.

I heard an Assembly of God Youth Pastor tell a South AL TV reporter during an interview that he had never given an altar call in the services he organized for his church's young people. He remarked, "Oh, there is no need for the traditional altar call. They do not need to be embarrassed or shamed into coming forward. A simple bowing of their heads and saying they are sorry is enough. I have to make sure that they know that God loves them, and he is proud of them just as they are, and God is not concerned with how they look or what they do!" I cried when I say this interview. I began to pray, "God, how can an evangelical youth pastor be this deceived? What is happening to the young people under his leadership? God, please have mercy on him and spare those children. Give them a chance to hear the real word of God!" This was my immediate prayer. People, we need to be praying for all churches, pastors, and ministry leaders. This same disease of ignorance has taken over so many churches. It is easier to ignore things and hope they will go away than to preach on sin! This is not what God wants for our churches.

We need a revival in America! But revival will never come until we convince the pastors of our churches that revival is needed. Once they are convinced, we have to educate them on planning and getting ready for revival. If your church is full of grumpy old Christians who find fault with everything that people do, judge them, and condemn them, how will you keep new converts? God cannot send you revival until you have revival with the current membership, and lifestyle changes are implemented. If God sent your church revival, the lazy, laid-back, allergic to prayer, and work members would run them off the first month!

Once a pastor and church are ready for revival, it will come. But while you are waiting for it to happen, you need to prepare materials and train workers to disciple the new converts. If you want

God to take you seriously that you want revival, you need to be ready! A person can dream of owning a grocery store and providing the best meats and produce in town. However, if the owner never rents the store or stocks it, how will he have customers? The same is true with the church!

a) ARE WE IN THE "LAST-DAY REVIVAL" TIME-FRAME NOW?

Most evangelical ministers believe that we are in the days that John was talking about in the book of Revelation. Some think we are about to enter into this pre-rapture revival. Others believe that we are already in the first year of the seven-year tribulation period. I will not debate the topics of pre-tribulation versus the mid-tribulation rapture of the church in this book. This book's focus is to "stir-up Churches" to desire revival and focus on soul-winning in these last days.

Numerous scriptures specifically outline when Christ will return and what we will see before his return. This topic is discussed in detail in "The Keys to Victorious Living Series" books coming out in 2021. If you have questions or feel confused about the return of Christ, I recommend that you secure a copy of that book.

b) THEN WHY DOES II THESSALONIANS SAY THAT THERE WILL BE A GREAT APOSTASY IN THE LAST DAYS?

In his letter to the Thessalonians, the apostle Paul reminded them of the teachings he had previously given to them. He told them that there would be wide-spread rebellions and riots in the last days, which indicates that this is a sign of the end of time.

II Thessalonians 2:3-5, 8-11: Let no man deceive you by any means; for that day shall not come, except there comes a falling away first, and that man of sin be revealed, the son of perdition; who opposeth and exalteth himself above all that is called God, or that is worshipped, so that he as God sitteth in the temple of God, shewing himself that he is God. And then shall that wicked be revealed, whom the Lord shall consume with the spirit of his mouth, and shall destroy with the brightness of his coming: Even him whose coming is after the working of Satan with all power and signs and lying wonders. And with all deceivableness of unrighteousness in them that perish; because they received not the love of the truth, that they might be saved. And for this course, God shall send them strong delusions, that they should believe a lie. That they all might be damned who believed not the truth but had pleasure in unrighteousness. (KJV, 2020).

This scripture is found in the letter that the apostle Paul wrote to the Thessalonians. This letter tried to clarify several misconceptions and false teachings that had been given to the Thessalonians. In the second verse of this chapter, Paul tells them not to be "shaken in mind, or be troubled…. that the day of Christ is at hand." In the third verse, he continues, "let no man deceive you by any means."

Paul did not want the Thessalonians to give up, quit their jobs, and sit around waiting for Christ to appear in the sky. He wanted them to continue spreading the good news of the gospel of Jesus Christ. He wanted them to work and prepare while looking for Christ's return. So, he gave them signs to look for to help them that would allow them to discern who was right or wrong and what would be in the last days.

In this verse, Paul is telling them not to worry. They will not be deceived if they continue to follow the teachings and instructions, he has given them. He said that they would recognize the son of perdition (the evil one, the beast in Revelation). They did not have to worry nor be deceived. Paul explains how the son of perdition (the Beast) will exalt himself above God and declare that he is God.

Paul instructed them that in the days that the evil one was setting up, there would be so much evil occurring and that there will be a "falling away first." To describe this falling away, let us look back to the time of Noah. Before the flood came, there was "drinking, marrying...and evil" that was continually present. The evil was so severe that it vexed Noah's soul. Paul is telling the Thessalonians that the same thing will occur in the end. That the world will become so evil that it will be easy for the son of perdition (the Beast) to rise-up, declare himself God, and take control.

Consider the condition of the world today. Look at the sick state of affairs in America. Life is no longer valuable with crimes, chaos, and confusion everywhere. People no longer show any shame. Evil and immorality are the new normal! We can easily conclude that we are living in the days that Paul is talking. It would be easy for the "beast" to appear and declare himself God, and the majority of the world's population would vote him in as long as he announced that he was tolerant of all faiths and lifestyles. That is all that it would take. We have desensitized the past two generations to the point that as long as someone wants peace, promotes tolerance, and free-choice, he would be accepted as the one! They would vote him in and give up their freedoms if he asked.

This scripture is not in conflict with the declaration of revival in the last days. It is not declaring a decline in the churches or the closing of the church doors. Although this may be something that we see, and evil begins to take over, our freedoms are removed. The answer to your question is that both scriptures are correct. Both events will happen because Paul and John are talking about two separate topics. I believe that this scripture is being fulfilled before our eyes this year!

XI. WHAT OR WHO IS A LAST-DAY MINISTER?

a) WHAT WILL AN END-TIME MINISTER, TEACHER, MISSIONARY, OR PROPHET LOOK LIKE ACCORDING TO SCRIPTURE?

An end-time or last days minister, teacher, missionary, or prophet will be living a dedicated life of integrity and have a passion for winning the lost. These individuals are continually prepping and preparing to help the new converts and lead them to a closer walk with Christ. These individuals have a heart for revival and a desire to see revival, no matter what the cost! This could be anyone willing to dedicate their lives to Christ's commission. God will accept any age group and educational background to carry the gospel of the good news of Jesus Christ to the world!

b) HOW WILL GOD USE THESE PEOPLE?

The primary duty will be soul winning. It may be from a pulpit, through music, teaching, Bible studies, intercessory prayer, one-on-one witnessing, writing a weekly blog, or writing articles and books. God will use your talents to his glory if you let him.

XII. WHAT THIS MESSAGE FROM GOD TO US IS SAYING?

I firmly believe that God gave me this message to wake up the church, starting with the pastors. Each time in the Old Testament that God wanted to get Israel's attention and deliver them from their captors, he would "stir-up" a prophet or king. They would see visions or have dreams. God dealt with one individual, and that person got others stirred-up. Then revival would begin.

Remember the story of how Elijah met the children of Israel on Mount Carmel? What did Elijah do when it was his time to offer a sacrifice? He began to pump and prime the crowd. Elijah reminded them of the promises of God. He got them to agree that if God answered by fire, they promised to serve God and Him alone with all of their hearts. When the children of Israel were willing to commit to God, God showed up! In this story, God showed up and answered by fire so that they could not deny that our Lord God Jehovah was the only true God!

The people were so committed to their promise to serve God that the people at Elijah's command killed the 300 plus false prophets and priests present that day! A revival began in Israel and lasted as long as they remained faithful to God's commitment and shared what God had done.

God is asking you to seek him, to desire to study His word more than anything else. God wants you to have him first, the fruits of the spirit in your life, and none of the works of the flesh present. God wants you to desire revival so much that revival starts in you! God wants you to have a passion and burden for lost souls! If you do these things, you will be rapture ready!

XII. WHAT SHOULD I DO IF THIS MESSAGE DESCRIBES MY PASTOR AND MY CHURCH?

If this word from God has shown you that you are in a church where the pastor is a false teacher/preacher or is not a true shepherd, you need to find a new church. It does not matter where your family or friends attends; you need to attend a church with the true move of God. A church without evil spirits and demons controlling or running the operations of the church. If you stay back with your family and friends, you run the risk of being left behind. The most important decision you will make today is to commit your heart and life to the truth of the gospel. Make the change needed for the sake of your family, home, and children or grandchildren.

If this word from God has shown you several problems in your church, consider whether or not your pastor is involved in those issues. If your pastor is not involved or a participant, then begin intercessory prayer for your pastor. Ask God to show you what to do to help him make the changes needed. Support your pastor, and God will move the hindrances, or he will move the pastor to a church that wants deliverances and revival. The most important thing for you to remember is not to be swayed or pulled by friends making you feel that you need to be politically correct by attending that church.

If you find that your pastor is involved in your church's problems and issues, you need to find a new church pronto! You do not need to be a part of a church that is defiling itself or is being led by immoral leadership.

XIV. WHAT SHOULD I DO IF THIS MESSAGE DESCRIBES MY LIFE AND MY FAMILY?

If this message shows you that you are being led by or oppressed by demonic spirits or that you have let sin creep into your life, like disobedience, talk with your pastor. Share with him what you have realized, and ask him to pray with you and counsel you. Being open is the first step to deliverance. Some oppressions are severe enough that you may need counseling or one-on-one training to help you get the victory and keep it. If you are part of the leadership team, a teacher, church worker, or church employee, you will need to step down from your position until you can get your spiritual life back in alignment with God's word. You need to be disciplined, not teaching others at this time.

If you openly and honestly confess to God and your pastor, you will be amazed at how quickly God will move on your behalf. Making that first step is the most challenging part! I pray that this chapter has helped open your eyes and helps you realize what God wants in your life and your church. God is waiting for you!

Now that we have laid some basic knowledge about this book, and its message, let us take a more in-depth look at the hindrances Satan puts in our path. Satan will send deceivers, apostates, and false prophets to influence us, causing us to miss God's will, way, and plans for our churches and us! The next few chapters will discuss topics that will help you to understand this word from God in more detail. I pray that the Holy Spirit will open your eyes to what it will take for you to be rapture ready and what needs to happen in your life, ministry, and church for revival to occur!

XV. WHAT CAN I DO TO HELP REVIVAL COME TO MY CHURCH?

1) Be rapture ready at all times with your sins confessed under the blood of Jesus Christ.

2) Demonstrate the fruits of the spirit in your life, home, communications, career, and the church.

3) Live a holy, dedicated life to Christ. (See the definition of holiness that was listed in previous chapters).

4) Live a daily life with the works of the flesh in operation in your life

5) Pray for souls and travail before the Lord for revival in your church

6) Witness to everyone you meet or feel let to contact

7) Pray at least two times per day

8) Read your Bible every morning and night, while reading through the Bible at least once per year

9) Ask God to show you who to help, who to witness to, and who you should show extra love toward each day.

10) Take communion at least weekly. Take daily if you are experiencing a spiritual battle or if you need physical healing.

11) Pray for God to show you what to do for your church.

12) Pray and ask God to show you what to do for the elders in your church and community.

13) Pray for your family, church, pastor, community, county, state, and federal government employees and leaders to do God's will.

14) Ask God for healing for our land and revival.

Be sincere with the fourteen steps above. Complete these steps every day and ask God to help you to control your tongue. You need to speak the word of God over your situations and problems, not grumble about them. It would be best if you spoke "good-positive" words each day, leaving bad, inadequate, and deficient words out of your vocabulary. Do not speak in anger or with resentment. Keep those out of your life! According to the Bible, if you are a preacher or teacher, speak God's word with boldness. Do not give your opinions as gospel. Do not compromise God's word to appease your church members or attract others to your church. Preach the true, unadulterated word of God and God will anoint you, bless your ministry, and help your church grow!

SUPPORTIVE SCRIPTURES FOR

EACH TOPIC DISCUSSED

Supportive Scriptures for
this message from God

*Here are scriptures by category to back-up
and support this word from the Lord:*

SEEK GOD

Leviticus 19:31: Regard not them that have familiar spirits, neither seek after wizards, to be defiled by them: I am the LORD your God. (KJV, 2020).

Deuteronomy 4:29: But if from thence thou shalt seek the LORD thy God, thou shalt find him, if thou seek him with all thy heart and with all thy soul. (KJV, 2020).

I Chronicles 28:9: And thou, Solomon, my son, know thou the God of thy father and serve him with a perfect heart and with a willing mind: for the LORD searcheth all hearts, and understandeth all the imaginations of the thoughts: if thou seek him, he will be found of thee; but if thou forsake him, he will cast thee off forever. (KJV, 2020).

Psalm 63:1: O God, thou *art* my God; early will I seek thee: my soul thirsteth for thee, my flesh longeth for thee in a dry and thirsty land, where no water is; (KJV, 2020).

Amos 5:14: Seek good, and not evil, that ye may live: and so, the LORD, the God of hosts, shall be with you, as ye have spoken. (KJV, 2020).

Matthew 6:33: But seek ye first the kingdom of God and his righteousness, and all these things shall be added unto you. (KJV, 2020).

Luke 12:31: But rather seek ye the kingdom of God; and all these things shall be added unto you. (KJV, 2020).

SEEK NOT MAN'S APPROVAL

John 5:44: How can ye believe, which receive honour one of another, and seek not the honour that *cometh* from God only? (KJV, 2020).

Galatians 1:10: For do I now persuade men or God? or do I seek to please men? for if I yet pleased men, I should not be the servant of Christ. (KJV, 2020).

FAITH IS NEEDED TO PLEASE GOD

Hebrews 11:6: But without faith, *it is* impossible to please *him*: for he that cometh to God must believe that he is and *that* he is a rewarder of them that diligently seek him. (KJV, 2020).

I Corinthians 10:13: There hath no temptation taken you but such as is common to man: but God *is* faithful, who will not suffer you to be tempted above that ye are able; but will with the temptation also make a way to escape, that ye may be able to bear *it*. (KJV, 2020).

Hebrews 10:23: Let us hold fast the profession of *our* faith without wavering; (for he *is* faithful that promised). (KJV, 2020).

Hebrews 11:1-3: Now faith is the substance of things hoped for, the evidence of things not seen…. Through faith, we understand that the worlds were framed by the word of God so that things which are seen were not made of things which do appear. (KJV, 2020).

Hebrews 11:6-7: But without faith, *it is* impossible to please *him*: for he that cometh to God must believe that he is and *that* he is a rewarder of them that diligently seek him. By faith Noah, being warned of God of things not seen as yet, moved with fear, prepared an ark to the saving of his house; by the which he condemned the world, and became heir of the righteousness which is by faith. (KJV, 2020).

James 1:5-6: If any of you lack wisdom, let him ask of God, that giveth to all *men* liberally, and upbraideth not; and it shall be given him. But let him ask in faith, nothing wavering. For he that wavereth is like a wave of the sea driven with the wind and tossed. (KJV, 2020).

---

1 Peter 1:7: That the trial of your faith, being much more precious than of gold that perisheth, though it be tried with fire, might be found unto praise and honour and glory at the appearing of Jesus Christ: (KJV, 2020).

DISOBEDIENCE

Ephesians 5:5-6: For this ye know, that no whoremonger, nor unclean person, nor covetous man, who is an idolater, hath any inheritance in the kingdom of Christ and God. Let no man deceive you with vain words: for because of these things cometh the wrath of God upon the children of disobedience. (KJV, 2020).

---

1 Kings 13:26-27: And when the prophet that brought him back from the way heard *thereof*, he said, it *is* the man of God, who was disobedient unto the word of the LORD: therefore, the LORD hath delivered him unto the lion, which hath torn him, and slain him, according to the word of the LORD, which he spoke unto him. And he spoke to his sons, saying, Saddle me the ass. And they saddled *him*. (KJV, 2020).

Romans 1:21-32: Because that, when they knew God, they glorified *him* not as God, neither were thankful; but became vain in their imaginations, and their foolish heart was darkened. Professing themselves to be wise, they became fools and changed the glory of the incorruptible God into an image made like to corruptible man, and to birds, and four-footed beasts, and creeping things. Wherefore God also gave them up to uncleanness through the lusts of their own hearts, to dishonour their own bodies between themselves: Who changed the truth of God into a lie, and worshipped and served the creature more than the Creator, who is blessed forever. Amen. For this cause God gave

221

them up unto vile affections: for even their women did change the natural use into that which is against nature: And likewise, also the men, leaving the natural use of the woman, burned in their lust one toward another; men with men working that which is unseemly, and receiving in themselves that recompense of their error which was meet. And even as they did not like to retain God in *their* knowledge, God gave them over to a reprobate mind, to do those things which are not convenient; Being filled with all unrighteousness, fornication, wickedness, covetousness, maliciousness; full of envy, murder, debate, deceit, malignity; whisperers, backbiters, haters of God, despiteful, proud, boasters, inventors of evil things, disobedient to parents, without understanding, covenant-breakers, without natural affection, implacable, unmerciful: who knowing the judgment of God, that they which commit such things are worthy of death, not only do the same but have pleasure in them that do them. (KJV, 2020).

Titus 1:15-16: Unto the pure, all things *are* pure: but unto them that are defiled and unbelieving *is* nothing pure, but even their mind and conscience is defiled. They profess that they know God; but in works they deny *him*, being abominable, and disobedient, and unto every good work reprobate. (KJV, 2020).

II Timothy 3:1-7 (KJV): This also knows that in the last days, perilous times shall come. For men shall be lovers of their own selves, covetous, boasters, proud, blasphemers, disobedient to parents, unthankful, unholy, without natural affection, trucebreakers, false accusers, incontinent, fierce, despisers of those that are good, traitors, heady, high minded, lovers of pleasures more than lovers of God; having a form of godliness, but denying the power thereof: from such turn away. For of this sort are they which creep into houses, and lead captive silly women laden with sins, led away with divers' lusts, ever learning, and never able to come to the knowledge of the truth. (KJV, 2020).

There is a chapter that deals with disobedience in more detail in the book: *Why am I not Living a Victorious Life?* If you have not read this book, and you feel that you need more reference materials on obedience and disobedience, secure a copy of this book and study that chapter.

SALVATION
(WHAT IS SALVATION?)

Luke 1:77-79: To give knowledge of salvation unto his people by the remission of their sins, Through the tender mercy of our God; whereby the dayspring from on high hath visited us, to give light to them that sit in darkness and *in* the shadow of death, to guide our feet into the way of peace. (KJV, 2020).

Acts 4:12: Neither is there salvation in any other: for there is none other name under heaven given among men, whereby we must be saved. (KJV, 2020).

Hebrews 5:9: And being made perfect, he became the author of eternal salvation unto all them that obey him; (KJV, 2020).

Hebrews 2:1-4: Therefore, we ought to give the more earnest heed to the things which we have heard, lest at any time we should let *them* slip. For if the word spoken by angels was steadfast, and every transgression and disobedience received a just recompense of reward; How shall we escape, if we neglect so great salvation; which at the first began to be spoken by the Lord, and was confirmed unto us by them that heard *him*; God also bearing *them* witness, both with signs and wonders, and with divers' miracles, and gifts of the Holy Ghost, according to his own will? (KJV, 2020).

Philippians 2:12-13: Wherefore, my beloved, as ye have always obeyed, not as in my presence only, but now much more in my absence, work out your own salvation with fear and trembling. For it is God which worketh in you both to will and to do of his good pleasure. (KJV, 2020).

Titus 2:11-14: For the grace of God that bringeth salvation hath appeared to all men, teaching us that, denying ungodliness and worldly lusts, we should live soberly, righteously, and godly, in this present world; looking for that blessed hope, and the glorious appearing of the great God and our Savior Jesus Christ; Who gave himself for us, that he might redeem us from all iniquity, and purify unto himself a peculiar people, zealous of good works. (KJV, 2020).

I Thessalonians 5:6-10: Therefore, let us not sleep, as *do* others; but let us watch and be sober. For they that sleep, sleep in the night; and they that be drunken are drunken in the night. But let us, who are of the day, be sober, putting on the breastplate of faith and love; and for an helmet, the hope of salvation. For God hath not appointed us to wrath, but to obtain salvation by our Lord Jesus Christ, who died for us, that, whether we wake or sleep, we should live together with him. (KJV, 2020).

HOW TO BE SAVED

John 3:16-17: For God so loved the world, that he gave his only begotten Son, that whosoever believeth in him should not perish, but have everlasting life. For God sent not his Son into the world to condemn the world; but that the world through him might be saved. (KJV, 2020).

Romans 10:9-10: That if thou shalt confess with thy mouth the Lord Jesus, and shalt believe in thine heart that God hath raised him from the dead, thou shalt be saved. For with the heart, man believeth unto righteousness; and with the mouth, confession is made unto salvation. (KJV, 2020).

Acts 2:21: And it shall come to pass, *that* whosoever shall call on the name of the Lord shall be saved. (KJV, 2020).

DECEPTION

Matthew 24:4-5: And Jesus answered and said unto them, take heed that no man deceives you. For many shall come in my name, saying, I am Christ; and shall deceive many. (KJV, 2020).

I John 4: 1-4: Beloved, believe not every spirit, but try the spirits whether they are of God: because many false prophets are gone out into the world. Hereby know ye the Spirit of God: every spirit that confesseth that Jesus Christ is come in the flesh is of God: and every spirit that confesseth not that Jesus Christ is come in the flesh is not of God: and this is that spirit of antichrist, whereof ye have heard that it should come; and even now already is it in the world. (KJV, 2020).

I John 2:21-22: Who is a liar but he that denieth that Jesus in the Christ? He is antichrist, that denieth the Father and the Son. Whosoever denieth the Son, the same hath not the Father: he that acknowledgeth the Son hath the Father also. (KJV, 2020).

II Peter 2:1- 10: But there were false prophets also among the people, even as there shall be false teachers among you, who privily shall bring in damnable heresies, even denying the Lord that brought them, and bring upon themselves swift destruction. And many shall follow their pernicious ways; by reason of whom, the way of truth shall be evil spoken of. And many shall follow their pernicious ways; by reason of whom, the way of truth shall be evil spoken of. And through covetousness shall they with feigned words make merchandise of you: whose judgment now of a long time lingereth not, and their damnation slumbereth not. For if God spared not the angels that sinned, but cast them down to hell, and delivered them into chains of darkness, to be reserved unto judgment; and spared not the old world; but saved Noah the eighth person, a preacher of righteousness, bringing in the flood upon the world of the ungodly; and turning the cities of Sodom and Gomorrah into ashes condemned them with and overthrow, making them an ensample unto those that after should live ungodly; and delivered just Lot, vexed with the filthy conversation of the wicked; for that righteous man dwelling among them, in seeing and hearing, vexed his righteous soul from day to day with their unlawful deeds;) The Lord knoweth how to deliver the godly out of temptations, and to reserve the unjust unto the day of judgment to be punished: But chiefly them that walk after the flesh in the lust of uncleanness, and despise government. Presumptuous are they, self-willed, they are not afraid to speak evil of dignities. (KJV, 2020).

BEING VICTORIOUS

Romans 8:35-39: Who shall separate us from the love of Christ? shall tribulation, or distress, or persecution, or famine, or nakedness, or peril, or sword? As it is written, for thy sake, we are killed all the day long; we are accounted as sheep for the slaughter. Nay, in all these things, we are more than conquerors through him that loved us. For I am *persuaded, that neither death, nor life, nor angels, nor principalities, nor powers, nor things present, nor things to come, nor height, nor depth, nor any other creature, shall be able to separate us from the love of God, which is in Christ Jesus our Lord. (KJV, 2020).*

I John 5:4: *For whatsoever is born of God overcometh the world: and this is the victory that overcometh the world, even our faith. (KJV, 2020).*

IDOL WORSHIP

Leviticus 26:1: *Ye shall make you no idols, nor graven image, neither rear you up a standing image, neither shall ye set up any image of stone in your land, to bow down unto it: for I am the LORD your God. (KJV, 2020).*

II Kings 17:12-18: *For they served idols, whereof the LORD had said unto them, Ye shall not do this thing. Yet the LORD testified against Israel, and against Judah, by all the prophets, and by all the seers, saying, turn ye from your evil ways, and keep my commandments and my statutes, according to all the law which I commanded your fathers, and which I sent to you by my servants the prophets. Notwithstanding, they would not hear, but hardened their necks, like to the neck of their fathers, that did not believe in the LORD their God. And they rejected* his statutes, and his covenant that he made with their fathers, and his testimonies which he testified against them; and they followed vanity, and became vain, and went after the heathen that *were* round about them, *concerning* whom the LORD had charged them, that they should not do like them. And they left all the commandments of the LORD their God, and made them molten images, *even* two calves, and made a grove, and worshipped all the host of heaven, and served Baal. And they caused their sons and their daughters to pass through the fire, and used divination and enchantments, and sold themselves to do evil in the sight of the LORD, to provoke him to anger. Therefore, the LORD was very angry with Israel and removed them out of his sight: there was none left but the tribe of Judah only. (KJV, 2020).

Acts 15:20: But that we write unto them, that they abstain from pollutions of idols, and *from* fornication, and *from* things strangled, and *from* the blood. (KJV, 2020).

REPENTANCE

II Peter 3:8-10: But, beloved, be not ignorant of this one thing, that one day *is* with the Lord as a thousand years, and a thousand years as one day. The Lord is not slack concerning his promise, as some men count slackness; but is longsuffering to us-ward, not willing that any should perish, but that all should come to repentance. But the day of the Lord will come as a thief in the night; in the which, the heavens shall pass away with a great noise, and the elements shall melt with fervent heat, the earth also and the works that are therein shall be burned up. (KJV, 2020).

HOLINESS

II Peter 3:11-18: *Seeing* then *that* all these things shall be dissolved, what manner *of persons* ought ye to be in *all* holy conversation and godliness, looking for and hasting unto the coming of the day of God, wherein the heavens being on fire shall be dissolved, and the elements shall melt with fervent heat?   Nevertheless, we, according to his promise, look for new heavens and a new earth, wherein dwelleth righteousness.   Wherefore, beloved, seeing that ye look for such things, be diligent that ye may be found of him in peace, without spot, and blameless.   And account *that* the longsuffering of our Lord *is* salvation; even as our beloved brother Paul also according to the wisdom given unto him hath written unto you; As also in all *his* epistles, speaking in them of these things; in which are some things hard to be understood, which they that are unlearned and unstable wrest, as *they do* also the other scriptures, unto their own destruction. Ye therefore, beloved, seeing ye know *these things* before, beware lest ye also, being led away with the error of the wicked, fall from your own steadfastness. But grow in grace and *in* the knowledge of our Lord and Saviour Jesus Christ. To him *be* glory both now and forever. Amen. (KJV, 2020).

Titus 2:1-6:   But speak thou the things which become sound doctrine: That the aged men be sober, grave, temperate, sound in faith, in charity, in patience.   The aged women likewise, that *they be* in behavior as becometh holiness, not false accusers, not given to much wine, teachers of good things; That they may teach the young women to be sober, to love their husbands, to love their children, *to be* discreet, chaste, keepers at home, good, obedient to their own husbands, that the word of God be not blasphemed. Young men likewise exhort to be sober-minded. (KJV, 2020).

HOW TO PRAY

THE LORD'S PRAYER

Luke 11:1-13: And it came to pass, that, as he was praying in a certain place, when he ceased, one of his disciples said unto him, Lord, teach us to pray, as John also taught his disciples. And he said unto them, when ye pray, say, Our Father which art in heaven, hallowed be thy name. Thy kingdom comes. Thy will be done, as in heaven, so in earth. Give us day by day our daily bread. And forgive us our sins; for we also forgive everyone that is indebted to us. And lead us not into temptation, but deliver us from evil. And he said unto them, which of you shall have a friend, and shall go unto him at midnight, and say unto him, Friend, lend me three loaves; For a friend of mine in his journey is come to me, and I have nothing to set before him? And he from within shall answer and say, Trouble me not: the door is now shut, and my children are with me in bed; I cannot rise and give thee. I say unto you, though he will not rise and give him, because he is his friend, yet because of his importunity he will rise and give him as many as he needeth. And I say unto you, Ask, and it shall be given you; seek, and ye shall find; knock, and it shall be opened unto you. For every one that asketh receiveth; and he that seeketh findeth, and to him that knocketh it shall be opened. If a son shall ask bread of any of you that is a father, will he give him a stone? or if *he asks* a fish, will he for a fish give him a serpent? Or if he shall ask an egg, will he offer him a scorpion? If ye then, being evil, know how to give good gifts unto your children: how much more shall *your* heavenly Father give the Holy Spirit to them that ask him? (KJV, 2020).

Matthew 7:7-11: Ask, and it shall be given you; seek, and ye shall find; knock, and it shall be opened unto you: For every one that asketh receiveth; and he that seeketh findeth, and to him that knocketh it shall be opened. Or what man is there of you, whom if his son ask bread, will he give him a stone? Or if he asks a fish, will he give him a serpent? If ye then, being evil, know how to give good gifts unto your children, how much more shall your Father which is in heaven give good things to them that ask him? (KJV, 2020).

DAILY READING AND PRAYING TOGETHER WILL KEEP A FAMILY INTACT AND YOUR MARRIAGE FLOURISHING. A MARRIAGE WITHOUT DAILY FAMILY DEVOTIONS WILL NOT WITHSTAND SATAN'S ATTACKS AND THE TRIALS OF THE 21ST CENTURY!

DUTIES/RESPONSIBILITIES OF PASTORS

I Timothy 3:1-7: This *is* a true saying if a man desires the office of a bishop, he desireth a good work. A bishop then must be blameless, the husband of one wife, vigilant, sober, of good behaviour, given to hospitality, apt to teach; Not given to wine, no striker, not greedy of filthy lucre; but patient, not a brawler, not covetous; One that ruleth well his own house, having his children in subjection with all gravity; (For if a man knows not how to rule his own house, how shall he take care of the church of God?) Not a novice, lest being lifted up with pride, he falls into the condemnation of the devil. Moreover, he must have a good report of them which are without; lest he falls into reproach and the snare of the devil. (KJV, 2020).

Titus 1:6-16: If any be blameless, the husband of one wife, having faithful children not accused of riot or unruly. For a bishop must be blameless, as the steward of God; not self-willed, not soon angry, not given to wine, no striker, not given to filthy lucre; But a lover of hospitality, a lover of good men, sober, just, holy, temperate; Holding fast the faithful word as he hath been taught, that he may be able by sound doctrine both to exhort and to convince the gainsayers. For there are many unruly and vain talkers and deceivers, especially they of the circumcision: Whose mouths must be stopped, who subvert whole houses, teaching things which they ought not, for filthy lucre's sake. One of themselves, even a prophet of their own, said, The Cretians are

233

always liars, evil beasts, slow bellies. This witness is true. Wherefore rebuke them sharply, that they may be sound in the faith; Not giving heed to Jewish fables, and commandments of men, that turn from the truth. Unto the pure, all things are pure: but unto them that are defiled and unbelieving is nothing pure, but even their mind and conscience is defiled. They profess that they know God; but in works they deny him, being abominable, and disobedient, and unto every good work reprobate. (KJV, 2020).

James 1:19-26: Wherefore, my beloved brethren, let every man be swift to hear, slow to speak, slow to wrath: For the wrath of man worketh not the righteousness of God. Wherefore lay apart all filthiness and superfluity of naughtiness, and receive with meekness the engrafted word, which is able to save your souls. But be ye doers of the word, and not hearers only, deceiving your own selves. For if any be a hearer of the word and not a doer, he is like unto a man beholding his natural face in a glass: For he beholdeth himself, and goeth his way, and straightway forgetteth what manner of man he was. But whoso looketh into the perfect law of liberty, and continueth *therein*, he being not a forgetful hearer, but a doer of the work, this man shall be blessed in his deed. If any man among you seem to be religious, and bridleth not his tongue, but deceiveth his own heart, this man's religion *is* vain. (KJV, 2020).

Jeremiah 23:1-2: Woe be unto the pastors that destroy and scatter the sheep of my pasture! saith the LORD. Therefore, thus saith the LORD God of Israel against the pastors that feed my people; Ye have scattered my flock, and driven them away, and have not visited them: behold, I will visit upon you the evil of your doings, saith the LORD. (KJV, 2020).

HOW TO REBUKE A PERSON

I Thessalonians 5:11-15: Wherefore comfort yourselves together, and edify one another, even as also ye do. And we beseech you, brethren, to know them which labour among you, and are over you in the Lord, and admonish you; And to esteem them very highly in love for their work's sake. And be at peace among yourselves. Now we exhort you, brethren, warn them that are unruly, comfort the feebleminded, support the weak, be patient toward all men. See that none render evil for evil unto any man; but ever follow that which is good, both among yourselves, and to all men. (KJV, 2020).

I Timothy 5:1-2: Rebuke not an elder, but entreat him as a father; and the younger men as brethren; The elder women as mothers; the younger as sisters, with all purity. (KJV, 2020).

II Timothy 4:2-5: Preach the word; be instant in season, out of season; reprove, rebuke, exhort with all longsuffering and doctrine. For the time will come when they will not endure sound doctrine; but after their own lusts shall they heap to themselves teachers, having itching ears; And they shall turn away their ears from the truth, and shall be turned unto fables. But watch thou in all things, endure afflictions, do the work of an evangelist, make full proof of thy ministry. (KJV, 2020).

Luke 17:3-4: Take heed to yourselves: If thy brother trespass against thee, rebuke him; and if he repents, forgive him. And if he trespasses against thee seven times in a day, and seven times in a day turn again to thee, saying, I repent; thou shalt forgive him. (KJV, 2020).

Matthew 7:1-6: Judge not, that ye be not judged. For with what judgment ye judge, ye shall be judged: and with what measure ye mete, it shall be measured to you again. And why beholdest thou the mote that is in thy brother's eye, but considerest not the beam that is in thine own eye? Or how wilt thou say to thy brother, let me pull out the mote out of thine eye; and, behold, a beam *is* in thine own eye? Thou hypocrite, first cast out the beam out of thine own eye; and then shalt thou see clearly to cast out the mote out of thy brother's eye. Give not that which is holy unto the dogs, neither cast ye your pearls before swine, lest they trample them under their feet, and turn again and rend you. (KJV, 2020).

Luke 6:36-38: Be ye therefore merciful, as your Father also is merciful. Judge not, and ye shall not be judged: condemn not, and ye shall not be condemned: forgive, and ye shall be forgiven: Give, and it shall be given unto you; good measure, pressed down, and shaken together, and running over, shall men give into your bosom. For with the same measure that ye mete withal, it shall be measured to you again. (KJV, 2020).

Matthew 7:1-5: Judge not, that ye be not judged. For with what judgment ye judge, ye shall be judged: and with what measure ye mete, it shall be measured to you again. And why beholdest thou the mote that is in thy brother's eye, but considerest not the beam that is in thine own eye? Or how wilt thou say to thy brother, let me pull out the mote out of thine eye; and, behold, a beam *is* in thine own eye? Thou hypocrite, first cast out the beam out of thine own eye; and then shalt thou see clearly to cast out the mote out of thy brother's eye. (KJV, 2020).

JUDGING VERSUS REBUKING ACCORDING TO PAUL'S TEACHING

James 4:11: Speak no evil one of another, brethren. He that speaketh evil of *his* brother, and judgeth his brother, speaketh evil of the law, and judgeth the law: but if thou judge the law, thou art not a doer of the law, but a judge. (KJV, 2020).

James 5:8-10: Be ye also patient; establish your hearts: for the coming of the Lord draweth nigh. Grudge not one against another, brethren, lest ye be condemned: behold, the judge standeth before the door. Take, my brethren, the prophets, who have spoken in the name of the Lord, for an example of suffering affliction, and of patience. (KJV, 2020).

TEN COMMANDMENTS

Exodus 20:1-17: And God spake all these words, saying, I am the LORD thy God, which have brought thee out of the land of Egypt, out of the house of bondage. Thou shalt have no other gods before me. Thou shalt not make unto thee any graven image or any likeness of anything that is in heaven above, or that is in the earth beneath, or that is in the water under the earth: Thou shalt not bow down thyself to them, nor serve them: for I the LORD thy God am a jealous God, visiting the iniquity of the fathers upon the children unto the third and fourth generation of them that hate me; And shewing mercy unto thousands of them that love me, and keep my commandments. Thou shalt not take the name of the LORD thy God in vain; for the LORD will not hold him guiltless that taketh his name in vain. Remember the sabbath day to keep it holy. Six days shalt thou labour, and do all thy work: But the seventh day is the sabbath of the LORD thy God: in it, thou shalt not do any work, thou, nor thy son, nor thy daughter, thy manservant, nor thy maidservant, nor thy cattle, nor thy stranger that is within thy gates: For in six days the LORD made heaven and earth, the sea, and all that in them is, and rested the seventh day: wherefore the LORD blessed the sabbath day and hallowed it. Honour thy father and thy mother: that thy days may be long upon the land which the LORD thy God giveth thee. Thou shalt not kill. Thou shalt not commit adultery. Thou shalt not steal. Thou shalt not bear false witness against thy neighbour. Thou shalt not covet thy neighbour's house, thou shalt not covet thy neighbour's wife, nor his manservant, nor his maidservant, nor his ox, nor his ass, nor anything that is thy neighbour's. (KJV, 2020).

JESUS' FIRST COMMANDMENT

Mark 12:28-30: And one of the scribes came and having heard them reasoning together, and perceiving that he had answered them well, asked him, which is the first commandment of all? And Jesus answered him, the first of all the commandments is, Hear, O Israel; The Lord our God is one Lord: And thou shalt love the Lord thy God with all thy heart, and with all thy soul, and with all thy mind, and with all thy strength: this is the first commandment. (KJV, 2020).

JESUS' SECOND COMMANDMENT

Mark 12:31: And the second is like, namely this, thou shalt love thy neighbour as thyself. There is none other commandment greater than these. (KJV, 2020).

FALSE MINISTRIES AND PREACHERS

Hosea 4:6-11: My people are destroyed for lack of knowledge: because thou hast rejected knowledge, I will also reject thee, that thou shalt be no priest to me: seeing thou hast forgotten the law of thy God, I will also forget thy children. As they were increased, so they sinned against me: *therefore,* will I change their glory into shame. They eat up the sin of my people, and they set their heart on their iniquity. And there shall be, like people, like priest: and I will punish them for their ways, and reward them their doings. For they shall eat, and not have enough: they shall commit whoredom, and shall not increase: because they have left off to take heed to the LORD. Whoredom and wine and new wine take away the heart. (KJV, 2020).

Matthew 7:15-20: Beware of false prophets, which come to you in sheep's clothing, but inwardly they are ravening wolves. Ye shall know them by their fruits. Do men gather grapes of thorns or figs of thistles? Even so, every good tree bringeth forth good fruit; but a corrupt tree bringeth forth evil fruit. A good tree cannot bring forth evil fruit; neither can a corrupt tree bring forth good fruit. Every tree that bringeth not forth good fruit is hewn down and cast into the fire. Wherefore by their fruits, ye shall know them. (KJV, 2020).

Matthew 24:11: And many false prophets shall rise, and shall deceive many. (KJV, 2020).

Matthew 24:23-27: Then if any man shall say unto you, Lo, here *is* Christ, or there; believe *it* not. For there shall arise false Christs, and false prophets, and shall shew great signs and wonders; insomuch that, if *it were* possible, they shall Behold, I have told you before. Wherefore if they shall say unto you, Behold, he is in the desert; go not forth: behold, *he is* in the secret chambers; believe *it* not. For as the lightning cometh out of the east, and shineth even unto the west; so, shall also the coming of the Son of man be. (KJV, 2020).

Mark 13:21-23: And then if any man shall say to you, Lo, here *is* Christ; or, lo, *he is* there; believe *him* not: For false Christs and false prophets shall rise, and shall shew signs and wonders, to seduce, if *it were* possible, even the elect. But take ye heed: behold, I have foretold you all things. (KJV, 2020).

II Peter 2:1-2: But there were false prophets also among the people, even as there shall be false teachers among you, who privily shall bring in damnable heresies, even denying the Lord that bought them, and bring upon themselves swift destruction. And many shall follow their pernicious ways; by reason of whom, the way of truth shall be evil spoken of. (KJV, 2020).

I John 4:1-3: Beloved, believe not every spirit, but try the spirits whether they are of God: because many false prophets are gone out into the world. Hereby know ye the Spirit of God: Every spirit that confesseth that Jesus Christ is come in the flesh is of God: And every spirit that confesseth not that Jesus Christ is come in the flesh is not of God, and this is that *spirit* of antichrist, whereof ye have heard that it should come; and even now already is it in the world. (LKV, 2020).

Jude 1:3-4: Beloved, when I gave all diligence to write unto you of the common salvation, it was needful for me to write unto you, and exhort *you* that ye should earnestly contend for the faith which was once delivered unto the saints. For there are certain men crept in unawares, who were before of old ordained to this condemnation, ungodly men, turning the grace of our God into lasciviousness, and denying the only Lord God, and our Lord Jesus Christ. (KJV, 2020).

FAITH IS NEEDED TO PLEASE GOD

James 2:14-26: What *doth it* profits, my brethren, though a man says he hath faith, and have not works? can faith save him? If a brother or sister be naked and destitute of daily food, and one of you say unto them, depart in peace, be *ye* warmed and filled; notwithstanding ye give them not those things which are needful to the body; what *doth it* profits? Even so, faith, if it hath not works, is dead, being alone. Yea, a man may say, thou hast faith, and I have works: shew me thy faith without thy works, and I will shew thee my faith by my works. Thou believe that there is one God; thou do well: the devils also believe, and

242

tremble. But wilt thou know, O vain man, that faith without works is dead? Was not Abraham our father justified by works when he had offered Isaac, his son upon the altar? Seest thou how faith wrought with his works, and by works was faith made perfect? And the scripture was fulfilled, which saith, Abraham believed God, and it was imputed unto him for righteousness: and he was called the Friend of God. Ye see then how that by works a man is justified, and not by faith only. Likewise, also was not Rahab the harlot justified by works, when she had received the messengers and had sent *them* out another way? For as the body without the spirit is dead, so faith without works is dead also. (KJV, 2020).

PURPOSE OF THE CHURCH AND MINISTRY

Acts 20:28-35: Take heed therefore unto yourselves, and to all the flock, over the which the Holy Ghost hath made you overseers, to feed the church of God, which he hath purchased with his own blood. For I know this, that after my departing shall grievous wolves enter in among you, not sparing the flock. Also, of your own selves shall men arise, speaking perverse things, to draw away disciples after them. Therefore watch, and remember, that by the space of three years, I ceased not to warn every one night and day with tears. And now, brethren, I commend you to God, and to the word of his grace, which is able to build you up and to give you an inheritance among all them which are sanctified. I have coveted no man's silver, or gold, or apparel. Yea, ye yourselves know, that these hands have ministered unto my necessities, and to them that were with me. I have shewed you all things, how that so labouring ye ought to support the weak, and to remember the words of the Lord Jesus, how he said, it is more blessed to give than to receive. (KJV, 2020).

Ephesians 5:21-33: Submitting yourselves one to another in the fear of God. Wives, submit yourselves unto your own husbands, as unto the Lord. For the husband is the head of the wife, even as Christ is the head of the church: and he is the saviour of the body. Therefore, as the church is subject unto Christ, so *let* the wives *be* to their own husbands in everything. Husbands, love your wives, even as Christ also loved the church, and gave himself for it; That he might sanctify and cleanse it with the washing of water by the word, that he might present it to himself a glorious church, not having spot, or wrinkle, or any such thing; but that it should be holy and without blemish. So, ought men to love their wives as their own bodies. He that loveth his wife loveth himself. For no man ever yet hated his own flesh; but nourisheth and cherisheth it, even as the Lord the church: For we are members of his body, of his flesh, and of his bones. For this, cause shall a man leave his father and mother and shall be joined unto his wife, and they two shall be one flesh. This is a great mystery: but I speak concerning Christ and the church. Nevertheless, let every one of you in particular so love his wife even as himself; and the wife *see* that she reverences *her* husband. (KJV, 2020).

SANCTIFICATION

I Thessalonians 4:1-8: Furthermore, then we beseech you, brethren, and exhort you by the Lord Jesus, that as ye have received of us how ye ought to walk and to please God, so ye would abound more and more. For ye know what commandments we gave you by the Lord Jesus. For this is the will of God, even your sanctification, that ye should abstain from fornication: That every one of you should know how to possess his vessel in sanctification and honour; Not in the lust of concupiscence, even as the Gentiles which know not God: That no man goes beyond and defraud his brother in any matter: because that the Lord is the avenger of all such, as we also have forewarned you and testified. For God hath not called us unto uncleanness, but unto holiness. He therefore that despiseth, despiseth not man, but God, who hath also given unto us his Holy Spirit. (KJV, 2020).

I Thessalonians 5:23-24: And the very God of peace sanctify you wholly; and I pray God your whole spirit and soul and body be preserved blameless unto the coming of our Lord Jesus Christ. Faithful is he that calleth you, who also will do it. (KJV, 2020).

WHAT DOES GOD LOOK LIKE?

Genesis 1:26-27: And God said, let us make man in our image, after our likeness: and let them have dominion over the fish of the sea, and over the fowl of the air, and over the cattle, and over all the earth, and over every creeping thing that creepeth upon the earth.   So, God created man in his own image, in the image of God created he him; male and female created he them. (KJV, 2020).

FLAMING SWORDS

Genesis 3:22-24: And the LORD God said, Behold, the man is become as one of us, to know good and evil: and now, lest he put forth his hand, and take also of the tree of life, and eat, and live forever: Therefore, the LORD God sent him forth from the garden of Eden, to till the ground from whence he was taken. So, he drove out the man; and he placed at the east of the garden of Eden Cherubims, and a flaming sword which turned every way, to keep the way of the tree of life. (KJV, 2020).

DANIEL'S SPIRITUAL WARFARE

Daniel 10:10-14: And, behold, an hand touched me, which set me upon my knees and *upon* the palms of my hands. And he said unto me, O Daniel, a man greatly beloved, understand the words that I speak unto thee, and stand upright: for unto thee am I now sent. And when he had spoken this word unto me, I stood trembling. Then said he unto me, fear not, Daniel: for from the first day that thou didst set thine heart to understand, and to chasten thyself before thy God, thy words were heard, and I am come for thy words. But the prince of the kingdom of Persia withstood me one and twenty days: but, lo, Michael, one of the chief princes, came to help me; and I remained there with the kings of Persia. Now I am come to make thee understand what shall befall thy people in the latter days: for yet the vision *is* for many days. (KJV, 2020).

KNOWING TO DO GOOD

James 4:16-17: But now ye rejoice in your boastings: all such rejoicing is evil. Therefore, to him, that knoweth to do good, and doeth *it* not, to him, it is a sin. (KJV, 2020).

247

HELPING THE WIDOWS

<u>James 1:27</u>:   Pure religion and undefiled before God and the Father is this, to visit the fatherless and widows in their affliction, *and* to keep himself unspotted from the world. (KJV, 2020).

HUMILITY

<u>I Peter 5:5-7</u>:   Likewise, ye younger, submit yourselves unto the elder. Yea, all *of you* be subject one to another and be clothed with humility: for God resisteth the proud, and giveth grace to the humble.   Humble yourselves therefore under the mighty hand of God, that he may exalt you in due time: Casting all your care upon him; for he careth for you. (KJV, 2020).

VISITING THOSE IN PRISON

<u>Matthew 25:35-45</u>:   For I was an hungred, and ye gave me meat: I was thirsty, and ye gave me drink: I was a stranger, and ye took me in:

Naked, and ye clothed me: I was sick, and ye visited me: I was in prison, and ye came unto me. Then shall the righteous answer him, saying, Lord, when saw we thee an hungred, and fed *thee*? or thirsty, and gave *thee* drink? When saw we thee a stranger, and took *thee* in? or naked, and clothed *thee*? Or when saw we thee sick, or in prison, and came unto thee? And the King shall answer and say unto them, Verily I say unto you, inasmuch as ye have done *it* unto one of the least of these my brethren, ye have done *it* unto me. Then shall he say also unto them on the left hand, depart from me, ye cursed, into everlasting fire, prepared for the devil and his angels: For I was an hungered, and ye gave me no meat: I was thirsty, and ye gave me no drink: I was a stranger, and ye took me not in: naked, and ye clothed me not: sick, and in prison, and ye visited me not. Then shall they also answer him, saying, Lord, when saw we thee an hungred, or athirst, or a stranger, or naked, or sick, or in prison, and did not minister unto thee? Then shall he answer them, saying, Verily I say unto you, inasmuch as ye did *it* not to one of the least of these, ye did *it* not to me. (KJV, 2020).

FRUITS OF THE SPIRIT

Galatians 5:16-18, 22-25: *This* I say then, walk in the Spirit, and ye shall not fulfill the lust of the flesh. For the flesh lusteth against the Spirit, and the Spirit against the flesh: and these are contrary the one to the other: so that ye cannot do the things that ye would. But if ye be led of the Spirit, ye are not under the law. But the fruit of the Spirit is love, joy, peace, longsuffering, gentleness, goodness, faith, Meekness, temperance: against such; there is no law. And they

249

that are Christ's have crucified the flesh with the affections and lusts. If we live in the Spirit, let us also walk in the Spirit. (KJV, 2020).

WORKS OF THE FLESH

Galatians 5:19-21: Now the works of the flesh are manifest, which are *these;* Adultery, fornication, uncleanness, lasciviousness, Idolatry, witchcraft, hatred, variance, emulations, wrath, strife, seditions, heresies, envyings, murders, drunkenness, revellings, and such like: of the which I tell you before, as I have also told *you* in time past, that they which do such things shall not inherit the kingdom of God. (KJV, 2020).

SIGNS OF THE END TIMES OR THE LAST DAYS

Matthew 24:4-31: And Jesus answered and said unto them, take heed that no man deceives you. For many shall come in my name, saying, I am Christ; and shall deceive many. And ye shall hear of wars and rumours of wars: see that ye be not troubled: for all *these things* must come to pass, but the end is not yet. For nation shall rise against nation, and kingdom against kingdom: and there shall be famines, and pestilences, and earthquakes, in divers' places. All these *are* the beginning of sorrows. Then shall they deliver you up to be afflicted, and shall kill you: and ye shall be hated of all nations for my name's sake. And then shall many be offended, and shall betray one another, and shall hate one another. And many false prophets shall rise, and shall deceive many. And because iniquity shall abound, the love of many shall wax cold. But he that shall endure unto the end, the same shall be saved. And this gospel of the kingdom shall be preached in all the world for a witness unto all nations; and then shall the end come. When ye, therefore, shall see the abomination of desolation, spoken of by Daniel the prophet, stand in the holy place, (whoso readeth, let him understand:) Then let them which be in Judaea flee into the mountains: Let him which is on the housetop not come down to take anything out of his house: Neither let him which is in the field return back to take his clothes. And woe unto them that are with child, and to them that give suck in those days! But pray ye that your flight be not in the winter, neither on the sabbath day: For then shall be great tribulation, such as was not since the beginning of the world to this time, no, nor ever shall be. And except those days should be shortened, there should no flesh be saved: but for the elect's sake, those days shall be shortened. Then if any man shall say unto you, lo here *is* Christ, or there; believe *it* not. For there shall arise false Christs, and false prophets, and shall shew great signs and wonders; insomuch that, if *it were* possible, they shall deceive the very elect. Behold, I have told you before. Wherefore if they shall say unto you, Behold, he is in the desert; go not forth: behold, *he is* in the secret chambers; believe *it* not. For as the lightning cometh out of the east, and shineth even unto the west; so, shall also the coming of the Son of man be. For wheresoever the carcass is, there will the eagles be gathered together. Immediately after the tribulation of those days shall the sun be darkened, and the moon shall not give

251

her light, and the stars shall fall from heaven, and the powers of the heavens shall be shaken: And then shall appear the sign of the Son of man in heaven: and then shall all the tribes of the earth mourn, and they shall see the Son of man coming in the clouds of heaven with power and great glory. And he shall send his angels with a great sound of a trumpet, and they shall gather together his elect from the four winds, from one end of heaven to the other. (KJV, 2020).

II Peter 3:3-7: Knowing this first, that there shall come in the last days scoffers, walking after their own lusts, and saying, where is the promise of his coming? For since the fathers fell asleep, all things continue as *they were* from the beginning of the creation. For this they willingly are ignorant of, that by the word of God the heavens were of old, and the earth standing out of the water and in the water: whereby the world that then was, being overflowed with water, perished: but the heavens and the earth, which are now, by the same word are kept in store, reserved unto fire against the day of judgment and perdition of ungodly men. (KJV, 2020).

II Timothy 3:1-9: This also know that in the last days, perilous times shall come. For men shall be lovers of their own selves, covetous, boasters, proud, blasphemers, disobedient to parents, unthankful, unholy, without natural affection, trucebreakers, false accusers, incontinent, fierce, despisers of those that are good, Traitors, heady, high-minded, lovers of pleasures more than lovers of God; Having a form of godliness, but denying the power thereof: from such turn away. For this sort, they creep into houses, lead captive silly women laden with sins, led away with divers' lusts, ever learning, and never come to the knowledge of the truth. As James and Jambres withstood Moses, so do these also resist the truth: men of corrupt minds, reprobate concerning the faith. But they shall proceed no further: for their folly shall be manifest unto all *men*, as theirs also was. (KJV, 2020).

Acts 2:15-20: For these are not drunken, as ye suppose, seeing it is *but* the third hour of the day. But this is that which was spoken by the prophet Joel, And it shall come to pass in the last days, saith God, I will pour out of my Spirit upon all flesh: and your sons and your daughters shall prophesy, and your young men shall see visions, and your old men shall dream dreams: And on my servants and on my handmaidens I will pour out in those days of my Spirit, and they shall prophesy: And I will shew wonders in heaven above, and signs in the earth beneath; blood, and fire, and vapour of smoke: The sun shall be turned into darkness, and the moon into blood, before that great and notable day of the Lord come: (KJV, 2020).

II Thessalonians 2:3-4: Let no man deceive you by any means: for that day shall not come, except there comes a falling away first, and that man of sin be revealed, the son of perdition; who opposeth and exalteth himself above all that is called God, or that is worshipped; so that he as God sitteth in the temple of God, shewing himself that he is God. (KJV, 2020).

II Thessalonians 2:8-12: And then shall that wicked be revealed, whom the Lord shall consume with the spirit of his mouth, and shall destroy with the brightness of his coming: even him, whose coming is after the working of Satan with all power and signs and lying wonders, and with all deceivableness of unrighteousness in them, that perish; because they received not the love of the truth, that they might be saved. And for this cause, God shall send them strong delusions, that they should believe a lie: that they all might be damned who believed not the truth but had pleasure in unrighteousness. (KJV, 2020).

253

I John 2: 18: Little children, it is the last time: and as ye have heard that antichrist shall come, even now are there many antichrists; whereby we know that it is the last time [last days]. (KJV, 2020).

MORE BLESSED TO GIVE
THAN RECEIVED

Acts 20:35: I have shewed you all things, how that so laboring ye ought to support the weak, and to remember the words of the Lord Jesus, how he said, it is more blessed to give than to receive. (KJV, 2020).

SERMON OUTLINE

OUTLINE FOR USE AS A SERMON, BIBLE STUDIES, OR SUNDAY SCHOOL LESSONS

I.   INTRODUCTION TO THIS TOPIC

1)   Share the dream given to Charlie O'Neal
2)   Layout the framework and outline for this study

II.   DISCUSS THE FOLLOWING TOPICS ABOUT GOD:

1) He is a jealous God;
2) A loving Father;
3) He gives blessings, honor, and favor to his children;
4) God loves to give gifts, especially healing, anointing, and inspiration to his children;
5) We are joint-heirs with Christ;
6) The church is compared to the Bride of Christ;
7) What is the tribulation period?
8) What is the coming of Christ?

255

III. ISSUES GOD DOES NOT TOLERATE FROM THE PULPIT OR THE CHURCH:

1) hypocrisy
2) deceitfulness
3) playhouse religion

IV. RIGHTEOUS PASTORS THAT LOVE GOD - HE WILL:

1) Open their eyes and give them a perfect vision to see what is happening in the church and the world.
2) Anoint them with power to preach God's word
3) Help them to rebuild the altars in the churches and call the people back to the cross
4) Preach like Jeremiah with boldness, humility, and a contrite spirit
5) Help them to lead their churches to a victorious lifestyle
6) Help them to live lives of integrity
7) Help them to lead their congregations toward lives of integrity

V. FOR THE FALSE PREACHERS, TEACHERS, AND PROPHETS, GOD WILL:

1) God will call the false preachers, teachers, and prophets to come to him in repentance; if they turn to God, he will treat them as the righteous pastors listed above. God will bless and anoint them.

2) If they refuse to turn to God, he will remove them

3) God is asking, "why have my children turned their backs on me?"

VI.   WHAT IS A FALSE PREACHER, TEACHER, OR PROPHET?

1)   A person who is about numbers and dollars
2)   A pastor more concerned with entertainment, numbers, offerings, programs, and fame than winning souls
3)   A person who leads the bride of Christ away from dedication
4)   A person who accepts everything, everyone, and does what the majority wants instead of following God's laws
5)   A person who refuses to listen to the Holy Spirit and does not preach on abortions, deceitfulness, sin, or repentance.
6)   A person who lets jealousy, greed, ego, and self-centeredness rule in their lives.
7)   A person who compromises for personal gain, church growth, fame, and fortune.
8)   A person without a burden for lost souls
9)   A person who prefers to play church instead of dedicating their lives to the truth and gospel of Christ
10) A person who is boastful, arrogant, prideful, haughty, and disobedient
11) A person who stands in the pulpit NOT prepared to deliver God's word
12) A person who does not have the fruits of the spirit in their lives.
13) A person who brags about the gifts of the spirit operating in their ministries
14) A person without a teachable spirit
15) A person who does not want to accept authority, instruction, church or organizational management, and leadership recommendations, or obey governmental regulations.
16) A person who feels that they have to be in control at all times and that God cannot use any other church in town or use any other preacher other than them!

VII. WHAT IS ICHABOD?

1)   Explain and define the word Ichabod

257

2) Explain why false preachers, teachers, and prophets allow the deceitful spirits, the spirits of Python, Leviathan, Jezebel, and Moloch, to operate in their churches
3) God's judgment
4) Destruction of the flesh for the saving of the soul
5) Pestilence

VIII. WHAT DOES IT MEAN TO BE RAPTURE READY?

1) What is a life of integrity?
2) What will keep you out of the rapture?
3) Why is it important that I strive daily to have the fruits of the spirit and none of the works of the flesh in my life?

IX. WHAT IS A LAST DAY REVIVAL?

1) Will there be a last day's revival?
2) Are we in this time period now?

X. WHAT OR WHO IS A LAST-DAY, MINISTER?

1) What will an end-time minister, teacher, missionary, or prophet look like according to scripture?
2) How will God use these people?

XI. WHAT IS THIS WORD FROM GOD ASKING OF ME?

1) Repentance

2) Dedication
3) Reading and praying
4) Discernment of the spirits
5) Living victoriously as a spiritual warrior on a mission to see souls saved
6) Rapture ready at all times

XII. WHAT DO I NEED TO DO?

a) <u>If this word describes me?</u>

1) Repent
2) Change
3) Get help

b) <u>If this word describes my pastor?</u>

1) Talk with my pastor(s)
2) If my pastor(s) refuses to accept this word from God—find another church that will accept it!

ABOUT THE AUTHOR

The author of this book series, Charlie O'Neal, felt God leading to write a seven-book series that would cover the keys to victorious living as a Christian. After much prayer and fasting over these seven-books' contents and outline for each, *The Keys to Victorious Living Series* was born. God also spoke that this author was to use a pen name for several reasons. God gave Charlie the outline for each book, the titles to each chapter, and specific steps for publication and marketing in a dream in January of 2017. With over two years of research and writing, Charlie began working on the first book, *Why am I not Living a Victorious Life,* in August 2019.

December 3rd, 2019, God gave Charlie a series of dreams and the message in this book. As Charlie began to share this word from God with churches in southern Alabama and northwest Florida from December 2019 through February 2020, God began to reveal that this word was written down and distributed worldwide, not just for Charlie's church. The reasons given in the 2017 dream for using a pen name are listed below.

1) God witnessed that he would provide the anointing to write this series of books as long as Charlie did not grow in pride or begin to feel that he was the author or the best person to deliver God's words.

2) God wanted a pen name utilized to ensure no publicity, fame, or recognition for these books' sales, the souls reached, or the churches and pastors delivered. God said that he would not allow anyone to take credit for the revival that this series would initiate worldwide.

3) God witnessed that the word of God needed to be shared from a raw, untainted perspective. God's word to Charlie was, "When an author utilizes his or her name on a book, they feel that they must consider all points, critique all statements and interpretations. Most authors write in a fashion to not offend their readers or embarrass their current congregations. If a preacher writes using his or her name, there will always be emotional and psychological critiquing

that occurs to the manuscript. However, if you will write these books as I give them to you, you will not be concerned with what anyone thinks, says, or publishes about these books, and you do not consider what others say, but follow my instructions precisely, I will give you more sales than your mind could imagine!"

4) Using a pen name will allow you to write without worrying if your congregation will be upset, mad, or leave because of your book. You will be able to give the true, unaffected, uncompromised interpretation of the word of God to this hungry, hurting world of people that are dying lost. You will be able to impact lives around the world, not just in your town or church.

5) Using a pen name will help you to write unbiased manuscripts and eliminate the need for controls or social checks on your writing due to the fear of negative publicity that your church might face or your family.

6) In the dream, God showed me my extended family reading this series. He said that they would never read the books with my name on the cover. However, if a pen name was used, they would read the books and would be touched. It is hard for the family to accept strong words and tough love from a family member. However, they will accept it from someone that they do not know.

7) God mentioned that it was not his desire for our church to be dragged into TV evangelism's limelight, which is where this book series would take the author. He stated that his ministry plan was not to be a Joel Osteen, Jensen Franklin, or a Jessie Duplantis, but to be a ministry that would reach people from the small, rural country communities, mission fields, jails, prisons, and one-on-one ministry. Some people will never attend a big church or a TV ministry affiliated church. If this book series brought media attention to our church, the local people he had plans to reach would never attend.

8) If the name of the church that you attend is mentioned, then the denomination will be indicated. That will keep people from other denominations from reading the book. I want this book series to be non-denominational and Bible-focused, not denominational affiliated.

9) The organization you are ordained with wants to review all manuscripts before publication to control negative publications or doctrinally incorrect books. When the organization gets through making the manuscript politically correct, the message will be lost. If you write with a pen name, then the manuscript will not be overcorrected by fearful organization leaders. Plus, the organization will not be embarrassed or have to deal with the media coverage and fall-out.

10) As the author, if you grow in fame and name recognition, it will draw people to your church that would overwhelm it and change the focus and purpose I have chosen for your church. So, I want you to humble yourself and obey me, and write without any recognition for your work. Then I will know that I can trust you to follow my directions. Then I can catapult your ministry to the next level.

The use of a pen name will also ensure that not only me, but no one individual, church member, family member, group, ministry licensing authority, or any other entities could receive recognition or financial gains for the success of this book series. To keep our church protected, I have chosen a publishing company from my home town, Brewton, Alabama, affiliated with a non-profit ministry to manage the publications, marketing, and distribution. Since I am not affiliated with this ministry, there cannot be any links back to me. To keep my identity "secret as God instructed," I have signed all contracts in the pen name and given all royalties to this organization. With no royalty checks being issued, my identity does not have to be verified. So, do not contact HFT Publishing, Inc., Heritage House Foundation, or Heritage House Bookstore for author identification. They cannot share information that they do not possess. I am trying my best to follow God's instructions for this book to the best of my ability.

I have made arrangements for profits from selling these books, e-books, audiobooks, and other promotional materials to go directly to HFT Publishing for distribution to Heritage House Foundation and Bookstore. The first project: secure a permanent ministry building and storage facility. The second project: a home for the minister who takes care of these retired ministers. (This home will provide lodging and food for the evangelist and missionaries preaching at So AL and NW FL area churches. Once those projects have been completed, I have instructed the foundation to take the profits and secure land and housing for retired ministers, missionaries, and church leaders who are homeless and need medical or financial assistance.

Heritage House Foundation has an extensive home and foreign mission plan that is dynamic. Once the two items that I felt led to fund have been accomplished, the Heritage House Foundation can utilize those ministry funds to complete their mission and vision if any donations are left. This non-profit organization assists missionaries worldwide, retired missionaries, plant churches, helps with the promotion and setup of prison ministries, children's homes, homes for unwed mothers, and other outreach programs to help with drug/alcohol rehabilitation and minister restoration.

AUTHOR'S CREDENTIALS AND EXPERIENCE:

To eliminate many readers' fears and skepticism, I will share my credentials and training with you. I fully understand that the Bible says that we should know those who work amongst us. Here are my earthly credentials in addition to my heavenly calling to preach and teach God's word that I heard over 40 years ago.

I am an ordained minister, happily married, with complete spousal and family support for my ministry. As a family, we are active with projects for home missions, foreign missions, domestic outreach programs, church, and other programs directed by God.

I am licensed with an evangelical organization that is internationally recognized with over 30 years of ministry experience ranging from assistant and associate pastor to senior pastor positions, teaching positions, international missions' positions, and jobs, including university professors. I have worked with other missionaries and helped with their missions, projects, etc., in numerous countries. I have been directly involved in missions on several continents.

When I began in ministry, I worked with several large ministry organizations that were televised. This gave my ministry a jump-start. Some of our ministry efforts have been recognized and covered on various Christian television broadcasting networks worldwide due to this exposure. However, I felt that God was calling me to the smaller to mid-size church, where I could work one-on-one with individuals, discipling them, helping them go forth as ministers and church leaders to impact the world for Jesus Christ!

In addition to local church work and missions, I have been the keynote speaker at international religious conferences across the United States and Internationally. I hold two master's degrees in my profession and love teaching part-time as a professor. My work training others to teach and preach is gratifying. I feel that I am impacting the world through more people than just my limited efforts. Planting into the lives of younger people, who will continue ministry when I am dead, leaves a living legacy for my ministry that glorifies God.

Now that you know where I have been, the exposures I have had in my ministry; hopefully, you will understand why God was so specific with his instructions not to get recognition for this series of books. With over 20 books written, and 12 books currently being used by colleges and universities as textbooks to my credit, you can understand why God gave me these instructions not to receive recognition for these books. God wanted *The Keys to Victorious Living Series and A Word from God for the Church* (a total of 64 books) donated to the ministry with no recognition for my church, ministry, the university, licensing organization, or myself.

I hope that you have enjoyed this book. I strongly encourage you to start reading *The Keys to Victorious Living Series.* It will take you the next three years to go through all of those books, but your life, home, family, ministry, and the church will never be the same…in Jesus' name! Take the books one at a time; focus on the content, not the author! Let God remove the blinds from your eyes and show you what you need to succeed in your life, marriage, career, and family. Learn how to have financial, emotional, physical, and spiritual freedom!

For more information on the Heritage House Foundation, this book series, or other questions you have, you can write to me at the address below. When the Heritage House Foundation receives the mail addressed as indicated below, they will scan it and email it to me, or you can email me directly at Charlie@minister.com. I will read your letter and answer your questions. You will get a response from me, not a computer, or a group of individuals trained to answer calls and mail at a call center. I care about your spiritual health. I will provide you with prayer support and guidance that I am qualified to give. If you have questions that I cannot answer, I will refer you to the best person to help you.

If you have gotten saved due to this book but do not have a home church to attend, contact us. I will help you locate a church in your area that preaches the "true word of God" and introduces the pastor there. We want you to have follow-up, spiritual assistance, and discipleship training. We can help you locate a local church regardless of whether you are in the United States or another country. Simply write to us or email.

If you want more information on the Heritage House Foundation, go to their website, www.heritagehousefoundation.org. For more information on HFT Publishing, including information about donating your next book's royalties or getting them to publish your next book for you, contact them at HFT-Publishing@post.com or go to their website, www.HFT-publishing.org. To ensure that you are always notified of new books coming out, go to the Heritage House Bookstore website and sign-up for their email list at www.heritagehousefoundationbookstore.org or send them an email at HeritageHouse@minister.com. You will be able to buy books at pre-publication reduced pricing or buy in bulk.

If you read a book and would love to use that book for teaching programs at your church or Sunday School classes, email your request to HFT-Publishing. Most of the books they publish for Charlie O'Neal have workbooks that can be used for Sunday School Books. The teacher uses the printed book as a textbook. You only have to purchase the workbooks (in bulk) for the classes. That helps to keep the ministry cost to a minimum. Imagine what you could do with an adult Sunday school class where the students have just spent 8-weeks learning to be a Spiritual Warrior or 6-weeks learning to be a Prayer Warrior?

Heritage House Foundation
Attention: *The Keys to Victorious Living Project*
P. O. Box 1801
Brewton, AL 36427-1801

HFT-Publishing, Inc.
P. O. Box 1863
Brewton, AL 36427-1863

CONTACT AND ORDER INFORMATION

If you need me to help you pray,
contact me directly at Charlie@minister.com

Thanks for reading this book. If you would like to donate money to help publish more books like this one or workbooks, send your tax-deductible contributions to the address below.

HFT-Publishing, Inc.
P. O. Box 1863
Brewton, AL 36427-1863

Email: HFT-Publishing@post.com

If you would like to help support the Heritage House Foundation and its outreach ministry to retired ministers and missionaries, write to them at the address below. We appreciate your prayers and financial support!

Heritage House Foundation
P. O. Box 1801
Brewton, AL 36427-1801

Email: HeritageHouse@minister.com

You can send money via credit card on the website below safely using PayPal's: www.heritagehousefoundationinc.org

267

BOOK STORE CONTACT INFORMATION

Heritage House Bookstore

Heritage House Book Store will be moving to a new physical location in 2021. The new location, once renovated, will be located at 6727 Appleton Road, Brewton, AL 36426

Website: www.heritagehousefoundationbookstore.org

If you do not have internet access or do not feel comfortable ordering online, send us a request by email to HFT-Publishing@post.com, and we will send you an order form. You can then order your books and attach your credit card information.

If you want to order more than five books at one-time, you will receive a 5% discount (there is a place on the order form to make the deduction). If you want to order ten or more books at one time, you will receive a 10% discount (this can also be deducted on the order form we will send you.

If you desire to order 11 or more copies of any book, you will need to send us an email for the discount amount. The price set for these books on our website only provides us with a $3 per book profit at the regular price. The only discount we can provide is the difference in the shipping cost for sending a bulk order to one address. To determine the discount amount, we will have to check with UPS for the exact shipping cost. Whatever we save on shipping, that savings will be forwarded to you as your discount. Our goal is not to make large profits but to get God's word to everyone that we can!

You can place an online at www.heritagehousefoundationbookstore.org

REFERENCES

Blackmon, L. (2020). *Getting to know God through the Old Testament: Genesis to Ezra.* Brewton, AL: HFT Publishing

Current-Argus, C. (April 5, 2018). *True holiness has true worth.* Retrieved from https://www.currentargus.com/faith

Franklin, J. & C. (2018). *Love like you have never been hurt: Hope, healing, and the power of an open heart.* Bloomington, MN: Chosen Books.

Gifford, J. (2014, Jan. 1). Sermon: Six signs we need to return to God-Jonah 1. Retrieved from https://www.lifeway.com/en/articles/sermon-returning-to-good-six-signs-Jonah-1

Google.com. (2020). *Google word searches.* Retrieved from https: // www.google.com/search

Google.com. (2020). *Google dictionary searches.* Retrieved from https: //www.google.com/dictionary

Hybel, B. (2008). *Too busy not to pray: Special Edition-20th Anniversary.* Downer Grove, IL: Intervarsity Press.

Jacobs, L. (2012, October 11). *Last days revival or end time apostasy?* Retrieved from https://www.shema.com/last-days-revival-or-end-time-apostasy-208/

Jakes, T. D. (2020). Quote from T.D. Jakes sermon on T

Jing, Z. (2019, June 23). *The last days are here: Are you prepared to meet God? Retrieved from* ttps://www.holyspiritspeaks.org/testimonies/prepare-to-meet-God/

KingJamesBibleDictionary.com. (2020). *King James Bible Dictionary.* (various definitions). Retrieved from: http://www.kingjamesbible dictionary.com

KJV. (2020). *The Holy Bible-King James Version.* Retrieved from https://www.biblestudytools.com

Min, L (2020, May 14). *How can we dine at the marriage supper of the lamb?* [website article]. Retrieved from ttps://www.holy spiritspeaks.org/testimoniesdine-at-marriage-supper-of-lamb/

Nall, L. (2020). *Living a Christian life in prison.* Repton, AL: Called-Out Ministries

O'Neal, C. (2020). *Why am I not living a Victorious Life?* Brewton, AL: HFT Publishing

Stone, P. (2013). *The Judas Goat.* Lake Mary, FL: Charisma House

www.ingramcontent.com/pod-product-compliance
Lightning Source LLC
Chambersburg PA
CBHW060009100426
42740CB00010B/1442